URBAN CHINA'S RURAL FRINGE

Bringing together scholars from China and the West, this study offers an innovative overview of the urbanization of China by focusing on the rural fringe and the centrality of its management in an attempt to ensure more sustainable paths of development. Challenging the current discourse on modernization in China that focuses solely on the urban rather than the rural, this book provides insights into the current massive urbanization that is taking place from a different angle. What is happening beyond the urban areas reveals the conflictive nature of the fast-changing Chinese society, still marked by a dual institutional urban-rural system, a growing income gap, a diverse life style and social status. However, the dense rural fringe of Chinese mega-city regions can also be conceived as an extraordinary laboratory where one can observe how the legacy of the old agricultural society coexists, in an original and rather unique way, with new forms of urbanity. Besides examining the evident urban-rural conflicts generated, this book looks at the prospective synergies of this linkage. A re-conceptualization of the rural dimensions of cities in a fast urbanizing context equips practitioners, scholars and students with new analytical tools to observe an unprecedented and complex great urban transition.

Giulio Verdini, PhD in Economics, Urban and Regional Development, from the University of Ferrara, is Associate Professor in Urban Planning and Design and Co-Director of the Research Institute of Urbanization at Xi'an Jiaotong-Liverpool University, People's Republic of China.

Dr. Yiwen Wang, PhD in Architecture from the University of Nottingham, is Lecturer in Urban Planning and Design at Xi'an Jiaotong-Liverpool University, People's Republic of China.

Dr. Xiaonan Zhang, PhD in Urban Geography at University of Salford, UK, is the former Head of the Department of Urban Planning and Design at Xi'an Jiaotong-Liverpool University, People's Republic of China.

Urban China's Rural Fringe
Actors, Dimensions and Management Challenges

Edited by

GIULIO VERDINI
YIWEN WANG
XIAONAN ZHANG
Xi'an Jiaotong-Liverpool University, People's Republic of China

LONDON AND NEW YORK

First published 2016
by Routledge
2 Park Square, Milton Park, Abingdon, Oxon OX14 4RN

and by Routledge
711 Third Avenue, New York, NY 10017

First issued in paperback 2018

Routledge is an imprint of the Taylor & Francis Group, an informa business

© 2016 Giulio Verdini, Yiwen Wang, Xiaonan Zhang and the contributors

The right of Giulio Verdini, Yiwen Wang, Xiaonan Zhang to be identified as the authors of the editorial material, and of the authors for their individual chapters, has been asserted in accordance with sections 77 and 78 of the Copyright, Designs and Patents Act 1988.

All rights reserved. No part of this publication may be reproduced, stored in a retrieval system or transmitted in any form or by any means, electronic, mechanical, photocopying, recording or otherwise without the prior permission of the publisher.

Trademark notice: Product or corporate names may be trademarks or registered trademarks, and are used only for identification and explanation without intent to infringe.

British Library Cataloguing in Publication Data
A catalogue record for this book is available from the British Library

Library of Congress Cataloging in Publication Data
Urban China's rural fringe : actors, dimensions and management
   challenges / by Giulio Verdini, Yiwen Wang and Xiaonan Zhang.
      pages cm
   Includes bibliographical references and index.
   ISBN 978-1-4724-4355-7 (hardback)—ISBN 978-1-4724-4356-4 (ebook)—
ISBN 978-1-4724-4357-1 (epub)   1. Rural-urban relations—China.
2. Wildland-urban interface—China.   3. Rural population—China.
4. Land use, Rural—China.   I. Verdini, Giulio, editor.
   HT384.C6U7176 2015
   307.760951—dc23
   2015018236

ISBN 13: 978-1-138-34200-2 (pbk)
ISBN 13: 978-1-4724-4355-7 (hbk)

Typeset in Times New Roman
by Apex CoVantage, LLC

Contents

List of Figures	*vii*
List of Tables	*xi*
Notes on Contributors	*xiii*
Preface	*xv*

1 The Rural Fringe in China: Existing Conflicts and Prospective
Urban-Rural Synergies   1
Giulio Verdini

2 Collaborative Approaches for Planning the Rural Areas of
Chinese Cities   17
Yu Guo and Sheng Zhong

3 The Rising Chinese Middle Class and the 'Construction' of a
New Countryside   33
John Sturzaker and Andrew Law

4 The Intermediate Role of Medium-Sized Cities in China
Between Ultra-Dense Rural Areas and Ultra-Large Cities   61
Abigaïl-Laure Kern, Marlène Leroux and Jean-Claude Bolay

5 Rural Regeneration in the Yangtze River Delta: The Challenge
and Potential for Rural Heritage Tourism Development   81
Yiwen Wang

6 Rural-Urban Edge: A Review of Spatial Planning Representation
and Policy Discourse in the Pearl River Delta   109
Francesca Frassoldati and Dongjin Qi

7 Preservation and Sustainable Development of Suburban
Historical Villages: A Case Study of Dayuwan Village in Wuhan   133
Shidan Cheng, Yang Yu and Rongbo Hu

8 Public Participation in Contested Spatial Planning: Learning
from a Failed Urban Development Project   147
Lei Sun and Xiaonan Zhang

9	A Pedagogical Approach to Designing the Future of China's Urban Fringe	175
	Rebecca Kiddle, Joon Sik Kim and Bing Chen	
	Point of View	195
	Paolo Ceccarelli	
	Conclusions	199
	Giulio Verdini	

Index   *201*

List of Figures

3.1	Windsor Island, Thames Town, Shanghai (Source: Andrew Law)	40
3.2	Photograph of advertisement for Eton flats (Source: Andrew Law)	42
3.3	The Han Mansions, Wuhan (Source: Andrew Law)	43
3.4	Han Road, Wuhan (Source: Andrew Law)	43
3.5	A Chinese theme park village, Jiangsu Province (Source: Andrew Law)	48
3.6	The 'new-old' water-town, September 2010 (Source: Qin Qianqian, permission of use granted)	50
3.7	Another perspective on the new-old water-town, September 2010 (Source: Qin Qianqian, permission of use granted)	51
3.8	'The creative space' connected to the Tiandi real estate development in Wuhan, May 2013 (Source: Andrew Law)	54
4.1	Typical Mount Song scenery (Source: Marlene Leroux)	68
4.2	Left: Dengfeng city (black). Right: Dujiangyan city (black). Existing new cities (white), planned new cities (dashed) (Source: Marlene Leroux)	69
4.3	District being destroyed, South Dengfeng (Source: Marlene Leroux)	70
4.4	New residential area, East Dengfeng (Source: Marlene Leroux)	71
4.5	50 km around Dengfeng: existing built area and water system (Source: Marlene Leroux)	74
4.6	50 km around Dujiangyan: existing built area and water system (Source: Marlene Leroux)	74
4.7	250 km around Dengfeng: existing built area and water system (Source: Marlene Leroux)	75
4.8	250 km around Dujiangyan: existing built area and water system (Source: Marlene Leroux)	75
5.1	The Yangtze River Delta generally refers to Shanghai, southern Jiangsu Province and northern Zhejiang Province of China (Source: Yiwen Wang)	88
5.2	Examples of recently refurbished and new-build houses in the countryside (Source: Yiwen Wang)	89

5.3	The routes of four field surveys and the locations of eight case studies (Source: Giulio Verdini)	91
5.4	The districts and counties in the Suzhou prefecture (Source: Giulio Verdini)	93
5.5	Aerial photo of the historical high street of Jinshi Village (Case Study 3) (Source: Google Satellite Image)	94
5.6	Unoccupied shop-houses in the high street and detached house (Source: Yiwen Wang)	95
5.7	Dilapidated and abandoned houses in the Jinshi Village (Source: Yiwen Wang)	96
5.8	Aerial photo of Nankun Village (Case Study 5) (Source: Google Satellite Image)	97
5.9	View towards the bay and the interlocking arrangement between the old and new houses in the area (Source: Yiwen Wang)	97
5.10	Dilapidated and abandoned houses in the Nankun Village (Source: Yiwen Wang)	98
5.11	View of Xitang Village (Case Study 1) (Source: Yiwen Wang)	99
5.12	View of Jinshi Village (Case Study 3) (Source: Yiwen Wang)	99
5.13	Aerial photos of Chuodunshan Village (Case Study 2) taken before and after the improvement of the public realm. The outer service road and the footpath on the south bank of the east-west canal were added (Source: Google Satellite Image)	101
5.14	The public spaces in Chuodunshan Village (Source: Yiwen Wang)	102
5.15	Canals and footpaths. Many daily activities of local residents, such as cleaning and chopping vegetables and washing up take place along the canal (Source: Yiwen Wang)	102
5.16	The restaurant provides customers a free cruise along the canal to the village by motor yacht (Source: Yiwen Wang)	103
6.1	Present rural-urban edge of Zhaoqing, one of the nine cities of the PRD (Source: Francesca Frassoldati)	115
6.2	The urban future of Zhaoqing, as displayed at the local Urban Planning Bureau (Source: Francesca Frassoldati)	116
6.3	Dwelling makeover and traditional building in a village that is now surrounded by Guangzhou city (Source: Francesca Frassoldati)	118
6.4	Distribution of the population in the PRD according to the *hukou* registration and long-term residents registers (Source: GSTJ 1997, 2001, 2005, 2012)	126
7.1	The Fengshui pattern of Dayuwan Village's site selection (Source: Shidan Cheng)	138

7.2	The architectural forms in Dayuwan Village (Source: Shidan Cheng)	139
7.3	Tourism activities in Dayuwan Village (Source: Shidan Cheng)	143
8.1	The location and spatial structure of the DTMD (Source: Lei Sun)	151
8.2	Local government-proposed plans in Sajinqiao Street area (Source: local official promulgation materials in 2005)	154
8.3	Run-down houses in the district (Source: Lei Sun)	154
8.4	The changes brought by the self-sponsored physical regeneration (Source: Lei Sun)	160
8.5	Passive chain reaction (Source: modified from Bao and Sun 2007)	166
9.1	Learning by doing during the intensive week of the workshop (Source: Giulio Verdini)	180
9.2	The field visit to Xishan Island in Tai Lake during the workshop (Source: Giulio Verdini)	181

List of Tables

3.1	Exhibitors at the Xi'an EXPO	52
5.1	National exemplary sites for rural tourism development	86
5.2	The list of eight case studies (Source: Verdini *et al.* 2011)	92
6.1	Rural-urban edge in the institutional bodies	119
6.2	The mechanisms of land use rights (Source: adapted from Wu *et al.* 2007: 37–47)	122
6.3	The lease of state-owned land compared to administrative allocation in the PRD (Source: GST 1999, 2001, 2003, 2005)	124
6.4	Administrative readjustment in Guangdong Province 1981–2011 (Source: GSTJ 1992, 2002, 2012; CSSB 1982)	125

Notes on Contributors

Jean-Claude Bolay is Director of the Cooperation & Development Center (CODEV) of École Polytechnique Fédérale de Lausanne, Director of the UNESCO Chair 'Technologies for Development' and Professor in the Laboratory of Urban Sociology (Institute of Territorial Development).

Paolo Ceccarelli is Director of the UNESCO Chair in 'Urban and Regional Planning for Sustainable Local Development' at the University of Ferrara and President of the International Laboratory of Architecture and Urban Design (ILAUD). He is Emeritus Professor of Urban Planning at the University of Ferrara.

Bing Chen has a PhD in Architecture from the University of Sheffield (UK) and is a Lecturer in Urban Planning and Design at Xi'an Jiaotong-Liverpool University.

Shidan Cheng has a PhD in Architecture from Chongqing University and is Professor and Head of Architecture Department in the School of Urban Design, Wuhan University.

Francesca Frassoldati has a PhD in Economics, Urban and Regional Development from the University of Ferrara and is Associate Professor at the South China University of Technology.

Yu Guo is a PhD candidate at the Department of Urban Planning and Design at Xi'an Jiaotong-Liverpool University.

Rongbu Hu is a PhD candidate at the Department of Architecture and Urban Design at Wuhan University.

Abigaïl-Laure Kern is Scientific Advisor for the Cooperation & Development Center at the École Polytechnique Fédérale de Lausanne and is a PhD candidate at the Laboratory of Urban Sociology of EPFL.

Rebecca Kiddle has a PhD in Urban Design from Oxford Brookes University and is a Lecturer in Environmental Studies and Geography at Victoria University of Wellington.

Joon Sik Kim has a PhD in Town and Regional Planning from the University of Liverpool and is Associate Professor in Urban Planning and Design at Xi'an Jiaotong-Liverpool University.

Andrew Law has a PhD in Human Geography from the University of Newcastle and is a Lecturer in Town Planning at the University of Newcastle.

Marlène Leroux is a PhD candidate at the Laboratory of Architecture and Urban Mobility (LAMU) at the École Polytechnique Fédérale de Lausanne.

Dongjin Qi is a Lecturer in Urban Planning and a PhD candidate at the South China University of Technology.

John Sturzaker has a PhD in Planning from Newcastle University and is a Lecturer in Civic Design at the University of Liverpool.

Lei Sun is a PhD candidate at the Department of Urban Planning and Design at Xi'an Jiaotong-Liverpool University.

Giulio Verdini has a PhD in Economics, Urban and Regional Development from the University of Ferrara and is Associate Professor in Urban Planning and Design and Co-Director of the Research Institute of Urbanisation at Xi'an Jiaotong-Liverpool University.

Yiwen Wang has a PhD in Architecture from the University of Nottingham and is a Lecturer in Urban Planning and Design at Xi'an Jiaotong-Liverpool University.

Yang Yu is a PhD candidate at the Department of Architecture and Urban Design of Wuhan University.

Xiaonan Zhang has a PhD in Urban Geography from the University of Salford, UK and is the former Head of the Department of Urban Planning and Design at Xi'an Jiaotong-Liverpool University.

Sheng Zhong has a PhD in Planning at the University of British Columbia and is a Lecturer in Urban Planning and Design at Xi'an Jiaotong-Liverpool University.

Preface

To understand the dynamics of the transformation of the rural fringe in contemporary China requires facing some of the most controversial issues of the current massive urbanization that is taking place in this part of the world. What is happening beyond the urban areas reveals the conflictive nature of a fast-changing Chinese society still marked by different institutional urban-rural conditions, a growing income gap, a diverse lifestyle and social status. The dense rural fringe of Chinese mega-city regions provides a unique opportunity to observe how the legacy of the old agricultural society coexists, in an original and rather unique way, with new forms of urbanity. Such complexity requires suitable and more sophisticated tools of analysis than the ones employed by planners for a long time (see the *Point of View* in the present volume). Traditionally inclined to consider the non-urban areas as an empty space to fill or a chaotic space to regiment, they have often (and sometimes deliberately) ignored its endogenous characteristics and social capital, especially in regions of relatively late development or in the context of the fast-growing metropolis of the 'Global South'.[1] Contemporary China is no exception. However, while the gap in research in other countries has been partially filled, the risk of misleading interpretations of the Chinese rural fringe is clearly present, being epitomized by the controversial implementation of the green belt(s) of Beijing.[2] Thus, the Chinese fringe requires a deep understanding of its intrinsic dynamism and the reading of its dense web of relationships in order to test suitable and innovative urban policies and design solutions.

While ad hoc analytical and operational tools for fringe management might already be considered granted (but not necessary appropriately faced and employed) in a Western context, they cannot be directly applied to China. The reason is partially due to the regional differences of the country, where an *underdeveloped* rural west in China coexists with a fast-changing and complex urban-rural east. In addition, regionalist policy approaches are also often prevented by the high

---

1 For example the 'Third Italy' few decades ago, or more recently in the so-called 'Desakota' regions of South-East Asia. The literature is ample but here the reference is to two seminal works: Bagnasco, A. (1977), *Tre Italie. La problematica territoriale dello sviluppo italiano* (Bologna: Il Mulino); and Ginsburg, N. et al. (1991), *The Extended Metropolis: Settlements in Transition in Asia* (Honolulu: University of Hawaii Press).

2 The problems faced in the implementation of the first green belt of Beijing has been interpreted as a lack of understanding of its characteristics of densely inhabited rural area near the city, as reported in Yang, J. and Z. Jinxing (2007), 'The failure and success of greenbelt program in Beijing', *Urban Forestry and Urban Greening* no. 6 (4): 287–96.

degree of centralization of the decision-making process. For this reason a different reconceptualization of the rural fringe, at least for some specific regions of urbanizing China both in the coast and in emerging urban clusters of the midland, could avoid the reproduction of policy and planning models still anchored to an obsolete idea of the country's urban-rural divide and incapable of capturing the peculiarity of local regional identity.

However, by assuming this incipient and deep urban-rural linkage in part of China as the underlying hypothesis of this research, the intention of the book is not purely descriptive. Conversely, emphasis is placed on conceptualizing the dense web of relations of the Chinese rural fringe by introducing an institutional framework of analysis. The reason is to deploy how state and market interacts in governing the fringe, and how emerging demands and practices of the rising Chinese middle class are already shaping new paths of development, requiring a new toolkit for planners. This focus can also help in reframing differently the obvious urban-rural conflicts today generated at the city fringe by looking at the prospective synergies inherent in such linkage. The reason for introducing those elements of distinctiveness, in respect to other diverse experiences across the world, should eventually prevent the easy shortcut of the sub-urbanization rhetoric as a natural one-way model of city expansion.

However, regardless of the country-specific issues, the challenge to ensure the utilization of appropriate conceptual and operational tools remains universal. They are in fact deeply interwoven with the innovation of practices, namely the policies and plans directly or indirectly influencing the rural fringe, and with the improvement of the curricula of the current planning programmes in China, where such topics are still scattered and poorly integrated with other mainstream disciplinary areas. It is a challenge that has been faced almost everywhere in the last years. For this reason, this book addresses in particular governmental officials, urban planners and architects, but also students from the relevant disciplines.

Under these considerations this book will provide evidence-based research material which conceives differently the rural fringe in urbanizing China, addressing both the research and the pedagogic challenge of such reconceptualization. A general introductory chapter (Chapter 1) is primarily focused on the definition of the actors and dimensions involved in the rural fringe, such as the conflicts and synergies embedded in the new urban-rural relationship. This is followed by a series of specific cutting-edge chapters based on case studies in China: the institutional innovation for managing the fringe adopting collaborative approaches in the city of Chongqing (Chapter 2); the conflicts between new, emerging societal demands affecting the fringe, namely the residential preferences of the rising Chinese middle class, utilizing examples in Shanghai, Xi'an and so on (Chapter 3); the intermediate role of emerging urban formations, between cities and dense peri-urban areas, and their specific management challenges, presenting the cases of Dengfeng in Henan and Dujiangyan in Sichuan (Chapter 4); rural regeneration projects in the Yangtze River Delta (Chapter 5); the planning practices and policies associated with the rural-urban edge in the Pearl River Delta (Chapter 6), a village regeneration in Wuhan (Chapter 7) and community participatory practices for local citizens' involvement in Chinese marginal areas, focussing on a case in Xi'an (Chapter 8). Afterwards, the outcome of an international student workshop held in 2012 as an innovative teaching experience, which took place at the fringe of Suzhou, is reported (Chapter 9). The international workshop has in fact been an opportunity to apply a comprehensive analytical framework for providing sustainable urban planning and design solutions, acknowledging the specific challenges and opportunities of a significant locality in the highly urbanized Jiangsu Province. The chapters are followed by a 'Point of View', tracing the main theoretical pathways for the preparation of this book, especially in relation to the pedagogic experience of the international workshop. A final conclusion completes the book's research findings and sets up a future research agenda on urban-rural linkages in China for the years to come.

The book is the outcome of a research programme concerning the rural fringe in China supported by the Suzhou Municipal Philosophy and Social Science Academy (2011 and 2012) and the Department of Education of the Jiangsu Province (2013).[3] XJTLU, moreover, provided the resources for organizing two International Workshops under the title Critical Planning for Chinese Cities (CPCC) and two International Seminars: 'Conceiving the rural in coastal China: the historic fringe and the contested fringe' in 2012 and 'Managing rural landscape in China' in 2013. The book collects selected research from Chinese and European scholars presented in our Department.

Mention must be made of the support received by Paolo Ceccarelli and Etra Connie Occhialini, from ILAUD, The International Laboratory of Architecture and Urban Design, an Italian association that promotes research and the formation in the field of architectural and urban design, founded by Giancarlo De Carlo in 1976. Over almost 40 years ILAUD has organized teaching and research programmes in collaboration with the most important European and North American schools of architecture and planning, expanding to emerging countries in recent years.

---

3   The list of research grants comprises: A) Research title: 'When local meets global: urban fringe planning and institutional arrangement' (2013–16). Research team: Giulio Verdini (PI), Yiwen Wang (CI), Yu Guo (Research Assistant). Funding body: Department of Education of the Jiangsu Province, 2013 Social Science Programme (2013SJD790052); B) Research title: 'Planning a local food system in Suzhou. Analysing the demand for quality of food and agriculture' (2012–13). Research team: Giulio Verdini (PI), Yiwen Wang (CI). Funding body: Suzhou Municipal Philosophy and Social Science Academy, 2012 Social Science Program (SSSP 12-D-56); C) Research title: 'Towards an effective integration of urban-rural tourism: mapping agro-tourism development on Suzhou urban fringe' (2012–13). Research team: Yiwen Wang (PI), Giulio Verdini (CI). Funding body: Suzhou Municipal Philosophy and Social Science Academy, 2012 Social Science Program of Suzhou (SSSP 12-D-57); D) Research title: 'Assigning open-space non market values as a tool for planning the urban-rural fringe in Suzhou' (2011–12). Research team: Giulio Verdini (PI), Yiwen Wang (CI). Funding body: Suzhou Municipal Philosophy and Social Science Academy, 2011 Social Science Program (SSSP 11-B-08).

Urban China's Rural Fringe

The principles at the base of ILAUD, who co-organized with us the above-mentioned two international workshops, namely the de-sectorialization of knowledge in designing the future of our contemporary cities and the 'learning by doing', have deeply inspired the teaching and research activities of a young department of Urban Planning and Design, established in 2010.

Giulio Verdini
Suzhou-Paris

Chapter 1

The Rural Fringe in China: Existing Conflicts and Prospective Urban-Rural Synergies

Giulio Verdini

Introduction

The rural fringe of Chinese cities is today a transitional place between urban and rural areas where several contradictions take place partly inherited from the past and partly due to recent trends of development. A consolidated body of international literature regarding the conceptualization of the fringe and the urban-rural interaction has already demonstrated that 'populations and activities described either as "rural" or "urban" are more closely linked both across space and across sectors than is usually thought, and that distinctions are often arbitrary' (Tacoli 1998). Thus peri-urban households may be 'multispatial', with some residents working in towns or others engaged in non-farm activities in the countryside. China, as other emerging countries in Asia, Latin America and Africa, featuring rapid urbanization, is no exception with similar 'complexities of changing peri-urban production and livelihood systems' (Simon 2008).

Focussing on the fringe means also to verify whether the current discourse of urbanization featuring China as a one-way urbanization country, converging towards a universal pattern of globalization, is still entirely applicable (Dick and Rimmer 1998). This assumption, which historically gained success especially among international organizations, is based on the recurring discourse of the 'urban age', statistically measured through the increasing volume of urban residents, but mainly inclined to prioritize urban agglomerations and to interpret the non-urban field as an empty field. Thus, Brenner and Schmidt (2014) advocate for a careful reading of the historic processes and socio-economic dimensions that play a fundamental role in shaping the fringe everywhere, which instead depict this empty field as a dense network of economic activities and social relations. However, in pursuing this goal, attempts to compare China and the West look similarly rather risky: *in primis*, for the substantially different nature of the rural society still residing at the city fringe and, moreover, as the urban encroachment into the rural areas in China has been mainly driven by employment-led urban development (Webster and Muller 2004), only recently shifting towards a predominantly residential-led development. Last but not least, China itself is a complex and diverse country featuring a very different pattern of development. This requires narrowing down the observation not only to some specific functional dimensions of the fringe, adopting an analytical framework already applied elsewhere to conceptualize the 'multiple fringe' (Gallent *et al.* 2006), but also to a spatial or regional one, in the attempt to distinguish between the multiple patterns of urbanization that China is experiencing.

Therefore the study of the singularity of the rural fringe *a la chinoise*, together with comparisons within the country, appears to be more interesting in the debate about peri-urbanity, developed almost everywhere in the last two decades. The interest is due in particular to the way its historic pattern of development, and the current institutional settings that regulate the fringe, interacts with the pursued modernity of the country, strongly and regionally unbalanced. This also depends on the way very different social formations, each with a different status, disposable income and lifestyle, cohabit in the most developed part of the country, increasingly finding at the fringe unavoidable tensions or beneficial opportunities of mutual interaction.

In this respect the urbanization process of the rural fringe, as a dense web of relations, will be observed primarily through the lens of the institutionalist approach, looking at the way Chinese localities are shaped by conflictive/ cooperative actors' behaviours within a given set of constrains (Healey 1999). Particular attention will be given to the residential 'hukou' system and the dual system of land ownership, collectively owned in rural areas and *de facto* privatized in urban areas.

Although the current 'rules of games' might change in the future, due to the recurring announcements of reforms coming from the central government, these transformations are very likely to be gradual. Therefore there is a need today to implement rapidly practical solutions for managing the fierce planning challenges of the rural fringe, embedded in the current system and, meanwhile, to figure out how to manage the unfinished transition of the country, which started with the 'opening up' policy in the late 1970s.

The Chinese Rural Fringe in Perspective

According to Friedmann in his book, *China's Urban Transition* (2005), the rapid urbanization of the country has been mainly characterized by a unique process of rural industrialization. The process has been boosted by the government, in some key coastal regions, like the lower Yangzi Delta or the Pearl River Delta, and has created a particular landscape of scattered industrial areas and new settlements surrounding dense urban areas. This new spatial structure has merged with the legacy of the previous socio-economic system, including agricultural activities, rural villages and ribbon developments.

For almost two decades, this model has reduced the pressure of mass migration towards the city centre, improving the living and economic conditions of large parts of the rural population in the coast. Yet, at the same time this has produced several social and environmental problems, denying the rural origin of these areas in transition. These areas have experienced the uncontrolled impact of pollution from a chaotic industrialization process and, later on, an increasing urbanization featuring a massive application of relocation schemes for farmers, resulting in unrest and a high level of social resistance due to perceived unfair compensation treatment. This trend, although embedded in the specific Chinese institutional setting and largely shaped by ad hoc top-down policies, can be associated with the Asian phenomenon of the industrialized/urbanized countryside, elsewhere addressed as 'desakota', an Indonesian word combining the term for villages, 'desa', and town, 'kota' (McGee 1991). This pattern relates to zones characterized by high population density, rapid growth of non-agricultural jobs, labour mobility and mixed, sometimes chaotic, land use (Xie *et al.* 2007).

Today urbanization continues unabated, moving from the coast to the west, driven by policies aimed at repositioning China from a purely manufacture-based country to an increasingly service- and knowledge-based one. This transition is characterized by the flourishing of new industrial parks and residential areas to accommodate the rising Chinese middle class. Primary activities are losing appeal and profitability especially if located within complex city-region systems, whereby the urban exerts a strong influence on the surrounding areas. Aside from the evident land use conflicts inherent in the process of 'metropolitanization', this generates an alteration of the peri-urban livelihood, elsewhere associated with the concept of 'de-ruralization' (Bryceson 1996), resulting in social costs that very often are not accounted for in the development process (Verdini 2014). The acknowledgement of the overall loss at the fringe, not just limited to farmlands, might highlight the existence of other systems of resources, like place-based economic activities, environmental assets or cultural and social capital, embedded in unique systems of organic rural settlements, today threatened by the urban growth.

Even if the conversion from rural to urban land has been massive, and is still ongoing, some important areas have been missed and a journey through those areas would reveal today that new forms of peri-urbanity are slowly growing at the fringe of the city of China. This trend, in some cases, seems to align to the Western trend where, since the 1990s, the rediscovery of different dimensions of rurality, labelled as post-productivist, around the city have played an important role in the diversification of some rural economic activities, such as those related to tourism and leisure time, or to the production of specific local food (Arnason *et al.* 2009).

These resources can play an important role for the future of China, strengthening prospective urban-rural synergies and configuring the Chinese fringe as a distinct and dynamic spatial organization. Thus the studying of these dense rural regions, part of complex and polycentric urban systems, will eventually contribute to the understanding of new emerging Asian Mega-city Regions (Qadeer 2000).

Actors, Dimensions and Management Challenges

Actors

There is still a clear demarcation line between those who reside in rural areas and those who are registered as urban citizens in China. As will be described in the next section covering the different 'dimensions' of the rural fringe, this line is reinforced by the residential 'hukou' system, where belonging determines a different status and access to welfare benefits. However, if we focus on rural households, the actors located at the rural fringe appear to be difficult to categorize. Besides their statistical classification as rural households, their livelihoods might derive from more or less profitable agricultural activities or from a variable combination of rural and urban jobs. Their status and their diverse pattern of income form an unexpected variety of social formations. The penetration of the capitalist form of production into Chinese agriculture has reshaped the once homogeneous peasant class, thus determining a growing divide between those increasingly working as capitalist agricultural producers and those gradually entering a condition of proletarianization (Zhang and Donaldson 2010). This process, which increasingly relies on commodification of the rural labour force, can partly explain the trend of in-migration towards the fringe areas for agricultural purposes.

In addition to this, the fringe can be seen as a suitable, temporary and affordable location for the 'floating population', mainly composed of the traditional migrants holding a rural hukou, finding job opportunities in the industrial sectors of the most urbanized part of the country (Zhu 2007). Especially in mega-cities like Shanghai, continuously shaped by inner redevelopments and strongly affected by rising real estate prices, the peri-urban areas have become the favourite destination of low-income people (J. Wu 2008), although migrants still prioritize the inner suburbs rather than the outer ones (W. Wu 2008). Regardless their origin, rural households located at the fringe might be involved in rural or urban jobs. As long as they are employed, taking advantage of both urban and rural opportunities, they share similar living conditions. Once the land is designated as urban, status determines the right to be compensated, creating new disparities between locals, entitled to land rights, and migrants: the latter being a category more seriously at risk of marginalization within the growing sector of the urban poor.

Rural households in China today number almost 200 million and recent estimations suggest that the total number of dispossessed farmers[1] will soon exceed 70 million, continuing at an annual rate of 2.5–3 million farmers (Ran 2012). On the other hand, the urban population grew by almost 20 million per year in the period 2000 to 2010, with official statistics declaring that, overall, the proportion of people living in urban areas rose from 17 per cent to almost 53 per

---

1 Normally this term refers to peri-urban famers who have been subject to compulsory purchase and then forcefully relocated into cities. They are 'dispossessed' as they have been deprived of their primary means of subsistence.

cent between 1978 and 2011 (OECD 2013). As reported in Frassoldati and Li in the present volume, this figure is very likely to be purely statistic, not considering the contribution of the floating population, *de facto* living in urban settings, to the extent that in fast-growing regions the rate of people involved in non-primary activities should today exceed 80 per cent. On the other hand, they also argue that in areas like the Pearl River Delta the frequent reclassification of towns and villages into urban areas, mainly due to political or economic reasons, have resulted in an unclear figure, where most of the new urban residents are located in these mid-ranking urban settings that form the dense Chinese rural regions.

Besides the issue of administrative readjustments, that warns us to consider the official statistics with caution, Chinese urban growth implies an important extension of the existing city boundary and new processes of peri-urbanization, both for residential and industrial development purposes. Taking Beijing as an example, China's metropolises are experiencing a complex urban-rural transition as the peri-urban areas attract temporary migrant residents, as in other dynamic metropolises, showing at the same time a residential demand from growing middle-class groups (Zhao 2012). Newcomers at the fringe express different housing needs. While the migrants mainly look for affordable temporary accommodation, the new Chinese middle class seeks spacious, low-density houses (see Law in the present volume). Low- or high-density gated community (Western) styles of urbanization are also flourishing (Wu 2007). Regardless, though, the typological preference of the recent trend of suburbanization determines an unprecedented socio-spatial fragmentation and polarization at the fringe, as already experienced in other emerging countries like Argentina, Brasil, Indonesia and so on.

However, what is still uncovered in literature is the contribution of the new Chinese cities (and citizens) in shaping a more mature and articulated demand for peri-urban areas, as already experienced in the developed world. A city demands not just new space for development (either affordable or elitist), but also quality rural places at the fringe for spending their leisure time, for enjoying tourist activities during the weekend, for purchasing local products and so on. As reported in Wang in the present volume, attempts to study this emerging trend and its implications are rather scattered today in China, while probably the south Jiangsu Province represents one of the most suitable regions to start with. Historically characterized by a rich agricultural tradition and a peculiar development of rural villages, some of these water towns have naturally become the object of interest of growing domestic tourism, like the water towns of Tongli and Zhouzhuang, near Suzhou, or Zhujiajiao in the suburbs of Shanghai. Similarly, some agricultural productions in peri-urban areas have converted to organic for feeding a niche, but increasingly urban, demand for quality food, mainly driven by the expat community and the wealthy Chinese bourgeoisie, like Dongshan Peninsula in Suzhou, in the residual agricultural areas of East Pudong or in Chongming Island, both in Shanghai.

Thus, this trend adds another component to the complex and multifaceted Chinese fringe as the emergence of the urban citizen (in some cases urban tourist) reshapes agricultural activities into a more service-oriented or quality-oriented manner, requesting contemporary reuse requesting contemporary and more sustainable reuse of the existing built environment (from single rural houses to entire historic rural villages) and open fields.

In this brief introduction we have outlined the contemporary emerging societal figures whose needs and demands will mostly determine the spatial configuration of the rural fringe of urbanizing China. We have purposely avoided mentioning those who act on behalf of the state (policymakers, local officials, local cadres and so on), although their beliefs and values, such as their behaviour, might determine a very different pattern of fringe development in light of the complex bureaucratic Chinese administration system and the relatively high level of local autonomy. This is because an important factor to consider is the performance benchmarking they have to achieve to fulfil their political duties, which are still mainly based on pure economic growth paradigms, leaving limited space for redesigning the fringe of Chinese cities, such as overall city transformation, based on principles of urban quality. These aspects, although extremely important, are often underestimated and would require ad hoc investigations. For this reason they will not be covered in this book, even if their implications have to be considered in outlining the challenge that future planners, urban designers and architects will face in the future when they are asked to deal with the fringe.

Dimensions

Studies regarding the rural-urban fringe in the West have been mainly attempted to consider the fringe from a multiplicity of different functional dimensions. This has led, for example, Gallent *et al.* (2006) to identify the main planning challenges according to five typologies of a fringe: historic, aesthetic, economic, socio-cultural and ecological.

In this book we will mainly focus on the institutional constrains, namely the rules of the games that shape planning practices at the fringe, due to their overwhelming importance in the current debate on Chinese urban issues and institutional reforms. This will not prevent us relating the specific Chinese institutional challenge to recurring and emerging dimensions, as they are perceived by the main actors or by the dominant political discourse. However, lack of systematic and comparative studies within China could easily bring us to an easy but dangerous shortcut. The risk would be to conceive of the Chinese fringe from a Western bias, assuming a similar pattern of development for both contexts. To avoid this hereinafter the institutional dimension of the Chinese fringe will be described and the regional dimension will be also taken in account, considering that trends of development at the fringe vary substantially based on geographic locational factors (the coast or midland China) and functions played by the Chinese urban networks (mega-cities or medium-sized cities, for example). Eventually, some emerging dimensions will be depicted, especially those related to raising environmental concerns and new economic dynamics.

Urban land in China constitutionally belongs to the state and is given in concession to urban households for a limited period of time, according to prevalent land use. Rural land, on the other hand, is collectively owned, belonging to the rural communes, who allocate land among the members of the community based on egalitarian principles (Hsing 2010). In urbanizing China, the rural fringe is the area where the conversion from rural to urban takes place, unless prohibited by specific planning restrictions, which aim to limit city size and preserve cultivated land (CPGPRC 1999).

Mechanisms for rural conversion to urban include the designation of areas of new development for residential or industrial purposes and the compulsory purchasing of the rural land from the state for public interest, based on the application of compensation schemes for dispossessed farmers. After the expropriation the land can be sold to private developers. Due to the ambiguity of property rights, determined by a dual system of land tenure, Chinese urban development is largely characterized by increasing types of grievance from peri-urban farmers, during the process of forceful urbanization. This is primarily due to the perception of unfair compensation that has led, in the last few years, to social unrest such as more articulated forms of resistance (Li and O'Brien 2008).

This is one of the main critical points of the current urban growth model which extracts the main resources for its reproduction from the capital gain obtained by selling land in the vigorous primary land market, deducting the very marginal farmers' compensation. Moreover, the Chinese devolution process, although not accompanied by adequate resource transfer from the centre, necessarily increases the appetite of city financing systems, resulting in land being consumed very quickly (Yanyun Man 2011). Thus local officials and policymakers, as mentioned before, play a fundamental role in fuelling a revenue-seeking urban development model, often resulting in unsustainable and unfair solutions.

Some steps forward have also been taken to establish a fairer system to protect farmers' land rights (CPGPRC, 2007), but only full tenure security is regarded as a way to reduce the widespread phenomenon of discretional allocation of land, curbing the risk of individual appropriation of urbanization capital gain (Ding 2007). Peri-urban farmers, moreover, affected by the urban development process might benefit from more or less rewarding compensation in monetary or urban real estate form (Zhao and Webster 2011). They eventually become urban citizens, not being exempted from problems bounded to their new status, however. The issue of 'passive urbanization' has in fact been well explored, pointing out how compensation does not acknowledge the deprivation of farming skills and often pushes the new citizens into the marginalized job sectors in the cities (He *et al.* 2009).

During the 1980s and 1990s the agricultural landscape of the fringe was transformed by the so-called industrialization of the countryside, driven by township enterprises. Advantages (mainly social) and disadvantages (mainly environmental) have been already discussed. Since the mid-1980s, moreover, efforts by the country to move fast from a purely manufacture-based economy to a more knowledge-based one materialized in the establishment of several new science parks, largely located at the urban fringe. The science park primarily aims to create development zones and new jobs (Zeng 2012), although very often it has assumed the form of a property-led residential investment. This is why new towns or new districts, increasingly mixed and diversified, appear, creating a magnet for high-profit industries, research institutions and real estate developments.

The last decade has finally witnessed, at least around the main mega-cities, a wave of residential development with the growing Chinese middle class determining, as in the West, the need for out-of-town retail centres, new infrastructures, dedicated services and so on. Yet in the peri-urban areas of the fast-growing regions of China, agricultural activities are still practiced. While the number of employees in the primary sector quickly declined in the last years, most Chinese cities (a part extreme cases like Shanghai or Shenzhen) still rely on their own regional production with a relatively high 'self-sufficiency ratio', namely the quota of local food consumed against the overall food consumption of the city (Lang and Miao 2013).

Besides the agricultural output transformation and management system innovation, due to the changing pattern of consumption of the new Chinese urban citizens (Huang 2011), the whole rural economy, especially at the city fringe, is changing. Multifunctional agriculture is flourishing together with attempts to raise the quality of food production, but overall rural tourism can be regarded as one of the main emerging and successful complementary activities to partially alleviate the decline that still characterized the Chinese countryside (Zeng and Ryan 2012).

These trends happened frequently in China but not everywhere with the same intensity due to the regional imbalance of the country. Thus it seems fundamental to introduce a geographic dimension to look at how the fringe can be conceived in different areas of the country. Ultimately the goal is to restrict our attention to the rural fringe of specific areas of urbanizing China, as mentioned in the title of this book, where distinct regional economic paths, spatial planning issues, environmental and societal challenges can be partially assimilated (Wheeler 2002). By introducing the lens of the regionalist approach, the intention is not to foster quantitative comparative studies but to provide examples in order to be able to catch, as much as possible, the current (and quickly mutating) situation of the Chinese fringe.

A useful study to start with and to determine a criteria to diversify rural China is the critique of the policy termed 'building a new countryside' by Long *et al.* (2010). From a geographical perspective they argue that the national policy aimed at modernizing agricultural production does not take into account different levels of regional development. If geographic specificity was applied to such a policy, a logical conclusion might be that rural areas within the dense and urbanized east of China are more suitable for diversifying the rural economy, while the western part of China might be more suitable for raising agricultural productivity. However a simple East-West dichotomy is probably no longer suitable to depict the changing urban dynamics of China, especially in light of the intention to develop inland China by the central government. Cities showing a positive economic trend and gradually readjusting their employment structure towards the most advanced parts of China might all express (if not now, very soon) a new relationship between the urban and rural areas, experiencing similar conflicts and synergies at the fringe. In addition to the regional pattern of development, the function and the physical dimension of the city might have an important implication in determining different degrees of conflicts or synergies as will be fully explained in the chapter by Kern *et al.* in the present book.

In summary, the rural-urban fringe zones, quoting the National Urbanization Plan (2014–20), are still very much conceived of as areas in which to improve planning, development, management and service provision, considering at the same time the fierce societal challenges (peri-urban farmers, migrants, urban households) directly related to the environmental issues of containing city growth and preserving the agricultural land surrounding the main cities (SCPRC 2014).

Besides this broad and urgent environmental concern (ecologic dimension of the fringe), the fringe is becoming a place where the diversification of economic activities are taking place, linked to a more mature demand emanating from an established or establishing Chinese middle class. In this respect the economic dimension of the fringe is assuming raised importance. Moreover, these economic activities are often embedded in particular morphologies that retain an historic (original or reinvented) and an aesthetic dimension. Thus the fringe is no longer perceived as an 'empty field', but conversely an area that mobilizes the growing interests of diverse urban stakeholders and a place with a more defined regional connotation.

Management Challenges

The main question related to the management challenges of the Chinese fringe has to do primarily with an issue of ownership or, in other words, with who is in charge of the fringe in a transitional socialist market system. The key problem is that the current trend of urbanization in China is producing unsustainable sprawling with the well-known associated issue of farmland reduction, particularly fertile in urbanized coastal areas, and typical urban planning problems such as congestion, stress on the provision of suitable infrastructures and services, alteration of landscape and so on. Worldwide urban sprawl is regarded as one of the main planning challenges of both developed and, more recently, emerging countries (Richardson and Bae 2004). The Western experience places increasing attention on the (controversial) way market-based mechanisms can enhance the efficiency of purely regulative approaches in the process of urban growth management, within neo-liberal systems (Van Dijk 2009). In general terms there is a consensus that regulative measures need to be supported by incentives and meaningful stakeholder participative processes in order to reduce the pressure of urban growth in the surrounding open spaces (Bengston et al. 2004).

Studies of peri-urbanization in China place more attention on the conflictive nature of the Chinese system of the governance of urban growth and on the role of government in fuelling these sprawls (Zhang 2000). Contradictions arise between the land-consuming needs of local authorities for supporting their local financing system that is still mainly based on land-sell and the rigid top-down measures to curb the sprawl, such as provincial quotas to preserve arable lands, planning restrictions for city growth and so on. Tensions moreover arise between the peri-urban citizens affected by the urbanization and those who handle the urban growth process (from local officials to private developers) due to the perceived corruption inherent in the current planning system. The growing mistrust generates high levels of social resistance and increasing costs during implementation of urban projects (see Sun and Zhang's argument in the present volume).

However, there are both potential and promising directions to explore in China, in order to reduce these conflicts, which cope effectively with these challenges, as will be explained in the next section: on the one hand, the effort, so far quite unsuccessful, to implement property taxation at the city level, thus reducing the appetite of local governments and the risks of growth per se, not bounded to a real demand; and, on the other hand, to test collaborative and market-based approaches for peri-urban planning, thus reducing the level of social resistance and ensuring a fairer system of compensation.

In addition to these two unavoidable issues, embedded in the current institutional model for urban growth is the question about what will be the vision of both planning and planners for the rural fringe in the future of Chinese cities. Does the fringe have to be conceived as a pure underdeveloped area, a reservoir for future residential suburban areas for the rising middle class? Or for new industrial parks or tourist attractions? Or a potential green and open space for raising the overall environmental quality of the Chinese cities?

Policy responses in this respect have been already put in place in the main Chinese cities, for example the programme of development of satellite cities as part of the strategies of the new Shanghai Master Plan (Den Hartog 2011) or the long-lasting (and not quite successful) attempts to implement a green belt in Beijing, in most of cases following models already applied in Western cities (Tan *et al.* 2011). However, emerging social practices at the fringe of Chinese cities, as already mentioned, bounded to a new urban lifestyle, are demanding for a different fringe, in continuity with the rural legacy of this environment. The policy response in this case has been scattered or, in some cases, inadequate and still driven by quantitative paradigms. Two evident examples, in this respect, are peri-urban agricultural parks and historic villages. The establishment of peri-urban agricultural parks, with the environmental intention of preserving fertile areas relatively close to urban areas, often hides a local wish to create a money machine for increasing the volume of domestic tourists (Lang and Miao 2013). The speculative intention is even more evident in the case of the rural regeneration of the historic villages of the South Jiangsu Province. While some villages, although retaining some historic characteristics, are simply abandoned and, in some extreme cases, demolished, others are designated as tourist attractions and, with the justification of cultural protection, are transformed into small-scale 'Disneylands' for weekend tourism trips.

Rural-Urban Interactions: Existing Conflicts and Prospective Synergies

The rural fringe in China, which was until recently the boundary between two different realms (urban vs. rural), is today the space where dense rural-urban interactions take place: these interactions might be determined by contentious demands for allocation of land use or, conversely, by prospective synergies, potentially fostering sustainable development paths at the fringe. The main driver of urban growth has been identified in the dangerous combination between the particular local financing system, strongly dependent on land-sell, and the particularly advantageous system of land requisition for public interest, due to the collective land system in rural areas. This led Tao (2012) to advocate for a coordinated property tax reform and collective ownership reform, capable of reducing abusive land requisition and distorted land leasing (Tao and Xu 2007). However, despite several attempts to employ property tax simulations at the city level, so far little has been done.

Instead, more margins of action, within the current Chinese planning systems, seem to exist regarding the application of innovative land management tools, as in the case of the land ticket of Chongqing, under the pilot programme for the urban-rural development reform of 2007. This experience basically aimed at ensuring higher compensation for peri-urban farmers, through market-based mechanism for land trading, and has been framed as a practical attempt to apply collaborative rural planning in China, tracing a promising path for a more socially balanced model of urban growth (see Guo and Zhong in the present volume).

Clearly a common argument behind the fierce urban-rural conflicts of the Chinese system of urban growth is the fact that lack of tenure security in rural areas discourages investments in agricultural improvement (Lichtenberg and Ding 2008). In peri-urban areas the situation is exacerbated by the proximity of the urban areas, as frequently happens even in Western countries, and by the aspiration of peri-urban farmers to become urban, achieving eventually better living conditions. However, this unfortunate combination of factors that might reinforce the assumption of a one-way urbanization model (who can resist the seductress of modernization) clashes with an emerging and probably still-minority trend of alternative rural activities flourishing at the fringe.

Although these rural activities are surviving mainly due to enforced rural land conservation areas that prevent the arbitrary conversion from rural into urban, these activities meet specific and growing market demands coming from the city. The spreading of non-agricultural jobs in peri-urban areas is becoming a reality in contemporary China, being comprised of the so-called happy farming houses (rural guest houses or agri-tourism), restaurants and fruit-picking activities, as well as scattered local handicraft or clusters of local production. The conservation of rural heritage is becoming a driver of unprecedented domestic tourism in rural areas. The reorganization of the production and commercialization chain of local food is timidly reinforcing new retail and logistic infrastructures for real urban food strategies.

Ultimately this new peri-urban landscape of social practices and economic activities is depicting a new scenario for planners, urban designers and architects to creatively rethink the rural fringe as a fundamental component of modern Chinese cities. As we have witnessed in the last years, most likely the Yangtze River Delta and, in particular, the fringe of new globalizing cities such as Shanghai and Suzhou are the ideal places to witness these transformations (see Wang in the present volume). However signals in this direction come from a variety of growing and changing contexts in coastal China or in the emerging midland urban clusters (see the case of Wuhan described by Cheng *et al.* in the present volume).

Preliminary Conclusion

Besides the evident conflicts lying behind the management of the Chinese rural fringe, this introductory chapter has attempted to show prospective synergies of this linkage. Future sustainable development scenarios for the fringe will be determined by the combination of an increasing demand for quality in these areas with successful attempts by institutional reforms aimed at reducing the purely financial need for municipal expansion. In the meantime, the way the fringe will be conceptualized, and consequently the way costs and benefits of its development or preservation will be accounted, opens potential avenues for further research requiring, along the way, in-depth theoretical study or experimentation on real case studies, as shown in the chapters in this book. This is an attempt to shed a light on an emerging broad planning issue, namely rural fringe management, for the study of sustainable ways to urbanize China.

References

Arnason, A., Shucksmith, M. and Vergunst, J. (eds) 2009. *Comparing Rural Development. Continuity and Change in the Countryside of Western Europe.* Farnham: Ashgate.

Bengston, D., Fletcher, J.O. and Nelson, K.C. 2004. 'Public policies for managing urban growth and protecting open space: policy instruments and lessons learned in the United States'. *Landscape and Urban Planning*, 69(2–3), 271–86.

Brenner, N. and Schmid, C. 2014. 'The "urban age" in question'. *International Journal of Urban and Regional Research*, 38(3), 731–55.

Bryceson, D.F. 1996. 'De-agrarianisation and rural employment in sub-Saharan Africa: a sectoral perspective'. *World Development*, 24(1), 97–111.

CPGPRC (Central People's Government of the People's Republic of China) 1999. Land Management Act, Amendment, Beijing (In Chinese).

CPGPRC (Central People's Government of the People's Republic of China) 2007. China's Property Rights Law, Beijing (In Chinese).

Den Hartog, H. (ed.) 2011. *Shanghai New Towns. Searching for Community and Identity in a Sprawling Metropolis*. Rotterdam: 010 Publishers.

Dick, H.W. and Rimmer, P.J. 1998. 'Beyond the third world city: the new urban geography of South-East Asia'. *Urban Studies*, 35(12), 2303–21.

Ding, C. 2007. 'Policy and praxis of land acquisition in China'. *Land Use Policy*, 24(1), 1–13.

Friedmann, J. 2005. *China's Urban Transition*. Minneapolis and London: University of Minnesota Press.

Gallent, N., Bianconi, M. and Andersson, J. 2006. *Planning on the Edge: The Context for Planning at the Rural-Urban Fringe*. London and New York: Routledge.

He, S., Liu, Y., Webster, C. and Wu, F. 2009. 'Property rights distribution, entitlement failure and the impoverishment of landless farmers in China'. *Urban Studies*, 46(9), 1925–49.

Healey, P. 'Institutionalist analysis, communicative planning, and shaping places'. *Journal of Planning Education and Research*, 19 (1999), 111–21.

Hsing, Y-T. 2010. *The Great Urban Transformation: Politics of Land and Property in China*. New York: Oxford University Press.

Huang, P.C. 1993. 'Public sphere/civil society in China?: The third realm between state and society'. *Modern China*, 19(2), 216–40.

Huang, P.C.C. 2011. 'China's new-age small farms and their vertical integration: agribusiness'. *Modern China*, 37(2), 107–34.

Hudala, D., Winarso, H. and Woltjer, J. 2007. 'Peri-urbanization in east Asia. A new challenge for planning?' *International Development Planning Review*, 29(4), 503–19.

Lang, G. and Miao, B. 2013. 'Food security for China's cities'. *International Planning Studies*, 18(1), 5–20.

Li, I. and O'Brien, K.J. 2008. 'Protest leadership in rural China'. *The China Quarterly*, 193, 1–23.

Lichtenberg, E. and Ding, C. 2006. 'Assessing farmland protection policy in China'. *Land Use Policy*, 25(1), 59–68.

Long, H., Liu, Y., Li, X. and Chen, Y. 2010. 'Building new countryside in China: a geographical perspective'. *Land Use Policy*, 27(2), 457–70.

McGee, T.G. 1991. 'The emergence of desakota regions in Asia: expanding a hypothesis', in *The Extended Metropolis: Settlements Transition in Asia*, edited by N. Ginsburg et al. Honolulu: University of Hawaii Press.

OECD 2013. *OECD Economic Surveys: China 2013*. Paris: OECD Publishing.

Qadeer, M.A. 2000. 'Ruralopolises: the spatial organisation and residential land economy of high-density rural regions in South Asia'. *Urban Studies*, 37(9), 1583–603.

Ran, T. and Xu, Z. 2007. 'Urbanization, rural land system and social security for migrant farmers in China'. *Journal of Development Studies*, 43(7), 1301–20.

Ran, T. 2012. The issue of land in China's transition and urbanization [Online: Lincoln Institute of Land Policy Working Paper, wp13tr1]. Available at: https://www.lincolninst.edu/pubs/dl/2225_1557_Ran_WP13TR1.pdf [accessed: 26 June 2014].

Richardson, H.W. and Bae, C.H.C. 2004. *Urban Sprawl in Western Europe and the United States*. Farnham: Ashgate.

Simon, D. 2008. 'Urban environments: issues on the peri-urban fringe'. *Annual Review of Environment and Resources*, 33, 167–85.

SCPRC (State Council of the People's Republic of China) 2014. New urbanization plan, 2014–2020, Beijing (In Chinese).

Tacoli, C. 1998. 'Rural-urban interactions: a guide to the literature'. *Environment and Urbanization*, 10(1), 147–66.

Tan, M., Robinson, G.M. and Li, X. 2011. 'Urban spatial development and land use in Beijing: implications from London's experiences'. *Journal of Geographical Sciences*, 21(1), 49–64.

Tomlinson, R. 2012. 'Does Shanghai have slums?' *International Development Planning Review*, 34(2), V–XVI.

Van Dijk, T. 2009. 'Who is in charge of the urban fringe? Neoliberalism, open space preservation and growth control'. *Planning Practice and Research*, 24(3), 343–61.

Verdini, G. 2014. 'The costs of urban growth at the fringe of a Chinese city. Evidence from Jinshi village in Suzhou'. *International Planning Development Review*, 36(4), 413–34.

Webster, D. and Muller, I. 2004. 'The challenges of peri-urban growth in East Asia: the case of China Hangzhou-Ningbo corridor', in *Enhancing Urban Management in East Asia*, edited by M. Freire and B. Yuen. Farnham: Ashgate, 23–54.

Wheeler, S. 2002. 'The new regionalism. Key characteristic of an emerging movement'. *Journal of the American Planning Association*, 68(3), 267–78.

Wu, F. 2007. 'Beyond gradualism: China's urban revolution and emerging cities', in *China's Emerging Cities. The Making of New Urbanism*, edited by F. Wu. New York: Routledge.

Wu, J. 2008. 'Global integration, growth patterns and sustainable development: a case study of the peri-urban areas of shanghai', in *World Cities and Urban Form. Fragmented, Polycentric, Sustainable?*, edited by M. Jenks et al. New York: Routledge.

Wu, W. 2008. 'Migrant settlement and spatial distribution in metropolitan Shanghai'. *The Professional Geographer*, 60(1), 101–20.

Xie, Y., Batty, M. and Zhao, K. 2007. 'Simulating emergent urban form using agent-based modelling: desakota in the Suzhou-Wuxian region in China'. *Annals of the Associations of American Geographers*, 97(3), 477–95.

Yanyun Man, J. 2011. 'Local public finance in China: an overview', in *China's Local Public Finance in Transition*, edited by J. Yanyun Man and Y. Hong. Cambridge: Lincoln Institute of Land Policy.

Zeng, B. and Ryan, C. 2012. 'Assisting the poor in China through tourism development: a review of research'. *Tourism Management*, 33(2), 239–48.

Zeng, D.Z. 2012. 'China's special economic zones and industrial clusters: the engines for growth'. *Journal of International Commerce, Economics and Policy*, 3(3), 1–28.

Zhang, T. 2000. 'Land market forces and government's role in sprawl. The case of China'. *Cities*, 17(2), 123–35.

Zhang, Q.F. and Donaldson, J.A. 2010. 'From peasants to farmers: peasant differentiation, labor regimes, and land-rights institutions in China's agrarian transition'. *Politics & Society*, 38(4), 458–90.

Zhao, P. 2012. 'Urban-rural transition in China's metropolises: new trends in peri-urbanisation in Beijing'. *International Development Planning Review*, 34(3), 269–94.

Zhu, Y. 2007. 'China's floating population and their settlements intention in the cities: beyond the hukou reform'. *Habitat International*, 31(1), 65–76.

Chapter 2

Collaborative Approaches for Planning the Rural Areas of Chinese Cities

Yu Guo and Sheng Zhong

The rapid urbanization process in China has posed significant threats to land resources not only in quantity but also in quality. In the peri-urban areas of Chinese cities, the pressures from urban sprawl have resulted in scattered construction lands mixed with cultivated lands. This highly inefficient use of rural construction, especially in peri-urban areas, has been identified as a major problem and, consequently, rural land consolidation has been increasingly considered as a priority for reaching more sustainable rural planning outcomes. Based on the existing experiences of land ticket reform, this chapter argues that market-based land ticket represents a promising approach to China's rural land consolidation practises and should be allowed to be used in a wider scope. However, reform of the existing land ticket and rural land consolidation processes is also needed to ensure better results. A perspective from participative and collaborative planning will shed light on how to achieve this outcome.

Rural Land Consolidation: an Urban Issue in China

Reform since the late 1970s has resulted in salient changes in China. In the past several decades, the growing population, accelerating pace of urbanization and degrading environment have posed significant threats to land resources not only in quantity but also in quality. Under the pressure of food security, urban expansion and the irregularity of the rural land management system, land consolidation, especially carried out in the rural areas, has become a hotly debated and urgent issue in contemporary China. Land consolidation is firstly put forward in the National Land Development and Consolidation Plan (2001–10) in the year of 2003, along with land reclamation and land development.

Each of the three factors that shaped the rural land consolidation process in China, namely food security, urban expansion and the irregularity of the rural land management system, has distinguished circumstances. According to the most recent result from the second national land survey published by the Ministry of Land and Resources (The Second National Land Survey Report 2013), the total amount of cultivated land in China was approximately 135.4 million hectares (2.03 billion mu) at the end of 2009. Even though the figure meets the 'red-line' requirement of 1.8 billion mu (120 million hectares) set by the central government, China's per capita cultivated land is only slightly above 0.1 hectares (1.52 mu), which is less than half of world average. Food security remains a central government concern, considering the miserable experience from the Great Famine from 1959 to 1961. In the former Premier Wen's government work report in 2007, the central government set the 1.8 billion mu (120 million hectares) cultivated land as a bottom line based on data of cultivated land, construction land, potential cultivated land resources, population and food demand. From the state's perspective, food self-sufficiency is necessary for both national food security and social stability. Based primarily on his observation of the rapid decline in cultivated land, Lester Brown (1995) predicted and warned that China would not be able to feed itself because the country had begun to lose the capacity to grow enough food. Notwithstanding, this concern has not yet come to reality, and a number of issues, such as maintaining a dynamic balance of cultivated land (as introduced as 'increasing and decreasing balance' in the following context) and improving farming technologies, have raised the public awareness (Yang and Li 2000; Zhu 2010). An equally astonishing result from the land surveys is that around 2 per cent of the country's cultivated land had been seriously polluted with heavy metals and, therefore, could not be used for growing safe food anymore (The Second National Land Survey Report 2013). Undeniably, the heavy metal contamination is by no means unrelated to the rapid industrialization process in China, mirroring the tension between food security and industrial development. According to another official report issued by the Ministry of Environment Protection, a total of 36,000 hectares of cultivated land had suffered from metal contamination, leading to 12 million tons of contaminated agricultural production and RMB 20 billion of economic loss. Due to different measurements and times of investigation, data from the Ministry of Land and Resources and from the Ministry of Environment Protection differ slightly. Nonetheless, a consensus has been reached that the tense relationship between land use and food security goes far beyond the quantitative bottom line, as qualitative land degradation due to soil pollution was extremely serious. What is more alarming, these two dimensions of cultivated land change tend to overlap spatially in the developed industrial areas such as the Pearl River Delta, the Yangtze River Delta and the Jingjinji Region, where industrialization and economic growth have been fast in the past several decades.

Apart from food security, pressures on land also stem from the huge urbanization process. China is witnessing the greatest urban transformation in contemporary times: the proportion of people living in the urban areas has climbed from 17 per cent to 53.7 per cent between 1978 and 2013(National Bureau of Statistics of China 2014). It has been predicted that by 2020, urbanization in China will reach 58 per cent and another 162 million people will become urban dwellers (Department Research Centre of the State Council 2010). Between 2000 and 2010, in the 515 metropolitan areas which cover most urbanized areas in China, the expansion speed of built-up areas was even higher than urban population growth, reported at 52 per cent and 44 per cent, respectively (OECD, 2013). Since the year

2000, public information shows the regional variation of land transformation from agricultural to urban use is significant, ranging from less than 5 per cent in the west to more than 10 per cent in the east (Liu 2008). Moreover, land has become a key instrument influencing the direction of the urbanization process in China. From one perspective, the demand for urban construction land is inflexibly and sharply increasing. According to Wei and Zhao (2009), the urban growth pattern of China's mega-cities can be considered as a hybrid of two forms. The first form is urban spill-over, defined as the significantly emerging 'development zones' that are often located in the vicinity of urban centres and the proliferation of residential developments in suburban areas. The second form is local urban sprawl which is seen as the other group of 'development zones' built by governments at district, township, and village levels, and often disconnected from the main urban area. On the other hand, as elaborated in the previous chapter, compared with the early days of economic reform where land use in the urban fringe was mainly industry-driven, there has been a shift to high-end residential development around the main mega-cities like Beijing and Shanghai. From another perspective, construction land for industrialization and residential use is supplied through two mechanisms. The first mechanism is land requisitioning. Since the land in the development of urban spill-over is transferred from collectively owned to state-owned land, this process is currently controlled and regulated by the state, although the implementation process in the real world is far from satisfactory. The other mechanism through which local urban sprawl takes place does not involve ownership transfer and this process in general lacks proper regulation partially due to the irregularity of the rural land management system. This situation brings more pressure to land supply. In addition, policy constraints on the transfer of rural land also aggravate China's land supply problems.

The encroachment of development zones, highways and roads, and rural settlements on agricultural land has dramatically altered the rural landscape (Ho and Lin, 2004). If food security and urban expansion are two exogenous reasons behind rural land consolidation, the irregularity of the rural land management system in terms of rural land ownership and use strategy can be seen as an endogenous one that makes rural land consolidation an imperative. In advanced economies, the property rights of land are clearly defined to ensure economic productivity and efficiency. As a counter-example in China, the Constitution stipulates that the state has the *de jure* ownership of urban land and rural land belongs to the local collectives; additionally, the Land Administration Law specifies that the state can requisition any land when it is in the ambiguously defined 'public interest' (Hsing 2010). In the name of 'public interest' and driven by pecuniary benefits, local governments in the rural area are able to expropriate farmland to urban constructions, even illegally (Hsing 2010). On the other hand, land that is kept rural is also poorly managed. The opposite direction of change in the rural population and rural construction land could be an interesting phenomenon to illustrate the inefficient use of rural land: from 1996 to 2007, the rural population decreased by 15.97 per cent while rural residential land increased by 18.28 per cent (China Statistical Book 2012; Long *et al.* 2012). In addition, this reverse variation can be even larger in some fast-developing regions such as Guangdong. Evidence also lies in the emerging 'hollow villages' (*kongxin cun*), or those villages with a large proportion of underused residential land. These villages have become increasingly and widely common in China nowadays (Ho and Lin 2004). Therefore, if land can be used more efficiently and rationally in the rural area, existing construction land can accommodate a larger number of people without sacrificing more cultivated land.

Increasing and Decreasing Balance: Is There a Way Out?

Increasing and decreasing balance (IDB) (*jianshe yongdi zengjian guagou*) is an innovative practice to enhance the developmental potential of land through intensification of rural construction land (often referred to as 'rural land consolidation') and the spatial transfer of development rights (Long *et al.* 2012). Basically, rural collectives are encouraged or pushed (and sometimes even coerced) to relocate to newly built villages of a higher density at another location. New villages may be built by government, villagers or developers and they may occupy cultivated land in their own villages or in another location following the merger process of two or more villages. But once relocation is complete, the old residential land in the original location is required to be reclaimed as cultivated land. As the land area of old residential land is larger than that of newly built residential areas due to land use intensification, a net increase of cultivated land is generated. The cultivated land red-line policy requires that total areas of cultivated land must not be decreased while the land use intensification of rural construction land and reclamation of old residential land can create a surplus of cultivated land (often temporary), which makes it possible to increase construction land by the amount of this surplus (often called 'the construction land use quota'). In addition, the IDB policy allows this land use quota to be transferred to urbanized areas within the same county-level jurisdiction to satisfy urbanization needs and the higher demand for construction land there. Although spatial quota transfer is possible, this policy was initially designed to help primarily rural communities. This means, in theory, local collectives should be able to decide on the use of the construction land use quota. For example, they may choose to retire the quota (in this case, no additional construction land is generated while total cultivated land is increased), use the quota themselves for township or village economic development (such as building factories, commercial venues or public facilities) or transfer it to another location (often urbanized areas).

IDB policy was not the result of grand design. Rather, it evolved gradually through a series of central government policy statements. As early as 2000, the Central Committee of the Communist Part of China and the State Council jointly issued 'A Few Opinions on Promoting Healthy Development of Small Cities and Towns' and for the first time it floated the idea of saving land through rural land consolidation and using the saved land to aid urban development. Later in 2004, another State Council policy document entitled 'Decisions about Deepening Reform and Tightening Land Management' articulated and encouraged the practice of linking increasing urban construction land use with decreasing construction land use in rural areas. Several ministries in subsequent years published a series of documents regulating operational details, culminating in the release of 'Management Methods for Pilot Programs of Increasing and Decreasing Balance of Urban-Rural Construction Land' by the Ministry of Land Resource (MLR) (Liu and Li 2012). Like other types of reforms, IDB was firstly implemented in a select small number of experimental localities and a larger scope for application took place later. For example, in 2006, Shandong, Tianjin, Jiangsu, Hubei and Sichuan were first authorized by MLR to implement IDB. In 2008 and 2009, 19 more provincial level units were added to the authorization list under the backdrop of the large-scale national economic stimulus plan. This triggered the large-scale and even problematic, uncontrolled IDB practises nationwide (Liu and Li 2012).

As mentioned earlier, extra land use quota does not have to be used for construction purposes, although in reality, it always is. In the Chinese context, the motivation behind large-scale rural land consolidation programs and IDB practice lies in the local government's insatiable thirst for urban construction land and the connected public revenue. Such motivation is urban-area-oriented and may not be aligned well with other rural-collective-oriented objectives of IDB such as the protection of cultivated land and socio-economic development for peasants and rural communities. These rural issues are often referred to as 'san-nong problems' (meaning agriculture, rural villages and peasants in Chinese). In the hierarchical Chinese political system, urban governments have much more power than rural collectives and hence the free will of rural communities to decide on the use of land use quota is more theoretical than real. As a matter of fact, local government frequently use coercive means to force villagers to undertake land consolidation programs and then grab the extra land use quota without rural collective consent or without fully compensating the land-losing villagers. This reality has led to mounting grievances from rural communities involved in land consolidation (Lu 2008; Xu 2012). And, ironically, such injustice may even be carried out under the lofty rhetoric of 'urban-rural integration'. Conventionally, land use planning for rural and urban areas in China has been done separately for various historical reasons. This has been identified as a consequence as well as a contributing factor to urban-rural duality. Facing the increasingly enlarged urban-rural disparity and the implicit social stability problems, in 2002, the 16th Party Congress raised the idea of coordinated urban-rural development (CURD, *chengxiang tongchou*). Subsequent slogans of 'socialist scientific development', 'harmonious society' and 'new socialist countryside' reverberate around this policy direction towards supporting rural communities and urban-rural integration (Zhong 2011). In land use planning practice, the CURD idea was interpreted by practitioners to mean coordinated planning of urban and rural land simultaneously or, simply put, covering urban and rural areas in one map (communication with planners).

As the transfer of the land use quota involves a sending rural area and a receiving urban area, an IDB plan has to put urban and rural land together into one map, as is often used in conventional Chinese planning, and this gives a superficial impression of 'coordination'. However, the irony is that IDB programs that were carried out under the CURD policy framework actually created or aggravated the exact 'san-nong problems' that CURD policies were meant to solve because the transfer of land use quota under asymmetric power is equivalent to the transfer of land and related development benefits from rural to urban areas. The ultimate result is unavoidably the enlarging urban-rural disparity. In other words, below the surface of the coordinated land use plan was the old story of exploiting rural communities by urban regimes.

A large number of IDB practises are intended for the eventual transfer of land use quota to urban areas. How the land quota is transferred impacts differently on the distribution of benefits to various IDB participants. Currently, two broad ways are used in the transfer: administrative transfer and market allocation. The former accounts for the majority of land involved and it gives local government control over the transfer process in terms of pace of change, compensation level and transfer price: and government can also get a larger share of the transfer benefit in this opaque process. Market allocation, which can be represented by land ticket (*dipiao*) trading in the formal rural land exchange, as has been implemented in the pioneering experience of Chongqing, is a more transparent process and can guarantee rural collectives and villagers more decision-making power and hence greater tangible benefits. In reality, in the case of Chongqing, the two means of construction land use quota circulation coexist. Although land ticket was a big innovation to improve land use efficiently, because local government wants to maintain control of IDB process, it imposes an annual limit on the amount of land use quota that can be transferred through the formal market (or land ticket). However, this policy creates a dual-track system which leads to unequal outcomes for rural communities involved in land consolidation and IDB practises (Huang 2013). The following section explains how land ticket trading in Chongqing has evolved and what opportunities and constraints this local innovation represents.

Chongqing Model: Opportunities and Constraints

Among the different cities of China, Chongqing is characterized by its distinguished development path which has received great attention under the name of 'Chongqing model' or 'Chongqing experience'. The revitalization of Chongqing can be traced back to the year 1997 when it was upgraded to the fourth and only centrally administered municipality in west China. Not much later, at the end of 1990s, the 4th Plenum of the 15th Communist Party of China Central Committee put forward the 'great development of Western region' with Chongqing being considered as the core city that could bring positive externalities to the surrounding cities and towns in west China. The period from 1996 to 2010 has witnessed a significant change in the urbanization rate in Chongqing and the rate of urban population increased from 29.5 per cent to 53.0 per cent (Statistic Yearbook 2010). The other distinguishing feature is that, in general, Chongqing is seen as an inland city of China, experiencing population outflow: in 2010, the number of people who moved out of Chongqing was 5.23 million, while this number declined to 945,200 if in-migration is considered.

In the year 2007, the State Council approved Chongqing as one of the two pilot cities for national coordinated urban-rural development reform, allowing it to embark on a series of institutional changes to reduce urban-rural gap in areas of social housing provision, the improvement of public service, reform of the household registration system, land management and so on. When Chongqing was selected, the city region had a large rural population and had experienced a widening urban-rural gap in the previous few years. For example, in 2007, about 80 per cent of the population lived in rural areas and the urban-rural income ratio increased from 3.1:1 in 1997 to 4:1 in 2006. In addition, the city also had large areas of remote mountainous regions in dire need of social-economic development (Zhang 2007). In addition to the boost from the central state, the Chongqing government also took a proactive role in designing and implementing local development strategies. At the same time, the role of government in the local development of Chongqing has been paid significant attention. According to the mayor of Chongqing, the source of government expenditure consists of three parts: government budget, land lease fees and budget of the state-owned assets. In comparison to other places in China, the third resource, state-owned assets, is rather a speciality in Chongqing which, according to the cadres, has enabled the government to spend more on social security, education, public health and public service (Huang 2009).

Although many areas of Chongqing's CURD development bears a socialist tint (for example higher reliance on state-owned enterprises, political mobilization, large-scale public housing programs and so on), the city somehow paradoxically pioneered the marketization of rural land use rights. In particular, in the recent half decade, development and reform in Chongqing's rural land management system have drawn increasing interest. On the 4th of December in 2008, the first 'rural land exchange' was established in Chongqing to facilitate the circulation of rural land use rights, including those for agricultural and construction land. The way of naming the land ticket (*di piao*), which can be traded in the rural land exchange, is borrowed from the Chinese term 'gu piao', which means shares in the stock market (Chen and Yao 2011). The intention of establishing the exchange is to trade the land use quota generated from consolidating rural construction land (Huang 2011). With official certification that formal rural construction land has been converted to cultivated land, the land ticket may be used for sale at the 'exchange' (Huang 2011).The key principle of land ticket is the 'increasing and decreasing balance' as discussed earlier.

From a theoretical perspective, the emergence of land ticket can be considered as an institutional innovation in land reform, bringing alternative solutions to social, economic and environmental problems. Since China launched the economic reform and opening-up policy in 1978, the income inequality between rural and urban area in China has been widely increasing. According to the official data, from 1990 to 2012, the urban-rural per capita net income gap has gradually increased from 824 to 16,648 Yuan (National Bureau of Statistics of China 2012). Meanwhile, urban regeneration and urban expansion processes occurring throughout China have also aggravated urban-rural disparity although severity of the situation varies among regions. For example, the transformation process of urban villages in Guangzhou has resulted in a number of millionaires because urban villages have become the new urban centres. Moreover, an empirical study based on 12 cities has found that the geographical proximity from rural village to urban centre plays a critical role in determining the compensation for demolished rural residential plots (Wang *et al.* 2012). That is to say, people living in the urban fringe area can benefit more from the urban expansion process than inhabitants living in the rural area. In the Chongqing case, the municipal government reiterated that, in theory, 85 per cent of pure profit in the land ticket sales should go to villagers and the remaining 15 per cent goes to collectives (Xue 2011). Considering land tickets are normally produced in the rural area far away from the city, the success in designing the land ticket lies in involving those peasants in periphery areas and allowing them to share in the profit from urban development. In addition, this economic advantage can directly make a contribution to the social environment. The dual land ownership system in China has determined a high value gap between rural and urban areas. Data show that in a group of 17 provinces in China, the amount of money used for compensating land-losing farmers was only 2.2 per cent of the sale price received by government due to the unfair compensating formula (Landesa, China Renmin University and Michigan State University 2012). Especially in recent years, the social instability caused by widespread grievances and increasing number of appeals by farmers has become a major concern for the central government as well as local cadres. The Chongqing government has set two preconditions in the implementation of land ticket to avoid such social problems: the first one is that individual projects have to get approval from at least two-thirds of affected land owners (collective members) before it goes to the land consolidation and reclamation process; the other one is that those peasants are expected to have stable incomes and a decent place to live before they leave their old homes (Chongqing Municipality 2008). Although land ticket has only been promoted in limited areas, its potential application throughout the country is huge. There are approximately 18 million hectares of rural construction land nationwide and that is 2.5 times more than the amount of urban construction land (Wang 2013). At the same time, a large number of former rural residents have migrated to urban areas. Therefore, land ticket trading offers great potential for improving land use efficiency and protecting the rural landscape.

In a recently released government work report, the mayor of Chongqing reiterated that the most important resource for promoting integrated rural-urban development is still rural land (Huang 2014). Referring to the official report, 8,800 hcctarcs (132,000 mu) of rural construction land had been traded in Chongqing through land ticket (Lian 2014). While acknowledging the great achievement that land ticket has made so far and the potential it may realize in the future, the report also remains cautious of land ticket's role in preserving cultivated land and supporting urban and rural development because of several perceived constraints to implementing the land ticket policy. The following discusses three constraints that are evident in the ticket transaction: the clarification of land ownership, profit distribution and the relocation of land-loss farmers.

The clarification of land ownership is crucially important in the production of land ticket. In the process of consolidating idle and underutilized rural construction land from farmers, villagers are often unclear about their right to rural collective land due to the ambiguous property right definition and villagers' general lack of legal knowledge. Some even believe that they own their residential plot as private property (Ho 2001). To some extent, the uncertainty stems from the emergence of 'private property' (*ziliudi*) introduced in the early 1960s which regulates that farmers can use the land for personal needs. However, the difference between *de facto* use right and *de jure* ownership right is significant. As written in the Constitution, apart from some specific defined state-owned land in the rural area, the local inhabitants collectively own the rural land. Thus, the land ticket policy touches on the interests of every household and each individual in the rural area. In turn, how to clarify land ownership becomes extremely difficult, but important.

The profit distribution of land ticket can be considered as the key innovation in this reform because the peasants can get higher compensation compared to previous policies. However, money is always a controversial issue and with land ticket there is no exception. Before land ticket was introduced, the financial compensation farmers can get back from land-loss simply depended on the value of attached agricultural products. Since the sale price of land is always significantly higher than the acquisition price, while the compensation farmers get is often inadequate for their livelihood, this results in potential threats to social stability in many rural areas of China. A key feature of the land ticket exchange process is the decisive role of market. As initially designed, after the consolidation of rural construction land, the produced quotas are expected to sell through auction. Although the pure profit is shared between villagers and collectives according to the clear division of 85 per cent and 15 per cent, the information released to the public mainly provides the sale price of the land ticket instead of just the pure profit. Then the underlying part is land reclamation, not only in terms of the payer of the fee but also about the assessment of reclamation quality. Even though the calculation of pure profit can be related to a series of processes and involves different groups of people, it is not easy to consider all the procedures and participants in real practice.

Last but not least, the relocation of land-loss farmers in this pilot land reform is a critical issue. The general approach is to densely build apartments in the towns or urban fringe nearby and then relocate the peasants in these dwellings. In some cases, several villages are merged into one village through coercive administrative and land readjustment. However, such practice is likely to break the existing social and cultural ties and does substantial harm to the local community. The alternative is that farmers are given sufficient compensation so that they can buy an individual house or apartment with their savings and received compensation. Nonetheless, either of the two ways can result in a large volume of population moving from rural to urban areas. In 2010, several places such as Guangdong, Shaanxi and Chongqing announced that rural collective owned land could be dealt with by an urban 'hukou' (household registration) for rural people. However, this swap was prohibited after only one year by the State Council (Zhang 2011). According to official calculations, RMB 130,000 is needed to cover public and private expenditure in order to enable a rural person to transfer to urban status (Chinese Academy of Social Science 2013). In addition to financial pressures, aggressively relocating land-losing villagers in densely built residential apartments provided by local government can lead to potential problems, such as drastic change of lifestyles as well as the conflicts between previous dwellers and newcomers.

Currently, the dual-track land system and related social-economic problems in transitional China have made the urbanization process extremely complicated and difficult. Considering the opportunities and constraints of the land ticket practice, this chapter argues that market-based land ticket represents a promising approach to China's rural land consolidation practises and should be allowed to be used in a wider scope. However, reform of the existing land ticket and rural land consolidation processes is also needed to ensure better results. The next section gives a few recommendations on land ticket and rural land consolidation reform in China from a participative and collaborative perspective.

Towards a Participative and Collaborative Planning: a Proposal for Land Ticket Reform in China

Urbanization and urban planning do not possess the characteristics of independence and self-determination (Dear and Scott 1981), and both are deeply embedded within society and historically develop with society as a whole (Scott and Roweis 1977). In line with the development of society, the tensions and conflicts among unequal power relations and competing interests groups impede the advancement of our contemporary world (Healey 2006). Recently, increasing attention has been paid to planning as a communicative or collaborative process within which political objectives and public participation can be absorbed (Healey 1999; Allmendinger 2002). According to Healey (2006), collaborative planning is oriented by an ethics of inclusion, asserting that 'all those with a stake in a place should have a right to give voice and be heard in the development of policies about what should happen there'. To prepare a proposal for rural land consolidation in China, collaborative planning is intended to be investigated from three mutually dependent elements: participation and communication within and among different groups of people, collaborative governance and respecting place identities and trajectories.

The prominence of participation and communication does not only mean that an agreement has to be reached on a particular issue, more importantly it recognizes multiple claims from different individuals and highlights the process of discussion and negotiation. Considering the collective ownership of rural land in China, one of the most distinguished features in the process of land ticket reform is the huge number of rural people influenced by the implementation of policies. Accordingly, to establish a participation model through which different stakeholders can be involved in the land consolidation process becomes critically important. A promising example can be seen in Liujie town located in the rural area of Chengdu (National School of Development at Peking University 2009). The process was initiated by local government, and after the local governors visited all the households to introduce the content and meaning of land consolidation, a 'villagers' discussion institute' (*cunmin yishi hui*) consisting of responsible elderly people was set up. Each of the institute members was elected by 5–15 households in the village, and they had the responsibility to clarify land right and discuss it with those villagers who had different opinions. Upon reaching the consensus of land right, local government started to implement the land consolidation process. This example is consistent with the two steps proposed by Healey (2006) – firstly, people are enabled to give voice to their concerns and needs; secondly, and more important, action should be taken through a series of clear and regulated procedures. In addition, based on an original study on the participative role of villagers in village planning, Yin and Chen (2013) also suggest that villagers' participation plays an extremely critical role in plan implementation. Apart from empowering the rural community, another important approach to encourage participation and communication among villagers is to improve their awareness of the right over land and other technical issues through long-term knowledge education and short-term skills training. Both rural land consolidation and land ticket are complex administrative mechanisms. Without stakeholders' full understanding of such processes and their potential benefits and pitfalls, it is hard to ensure true and effective participation. Participation is not just about allowing participants to be physically present at the negotiation table, but, more importantly, it means that all stakeholders are fully aware of their potential and constraints and have the capacity and skills to advance their interests on an equal footing. Lack of knowledge by certain participants would place them in a disadvantageous position against others, hence reproducing power asymmetry in the existing system. As technical experts, local planners can possibly assume the role of imparting knowledge and training villagers. If that happens, it would signify a fundamental transformation of the planning profession in China.

Ensuring all relevant stakeholders are present and allowing them to raise all potential concerns and share benefits is key in a collaborative process. However, to make this process more just and sustainable, formal governance is also important (Healey 2006). To alleviate the conflicts between uneven power relations that cause much existing grievance, institutionalized rules and regulations from higher levels of government (for example national or provincial level) are necessary. Moreover, collaborative governance from both horizontal and vertical perspectives becomes difficult. The rationale behind horizontal collaboration is to prevent territorial competition and promote efficient cooperation. In the case of land ticket reform, vertical coordination in policy-making is crucial from an institutional perspective. Since land ticket policy is a trial reform carried out only in a limited number of places, the critical challenge lies in how to allow localities to experiment with innovative approaches while keeping all practises within the framework of central policies. As already mentioned, rural land reform cannot be separated from the existing land ownership regime or the household registration system. While central rules or policies should allow flexibility in local practises, it is also important for localities to make detailed guidelines and plans for land ticket reform within the scope of national legal and administrative frameworks. In addition, the making of such guidelines or plans at the local level should also be participative and, therefore, a wider public, in particular including rural communities, must be consulted in order to ensure political support of these initiatives and subsequent successful implementation. At the same time, different localities may learn from the Chongqing experience by drawing strength from the Chongqing model while trying to resolve the problems encountered there, such as lack of transparency in cost-accounting of rural land consolidation projects or poor quality control of land reclamation. For example, in the local plan for land ticket reform, procedures for stakeholder participation, cost-accounting for different collaborative project participants and steps to check land quality must be clearly spelled out and strictly regulated. If clear cost-counting can be ensured, a formula for benefit distribution based on land ticket trading price may be replaced by those based on land ticket profit after taking into consideration land consolidation costs. Profit-based formulas are expected to better compensate project participants who have contributed various types of resources for the rural land consolidation processes and enhance the attractiveness of participation in such projects.

In the longer term, the success of land ticket reform is also dependent on the attractiveness or demand for the land tickets. Higher desirability for land ticket would clearly draw more participants, including local villagers, into rural land consolidation processes. To increase demand for land tickets, the government may consider increasing the types of uses for land tickets. For example, the geographic constraints of land ticket trading may be relaxed so that it can be traded within prefecture-level cities or within the provinces. It may also be possible to allow land tickets to be used for purposes other than obtaining extra construction land. For instance, land ticket may also be used for obtaining extra building density in urban redevelopment projects. In that sense, land ticket will not just represent a land use quota, but, more accurately, a development right. These long-term changes towards more land ticket flexibility at the institutional level can only be done after short-term reform to improve existing land use quota trading is successfully carried out.

Even though experimental land ticket reform has not yet become a nationwide project, it is likely that this pilot can be extended to the whole country. It does not mean that the specified policies have to be exactly the same from region to region; on the contrary, the significance of local identities should be acknowledged and adapted. The qualities and trajectories of places is the long-term implication of local development, created by the interaction between economic, social, environmental and political relations (Healey 2006). Moreover, place can be seen as a material and social space in which cultural capitals are formed and transformed (Healey 1997). Respecting the qualities and trajectories of places can facilitate in creating a place-focused understanding and in further promoting the participation of all stakeholders within a place. For example, the rural cultures in China diverge in different regions. In the coastal cities, villagers acknowledge traditional clan and family structures and people in a village rooted from one family tend to reach consensus through peaceful means. In terms of land ticket, which includes many procedures like land ownership clarification and land-loss farmer relocation, it is crucial to respect the local identity, such as people's lifestyles and the way through which people can pool ideas and information.

In conclusion, reform towards a participative and collaborative planning model, though not conceived as a panacea, can somehow help to address the many problems of existing rural land consolidation and land ticket trading in China. In particular, an appropriate classification of villages in the rural area such as central villages, relocation villages and preservation villages can make rural land use more efficient and environment-friendly. These efforts will help China meet the multiple challenges of economic development, cultivated land conservation and urbanization in the years to come. Given the diversity of localities nationwide, a creative and flexible mechanism, through which land tickets are used and traded, can be established if local stakeholders are well prepared and empowered, fundamental institutional frameworks are established and rich local traditions are respected.

References

Allmendinger, P. 2009. *Planning Theory*. Palgrave Macmillan.

Brown, L.R. 1995. *Who Will Feed China?: Wake-Up Call for a Small Planet*. WW Norton & Company.

Chen, Y. and Yao, J.W. 2011. 'Chongqing's "land certificate" trial is to be continued' ('chongqing 'dipiao' jixushi'). Caijing. [Online, 17 January] Available at: http://magazine.caijing.com.cn/2011–01–16/110620709.html [accessed: 16 February 2014].

Chinese Academy of Social Science, 2013. 'Blue book of cities in China' ('Chengshi Lanpishu'). Social Sciences Academic Press. [Online, 16 January] Available at: http://magazine.caijing.com.cn/2011–01–16/110620709.html [accessed: 16 February 2014].

Chongqing Municipality, 2008. 'Trial regulation on rural land trade house management in Chongqing' ('chongqing nongcun tudi jiaoyisuo guanli zanxing banfa'). [Online, 1 December]. Available at: http://www.doc88.com/ p-299203255825.html [accessed: 16 February 2014].

Dear, M. and Scott, A.J. 1981. *Urbanization and Urban Planning in Capitalist Society*. Routledge Kegan & Paul.

Development Research Center of the State Council, 2010. *China's Urbanization: Prospects, Strategies and Policies*. China Development Press.

Healey, P. 1997. *Collaborative Planning: Shaping Places in Fragmented Societies*. UBc Press.

Healey, P. 1999. 'Institutionalist analysis, communicative planning, and shaping places'. *Journal of Planning Education and Research*, 19, 111–21.

Ho, P. 2001. 'Who owns China's land? Policies, property rights and deliberate institutional ambiguity'. *The China Quarterly*, 166, 394–421.

Ho, S.P. and Lin, G.C. 2004. 'Converting Land to Nonagricultural Use in China's Coastal Provinces Evidence from Jiangsu'. *Modern China*, 30(1), 81–112.

Hsing, Y. 2010. *The Great Urban Transformation: Politics of Land and Property in China*. OUP Catalogue.

Huang, P.C. 2011. 'Chongqing Equitable Development Driven by a "Third Hand"?'. *Modern China*, 37(6), 569–622.

Huang, Q.F. 2009. 'Building the third finance, the globalisation of state-owned enterprises operation in Chongqing' ('daozao disan caizheng, chongqing guozi yunyin quanqiuhua'). China Business News. [Online, 17 June]. Available at: http://finance.ifeng.com/news/hgjj/20090617/801264.shtml [accessed: 16 February 2014].

Huang, Q.F. 2014. 'Government work report' ('zhengfu gongzuo baogao'). Chongqing Daily. [Online, 1 January]. Available at: http://cqrbepaper.cqnews.net/ cqrb/html/2014–01/20/content_1712625.htm [accessed: 16 February 2014].

Huang, Z. 2013. 'Let Market Play a Bigger Role: Rethinking of Innovation of Land Ticket System' ('Rang shichang fahui gengda nengliang – dipiao zhidu zaichuangxin de sikao'). *China Land* (2), 19–21.

Landesa, China Renmin University and Michigan State University, 2012. 'Findings from Landesa's survey of rural China published'. [Online, 6 February. Available at: http://www.landesa.org/news/6th-china-survey/ [accessed: 16 February 2014].

Lian, X. 2014. 'Brain tank from the Chinese People's Political Consultative Conference in Chongqing interpret rural land and financial reform' ('Chongqing zhengxie zhinangtuan jiedu Chongqing nongcun tudi yu jinrong gaige'). China News Service. [Online, 19 January] Available at: http://www.chinanews.com/ df/2014/01–19/5753416.shtml [accessed: 16 February 2014].

Liu, S.Y. 2008. 'The land property right in China and land market development. Ministry of Education'. Available at: http://www.civillaw.com.cn/wqf/weiz hang.asp?id=41228 [accessed: 28 January 2014].

Liu, X. and Li, X. 2012. 'Study on Issues of Urban-Rural Construction Land Increasing vs. Decreasing Balance' ('Chengxiang jianshe yongdi zengjian guagou wenti yanjiu'). *Shanghai Real Estate* (Shanghai fangdi), Aug. 2012, 25–6.

Long, H. Li, Y., Liu, Y., Woods, M. and Zou, J., 2012. 'Accelerated restructuring in rural China fueled by "increasing vs. decreasing balance" land-use policy for dealing with hollowed villages'. *Land Use Policy*, 29(1), 11–22.

Lu, X., 2008. 'Interest Game in Village Relocation and Combination – A Study Based on Questionnaire Surveys to Villagers'. *Urban Planning Forum*, 174, 45–8.

Ministry of Environment Protection, 2013. National Solid Pollution Investigation.

Ministry of Land and Resources, 2003. National land development and consolidation plan (2001–10).

Ministry of Land and Resources, 2013. The second national land survey report.

National Bureau of Statistics of China, China Statistical Yearbook 2010.

National Bureau of Statistics of China, China Statistical Yearbook 2012.

National Bureau of Statistics of China, China Statistical Yearbook 2014.

National School of Development at Peking University. 2009. Investigation Report: Reform on Chengdu Land System.

OECD, 2013. OECD Economic Surveys: China 2013, OECD Publishing.

Scott, A.J. and Roweis, S.T. 1977. 'Urban planning in theory and practice: a reappraisal'. *Environment and Planning A*, 9(10), 1097–119.

Wang, L.L., Wang, H. and Tao, R. 2012. 'Empirical study on the compensation to expropriated rural residential properties in China' ('zhaijidi chaiqian peichang de diyu chayi'). *Economic Theory and Economic Management* (*Jingji Lilun yu Jingji Guanli*) (7), 104–12.

Wang, S. 2013. 'Why Land Reform Efforts Remain on the Back Burner'. Caixin Online. [Online, 19 September] Available at: http://english.caixin.com/2013–09–19/100584273.html [accessed: 16 February 2014].

Wei, Y.P. and Zhao, M. 2009. 'Urban spill over vs. local urban sprawl: Entangling land-use regulations in the urban growth of China's megacities'. *Land use policy*, 26(4), 1031–45.

Wen, J.B. 2007. 'Government Work Report'. [Online, 5 March] Available at: http://news.sina.com.cn/c/2007–03–05/101312432260.shtml [accessed: 16 February 2014].

Xue, Z. 2011. '85% pure benefit of land ticket belongs to farmers, at least RMB 96,000 per mu' ('dipiao jingshouyi 85% gei nonghu, meimu zuishao 9.6wan'). Chongqing Business News. [Online, 29 June] Available at: http://www.chinacqsb.com/Get/News/Chongqing/Yaowen/1172904524346209.shtml [accessed: 16 February 2014].

Xu, D. 2012. 'Discussion on Resistance of Village Relocation and Recombination' ('Qianxi cunzhen jianshezhong qiancunbindian de zuli'). *China Urban Economy* (*Zhongguo chengshi jingji*), (2), 282–5.

Yang, H. and Li, X. 2000. 'Cultivated land and food supply in China'. *Land Use Policy*, 17(2), 73–88.

Yin, C.Z. and Chen, H.T. 2013. 'The participation role of villagers in village plan implementation: a comparative study on two villages in Guangxi Zhuang Autonomous region, China'. *China City Planning Review*, 22(2), 56–63.

Zhang, G.S. 2007. 'Chongqing experimental zone: three steps towards urban rural integration' ('chongqing shiyanqu: fensanbu shixian chengxiang tongchou'). Guangming Daily. [Online, 12 June]. Available at: http://www.gmw.cn/content/2007–06/12/content_621904.htm [accessed: 16 February 2014].

Zhang, Y.L. 2011. 'Prohibition of exchange between rural land and urban household registration' ('tudi huan huji'). Caixin Online. [Online, 1 January]. Available at: http://finance.sina.com.cn/roll/20110129/16039330677.shtml [Accessed 16 February 2014].

Zhong, S. 2011. 'Toward China's urban-rural integration: Issues and options'. *International Journal of China Studies*, 2, 345–67.

Zhu, L. 2010. 'Grain Production and Food Security in the Course of China's Urbanization'. *Economics Perspective*, 9, 7–14. <in Chinese>.

Chapter 3

The Rising Chinese Middle Class and the 'Construction' of a New Countryside

John Sturzaker and Andrew Law

Introduction

The idea that 'the countryside' is a multifaceted concept subject to a range of discursive 'constructions' has been well established in Western contexts, with their long history of urbanization, for a number of years (cf. Murdoch *et al.* 2003). In contexts such as China, where mass urbanization is a more recent phenomenon, there has been little if any discussion of these issues. The massive scale of recent Chinese urbanization and the implications of that urbanization for the countryside around cities means that it is vitally important that we develop an understanding of how concepts such as (sub)urbanization and the relationship between the urban and the rural are playing out in the Chinese context.

This chapter takes up this challenge, and focuses on the processes at work in the areas of countryside around China's cities and conurbations, subject to substantial pressure as the population of those urban centres grow. Much of this pressure results from the demands of the middle class in China, itself perhaps the most rapidly growing segment of the Chinese population. Most obviously, the demand of this new middle class for suburban housing at lower densities threatens to echo the problems inherent to urban sprawl around cities in the US and UK, as others have noted (Wu *et al.* 2007). At the same time, the tourism industry in China is expanding at a remarkable rate, with many of these new domestic tourists keen to visit what have been described as 'theme park' villages (Oakes 2006), placing very different pressures on the Chinese countryside.

The chapter seeks to combine these understandings of the growth of both China's suburbs and its rural tourism industry with Murdoch's concept of the differentiated countryside, to begin to develop an understanding of the constructions/ discourses which are operating in and around the Chinese countryside, and the implications these have for planning practice and scholarship. It will discuss similarities between China and the UK/US, including the tendency to construct the countryside in pastoral, idyllic terms, and the consequent development of a sharp urban-rural dichotomy, which might suggest that China is following a similar path of suburbanization and urban sprawl to that followed by Western nations. Crucially it will also point to fundamental differences, including the different legal status which applies to land and its ownership between urban and rural areas in China, which illustrate that policy transfer to the Chinese context is by no means straightforward.

The Differentiated Countryside – Comparing China and 'the West'

As discussed in the introduction, a major difference between China and what are called, variously, 'developed' or 'Western' nations, is that, generally speaking, the latter have been 'urbanized' for much longer – in most such nations the majority of the population has been living in urban areas for much longer than China, which only reached this state in the very recent past. For example, in 2011, the United Nations estimated that the UK had an urban population of 79 per cent, a figure which has been relatively constant since 1950. The United States, meanwhile, had an urban population of 64 per cent in 1950, which has now increased to 82 per cent. As is now well established, China's urban population has increased rapidly in recent years – whilst most commentators agree it is now around 50 per cent, in 1950 it was only 12 per cent (all figures from United Nations 2012).

Alongside the mass urbanization seen in countries such as the UK and USA has been a change in the role, function and perception of the countryside, from it being seen as a purely agricultural space to a recognition that there are a range of (often competing) uses and users in modern rural spaces, with commensurately different needs and understandings of what the countryside 'is' and is 'for'. The English countryside has been particularly well studied in this context, with Murdoch *et al.*'s *The Differentiated Countryside* (2003) an important text.

The Differentiated Countryside in England

Murdoch *et al.* observed that there are two main narratives acting to shape perceptions of the English countryside, tending to be in opposition to each other – pastoralism and modernism. 'The relationship between these two narratives varies according to the structural and spatial context' (Murdoch *et al.* 2003, p. 133). Pastoralism has its roots in the eighteenth and nineteenth centuries, as the urban areas of England grew very rapidly. This growth in urban areas was accompanied by a decline in rural areas, and agriculture in particular was in depression in the late nineteenth century. This dual process of industrialization and agricultural decline provoked some urban dwellers to feel nostalgic for the idyllic countryside they had left behind. Pastoralists seek to protect their romantic notion of rural life from outside influences, primarily new development (roads, new homes, industry and so on). Modernism, on the other hand, embraces new development in the countryside on the basis that the benefits of urban society (that is, access to jobs, services, a range of housing and so on) should also be available to those who live in rural areas. Modernists see the urbanization of the nineteenth century as an escape from 'a backward and isolated world where boredom vies with boorishness, inducing melancholia and a suspicion of boorishness' (Newby 1985, p. 13) and a move 'into the dynamic powerhouses of the modern world' (Murdoch *et al.* 2003, p. 2). Later in this chapter we identify both pastoralism and modernism in contemporary constructions of the Chinese countryside.

Murdoch *et al.* contrasted four different 'types' of the English countryside, the differentiation of which was partly caused by the presence or otherwise of middle class in-migrants: 1) the preserved countryside was usually the most accessible, in which decision-making processes are dominated by pastoral and preservationist attitudes. These attitudes mainly come from 'middle-class social groups living in the countryside, employed primarily in the service sector, and often working in nearby urban centres' (p. 12). Murdoch *et al.* contrasted this; with 2) the contested countryside, lying outside the main commuter zones, where incomers are less dominant but are increasingly in conflict with local agricultural, commercial and development interests who will tend to favour development for local needs; in the third type, 3) the paternalistic countryside, large landowners (in the form of private estates and big farms) dominate both in terms of ownership and the development process. These areas are typically more remote and hence less subject to the pressures of middle-class commuting; in the fourth type, 4) the clientelist countryside, the greater level of remoteness means that 'agriculture and its associated political institutions still hold sway' (p. 13). The reliance of that agriculture on state support means that agricultural interest groups work closely with state agencies and 'local politics is dominated by employment concerns and the welfare of the "community"' (Murdoch *et al.* 2003, p. 13).

Given this book's focus on the rural-urban fringe, Murdoch *et al.*'s preserved and contested countrysides are of particular interest to us – and they are perhaps the most transferable to the Chinese context, though perhaps inverted in terms of their relationship to China's urban centres. Others have noted the tendency of tourists in China to seek preserved, or 'authentic' rural experiences (Oakes 2006), and these tend to be further away, and hence less influenced by, urban centres; whereas the most contested areas of China are arguably those in the rural-urban fringe, where the different land ownership statuses, issues of migration, hukou and 'private space' converge. These issues are covered in more depth by other chapters in this book, but it is worthwhile briefly considering some of the contextual factors that influence the pace, shape and style of Chinese urbanization.

The Hukou, Migration and Spatial Patterns of Development in Urbanizing China

The hukou is the registration system which requires that 'all citizens must register themselves to relevant authorities at the place of their permanent residence ... the transfer of one's household registration from a rural to an urban place needs to be approved. All people are assigned a registration status as either "agricultural" or "nonagricultural"' (Zhu 2004, p. 208). The hukou has been used as a tool in China to attempt to control migration – without an urban hukou, migrants cannot access state housing, health and social care. In many cases, however, the lack of an urban hukou does not stop people migrating to urban areas, for either short- or long-term stays – Yuan Ren (2008b), in a study of the Yangtze River Delta Area (which includes Shanghai), found that 75 per cent of migrants without the hukou could be categorized as long-term residents.

As discussed elsewhere in this volume, the disparity in access to state benefits can cause dissatisfaction amongst migrants (Chen *et al.* 2013, p. 216), and amongst those who have been subject to what has been called 'in-situ urbanization' – when 'rural settlements and their populations transform themselves into urban or quasi-urban areas without much geographical relocation of the residents … [this is] caused by the massive development of rural nonagricultural activities, and the permeation of urban and quasi-urban facilities into the Chinese countryside since the 1980s' (Zhu 2004, p. 207). An example of the latter permeation is when urban areas swallow up surrounding rural land, transferring its status from rural-to-urban (with the corresponding change in tenure system from collectively owned to state owned land). As discussed in the preceding chapter, those living on this land are often forcibly relocated, and whilst offered compensation, may not be given an urban hukou.

Migration is one of the primary drivers for the changing spatial structure of China, in a number of ways. Firstly, as a result of migration, 'hundreds of "new villages", "new towns" and "new cities" are now replacing agricultural land all over the country' (den Hartog 2010, p. 8). Secondly, urban sprawl, often at a very high density, is a feature of Chinese cities such as Shanghai. Shanghai is very dense – 'Some parts of the "Central City" have densities of more than 50,000 residents per km[2] (more than 10 times that of Amsterdam). Its suburban area has expanded enormously and features a particularly high population density, that is even greater than most western city centres' (den Hartog 2010, p. 12). As noted by several authors, this sprawl has been, at least until recently, not as a result of residential preference but largely due to the policy of fiscal decentralization, through which local government officials are incentivized to pursue economic growth (Wu *et al.* 2007; Zhao *et al.* 2010). Land has tended to be cheaper in the suburban ring around cities than in the core, so 'The inner suburban ring has become the primary site receiving rural migrants' (Wu *et al.* 2007, p. 281). However, as we go on to discuss below, there is increasing evidence of middle-class 'colonization' of some suburban areas, which, based on the evidence from elsewhere, may bring conflict. The interactions of different sections of society, often categorized by their class, is seen as an important factor by many authors – Murdoch *et al.* note that the preserved countryside in England is dominated by middle-class incomers, who often commute into nearby urban areas to work; and that the contested countryside sees this group in conflict with longer established 'traditional' rural groups, who might be typified as falling into the working (or peasant) or upper (land owning) classes. As the middle class in China grow in number and influence, it seems fair to assume that their demands on rural and peri-urban areas, whether for tourism, recreation or housing, may bring them into more sharply defined conflict with existing rural populations. The next section of this chapter discusses the rising middle class in China.

The Rising Middle Class in China

Defining and researching the middle class in China has been the subject of increasing investigation in recent years (Pow 2007; Ren 2013; Shen and Wu 2011; Wang 2010; Wang and Siu Lu Lau 2009; Wu 2004; 2010; Zhang 2010). In general there has been little agreement over who constitutes the Chinese middle class, since it would appear that the idea of class – and therefore a middle class – still seems slightly vague to Chinese subjects (Zhang 2010).

Nevertheless, despite this confusion various Chinese and Western social theorists and researchers have often discussed ideas of class in China through five broad theoretical perspectives; crudely speaking we can describe these five schools as the: statistical-survey, Marxist, Weberian, combinationist and post-structuralist schools.

The statistical-survey school mainly comes from Chinese-based research on class and can be associated with the work of sociologists from research institutions in Beijing, Nanjing and Shanghai, who from the late 1990s produced a number of large-scale empirical studies. Pioneers in this field include Zhou Xiaohong from Nanjing University who (led a group of scholars that) produced a large-scale quantitative survey that defines the Chinese middle class as the 'middle-income strata'; interestingly, whilst suggesting that whilst middle-income groups now exist in China, Zhou holds back from the suggestion that China has become a 'middle class society', where the middle classes make up the general character of the total population (see Zhou 2005 in Ren 2013, pp. 8–9).

The Marxist model emerges out of sociological and urban studies. In relation to the former, writers such as Yan (2008) make reference to domestic helpers (usually rural migrants working for middle-class families) and their role in wider social relations. Moreover, writers such as Pow (2007) and Zhang (2010) in their studies of gated communities in Shanghai and Kunming have pointed to the production of new class exclusions via a policing of rural migrant outsiders and other 'low paid' persons; as Pow notes in relation to a story about a childcare facility being built within a middle-class enclave, residents were horrified at the thought of 'ah yis (nannies or domestic maids usually from rural provinces), with their "uncouth manners" and "unhygienic" habits swarming into their neighbourhood with their young charges' (Pow 2007, p. 1540); likewise, Zhang in her ethnography of Kunming luxury neighbourhoods also found that 'low-paid community and domestic service staff [were] treated as "servants"' (Zhang 2010, p. 131); importantly as Zhang points out, these staff were 'crucial to keeping the community safe and clean ... ensuring the quality of domestic life and well-being, yet they remain invisible and criminalised because most of them are migrants and [are] seen as being untrustworthy "outsiders" with low *suzhi* [civility]' (Zhang 2010, p. 132).

The second Marxist school then emerges out of urban studies and in many respects this deals with the question of the Chinese middle class indirectly. Drawing upon the ideas of David Harvey, scholars in this school have pointed to the role of local urban growth coalitions and developers in the construction of new urbanisms (characterized by heterogeneity and individualism) and gated urban communities: characterized by signifiers of 'globalization', 'Westernization' and 'cosmopolitanism' (Wu 2004, 2010). In relation to the latter, Wu points out the symbolisms and signifiers of these spaces connote ideas of 'magnificence', 'status' and a form of (middle class) 'niceness' (Wu 2010, p. 385, pp. 393–4).

Moving from Marxism, another school of researchers have taken up more Weberian and Bourdieuian approaches. Interestingly, writers in this theoretical movement reject the idea that 'middle-class' identity (or class itself) is taken up by subjects in any neat way. For instance writers such as Donald and Zheng (2008, 2009a, 2009b), adopting Bourdieu's idea of distinction (1989), explore the way in which 'middle-class' Chinese subjects have drawn upon self-betterment manuals, travel experience and tourism as new sites of identity production. Interestingly, Donald and Zheng view class (and intersected narratives of gender, 2009b) as a matter of becoming through the construction of ideas of the past and particularly the pre-PRC past; thus discussing imaginaries of an urban bourgeois era (particularly in 1920–30s Shanghai), Donald and Zheng write:

> The Grandmas [actresses from the 1920–40s] who have previously been disparaged as politically incorrect residues, resurface as the perfect avant-garde avatars of transhistorical taste. They are evoked as the leaders of everyday class practice, the very incarnations of sensibility. And in this sense these women are upheld as embodied class examples, even though they do not, in their contemporary selves, possess class. Rather, they function as links between past and present for younger aspirants of class and for those who would profit from molding taste in the present (Donald and Zheng 2009b).

A fourth school of writers has also sought to combine Marxist, Weberian and Bourdieuian perspectives. Here in this camp, the anthropologist Zhang Li in particular can be credited with combining these theoretical approaches. Indeed, whilst we have mentioned her earlier in relation to a specific Marxist position, in her excellent *In search of Paradise: Middle-Class Living in a Chinese Metropolis* (2010), Zhang also manages to weave Marxism and more status-based ideas of class together. Thus, like Wu (2004), Zhang sites neo-liberal growth regimes as having a key role in the production of class identity; however, and moving on from this stance, Zhang also discusses the role that 'homeownership' has played in the 'formation of a new propertied social group and a popular indicator of one's economic status' (Zhang 2010, p. 6). Zhang suggests that a new movement of propertied social actors has begun to develop various forms of taste and/or ideas of self-cultivation.[1]

---

1 In developing this theory, however, Zhang is very explicit in her insistence that rather than the revival of a traditional signifier and ideas of class, what is at stake here is a contemporary notion of *jieceng* (strata) which has strong stratifying symbolic connotations. Indeed, as Zhang points out, the Mandarin word for class (*jieji*) holds

The Rising Chinese Middle Class and the 'Construction' of a New Countryside 39

Finally, a fifth position in contemporary work on class concerns those scholars who have utilized post-structuralist ideas; the strongest figure in this movement is Hai Ren, whose book *The Middle Class in Neo-Liberal China, Governing Risk, Life-Building and Themed Spaces* (2013) develops a Foucauldian and Deleuzian approach to the way in which ideas of class have been constructed in the contemporary moment; rather than starting with the economy, or identity, Ren starts from the idea of the dispotif (a Foucauldian concept), that alludes to 'a configuration of arrangement of elements and forces, practices and discourses, power and knowledge, that is both strategic and technical' (Foucault, quoted in Ren 2013, p. 12); as Ren argues then, the production of an idea of the middle class in China has come about as an assemblage of forces that have worked in tandem to stave off perceived crises in the Chinese state: particularly as Ren purports the shift from a socialist to a neo-liberal market state system[2] has produced a series of perceived social crises and moments of precariousness. To avoid social problems and to govern problematic behaviour, Ren argues that 'the middle class dispotif is a mechanism of power by which the state polices the order of things for the purposes of developing a harmonious society' (Ren 2013, p. 141).

Developing this argument, Ren sees the middle class as a value-based subject position which has come to symbolize values of self-reliance and entrepreneurialism (see Chapter 6 in particular). Moreover, as Ren points out, the construction of middle-class neo-liberal subjects has also taken place to acclimatize subjects – both 'winners' and 'losers' in the system – to risk; thus, where the risks of neo-liberal living were generally unknown to pre-reform Chinese subjects, in the contemporary moment, as Ren suggests, new discourses of middle-class values and living have also enculturated individuals to a precarious world:

> As a consequence of China's neo-liberalization, a citizen, while acquiring values of harmony and stability and relevant skills, must navigate unforeseeable incidents of social unrest such as those caused by increasing gaps between rich and the poor, or between the Han and ethnic minorities (Ren 2013, p. 148).

---

historic links to a language of the pre-reform period (and particularly the Cultural Revolution) where notions of class carried strong and explicit pejorative associations. Thus, whilst the word for class seems outdated, a new narrative of distinction and status has certainly entered contemporary Chinese life; although interesting in her study of propertied groups, Zhang maintains that often the production of cultural and symbolic capitals (indicators of status) amongst Chinese groups is relatively insecure. Thus, for Zhang, *jieceng* is not something clear or concrete in the minds of Chinese subjects; rather ideas of *jieceng* and/or strata are relatively fragile and are seen as aspirational ideas with symbolic qualities.

2   A shift that was reinforced by the return of Hong Kong to China in 1997.

The Rising Middle Class, Development and the Production of Space

Urban-fringe Development

Whether the middle classes have emerged in China as a result of the economy, social movements or indeed strategic state practices, writers have been sure that the rise of a new middle class (or middle stratum) has had many social and spatial effects; indeed, as Wu (2004, 2010), Wang and Lau (2009) and Zhang (2010) have argued, the emergence of a new property market for middle class subjects has brought with it a new culture of urban-fringe land development and urban sprawl; indeed, with the rise of a middle-class property machine, the edges of Chinese cities have changed dramatically with the increasing rise of more and more gated communities and luxury residential estates (see Ballantyne and Law 2011; Wu 2004, 2009, 2010).

As Wu has argued, these new developments, and particularly niche towns, are often constructed through the notion of a 'small-town' discourse (an ideal somewhat similar to the values found within the new urbanism/neo-traditionalist movement of 1980s America, Wu (2010, p. 393)); as Wu states, these small self-contained towns, which consist mainly of low-rise houses, are often based on nostalgic ideas of a traditional community, small town or village; moreover, as Wu (2010) maintains, these new small towns are often constructed to have centres, streets, natural amenities, civil squares and possibly even religious sites rather than a town based on a mixed social community; however, these spaces are available only to the successful people who 'seek privacy and seclusion' (Wu 2010, p. 393).

Figure 3.1 **Windsor Island, Thames Town, Shanghai**

The Rising Chinese Middle Class and the 'Construction' of a New Countryside   41

Perhaps of all these new niche town developments, the Songjiang new city (nine towns) development which exists on the outskirts of Shanghai is possibly the most striking; interestingly the nine towns project has included the construction of: a faux Dutch town, a faux Swedish town, a faux German town (Anting), a faux American town, a faux English town (Thames Town – see Figure 3.1), a faux Italian town, a Faux Spanish town, a faux Chinese town and a faux eco-town (which has still not been built).

Remarkably, however, these ersatz-Western towns are mainly purchased by businessmen, entrepreneurs and officials; in this regard often these spaces are left empty as their actual residents own high-rise apartments in the centre of Shanghai (closer to their places of work); moreover, whilst often regarded as second homes, these ersatz houses are also being bought by their owners as long-term financial investments (see Ballantyne and Law 2011). Thus, all in all, these niche small towns are relatively underpopulated, serving more as venues for visiting Chinese tourists and newlyweds who are looking for 'Westernized' zones and 'hyper real "holiday space"[s]' to have their wedding photos taken (see Ballantyne and Law 2011, p. 177).

New Inner City Gentrification

But as well as urban fringe housing, research has pointed to the rise of a new era of elite inner city development that has also had a transformative effect on the construction of urban space. Indeed, and discussing Shanghai, writers such as Wang and Siu Lu Lau (2009) have contended that shifts in the use of space came about with government attempts to renew and renovate old towns. Thus, in the early 1990s, urban redevelopment projects grew in number with the effect that 'land parcels were released for development' which were then bought up 'by the so-called international new middle-class' (Wang and Siu Lu Lau 2009, p. 58). However, as Wang and Lau suggest, this large 'reshaping' of the 'socio-spatial structure of [the] urban landscape' led to the construction of 'many high-end estates' and the 'massive displacement of inhabitants by the affluent' (Wang and Siu Lu Lau 2009, p. 58). As Wang and Lau contend, then, these early government-led redevelopment projects set the foundations for a new era of middle-class urban gentrification.

Moreover, as Ren has demonstrated, new government development strategies to preserve old housing has also brought with it further gentrification (X. Ren 2008). Specifically in Shanghai, Ren notes that government-led development projects have rehabilitated old 1930s Shikumen houses into 'a quarter of coffee shops, restaurants and nightclubs' (Ren 2013, p. 32) for 'foreign expatriates and wealthy Chinese' (p. 36). But like the demolition and renewal strategies sited above, the preservation strategies of the contemporary government development coalition has also led to the massive displacement of 'lower-income residents' (X. Ren 2008, p. 31).

Figure 3.2 Photograph of advertisement for Eton flats

Furthermore, new middle-class communities (and also upper-class affluent communities) are also buying new kinds of luxury high-rise apartments in and around city centres. Here notably these new luxury apartments are also heavily marketed through Westernized themes – and sometimes even explicit signifiers of class. Thus, in the centre of Wuhan, it is noticed a series of elite high-rise apartments that were marketed as 'Eton'; Eton, which is a small and wealthy town in Berkshire, is home to the highly elitist English boarding school, Eton College.[3] And as the developers seem to be implying here, the spirit of Eton and indeed the classiness of this boarding school is alive and well on the lakes of Wuhan (see Figure 3.2)

Finally, it is noteworthy that these spaces are also connected (whether physically or symbolically) to new forms of luxurious public (as opposed to sealed off or gated) shopping zones that are often situated near or alongside the residential communities: an example being The Han Mansions, currently being built in the centre of Wuhan. The Han Mansions development is connected to Han Street, which is a luxurious shopping street, containing various Westernized shops (including Marks and Spencer) and high street brands; interestingly, one end of Han Street contains a replica of Tower Bridge in London, which serves to solidify the developers' imaginary of the area as both exotic and modern. Moreover, the shops which include many English firms, combined with the faux Tower Bridge, speak to customers of an urban-English (or Londonesque) imaginary of the cosmopolitan and the financially successful (see Figures 3.3 and 3.4).

---

3 Eton College is located near Windsor in England.

Figure 3.3 The Han Mansions, Wuhan

Figure 3.4 Han Road, Wuhan

Whilst there are few studies on the socio-economic status of consumers, no doubt these spaces are very likely to be economically inaccessible to a broad range of Chinese citizens, and no doubt like luxurious shopping spaces in the West, these zones also damage traditional businesses and more local forms of economic community. Notably, these shopping centres are often poorly made and, as we have said, have very little connection to the communities and locals that traditionally inhabit these spaces.

How the Countryside Has Been and is Perceived in China – a Historical Review

To contextualize our discussion in the final sections of this chapter, where we consider the possible future(s) for the Chinese countryside, it is essential to first review how the countryside has traditionally been perceived (or constructed) in China, as this is one area where the experience is very different to Europe or elsewhere. Even at the level of language, there are differences between the West and China – in English, '[the word] city is derived from the Latin civitas (city-state), closely associated with civilization, whereas the term country is derived from contra (against, opposite side), referring to land set off from the observer ... The Chinese terms for city and country refer to various levels of activity or administration on an urban-rural continuum' (Visser 2010, pp. 10–11). We would argue that this sort of etymological difference reflects and/or contributes to how the countryside has been and is perceived.

This section of the chapter is subdivided into three historical periods – Dynastic, covering the period up to the end of the nineteenth century (although the Qing dynasty ruled until the Xinhai Revolution in 1911); the period from the Opium Wars through to the 1949 Communist Revolution; and 1949 to today.

Dynastic

It is common to categorize countries such as the UK and the USA as featuring a strong divide (in both physical and sociological terms) between the urban and the rural. In part this is due to the development in Europe of walled cities, often standalone 'city states'. Friedmann (2005) is one of a number of authors who have argued that in China the 'open cities were never thought of as standing apart from the countryside' (p. 95). This certainly seems to be the case from at least the middle to latter part of the Zhou dynasty, which ended around 200 B.C. Prior to this, however, China did feature walled towns to at least some extent – 'In early Chou [Zhou] times the kuo, which in modern Chinese means "state" was actually the walled or stockade town seat of the head of a fief. From the social history of the period we can gain some awareness of the kuo town as an island of civilization surrounded and threatened by a sea of less-civilized and often hostile peasantry' (Mote 1977, pp. 102–3). This state of affairs appears not to have continued for long, and Mote goes on to contrast 'the attitudes associated with the city in the West, especially prior to the Industrial Revolution', wherein 'we may think first of the city as the symbol of safety'; with the Chinese saying '"In times of minor disorders, flee the countryside; in times of major disasters, flee the cities"' (Mote 1977, p. 104).

This cultural change accompanied trading between the walled towns and cities and the rural areas around them. Such trade 'resulted in the gradual blurring of the strongly divided rural and urban areas and was replaced by what is now referred to as the "rural-urban continuum"' (Nieuwenhuis 2010, p. 294). In addition to this physical and social 'continuum', it is also fair to say that unlike, say, England or France, no one city was powerful enough to dominate China – perhaps unsurprisingly given the great size of the country. This meant that whilst in England, London was the artistic and cultural centre of the country (and in France, Paris), in China there was no such centre, and hence hotspots of vibrancy in art and culture were dispersed across the country, often in the countryside. Mote (1977) has argued that 'The rural component of Chinese civilization … and not the cities, defined the Chinese way of life. It was like the net in which the cities and towns of China were suspended' (p. 105).

The countryside has been described as 'the source of the Chinese culture' (Nieuwenhuis 2010, p. 294), and the well-known Chinese author Fei Xiatong 'characterizes fundamental aspects of Chinese society in relation to its uniquely rural features, in opposition to Western culture, which equates civilization with the metropolis' (Visser 2010, p. 10, citing Fei 1947).

All these factors, along with the fact that China's population was predominantly rural until very recently, led to what became the dominant view in traditional Chinese society, that of 'a certain anti-urban sentiment on the part of the majority of China's population, the peasants … the urban-based merchant and artisan classes occupied a lesser status, and were thus "less virtuous" than the peasantry in general and the scholar-gentry in particular' (Kirkby 1985, p. 6).

This reification of the rural was exacerbated by the changes which took place in China in the nineteenth century.

Opium Wars to Revolution

The middle of the nineteenth century brought rapid change to China, and to the relationship between the urban and rural parts of the country. In no small part this was due to the influence of Western countries. The Opium Wars of the 1840s and 1850s resulted in the establishment of 'treaty ports' in cities, including Shanghai, which featured 'extraterritoriality', that is, they were not subject to the usual laws of the Chinese state. The development of the treaty ports 'resulted solely from Western exploitation and at the expense of the hinterlands' (Visser 2010, p. 11), leading to ' the concept of the city … acquiring a number of predominantly negative qualities' (Visser 2010, p. 12).

Early twentieth-century writing in China contrasted Beijing, where 'with its emphasis on nature, traditional rural values prevail' (Visser 2010, p. 13) with cities like Shanghai. Here we see an example of constructivism in action: 'Rather than simply indicating a certain population density, the "urban" that dominated early 20th Century cultural debates referred primarily to the China of the treaty ports ... such polemics cast the urban as inauthentic, implying that rural China was a metaphor for genuine Chinese society' (Visser 2010, p. 14).

This 'semi-colonization of Chinese cities' (Nieuwenhuis 2010, p. 296) was part of the 50 years or more of turmoil which enveloped China through the first half of the twentieth century, culminating in Mao Zedong proclaiming the People's Republic of China in 1949.

1949–80s

Mao is 'believed to have "viewed city life as too soft, lacking revolutionary vigour and labelled urban bureaucrats and intellectuals as 'lords and masters' (chengshi laoye) whose bodies and minds should be toughened"' (Meisner 1982, cited in Nieuwenhuis 2010, p. 296). In part this can be ascribed to the forced retreat of the Communist Party of China (CPC) from their urban bases in the 1920s/1930s, followed by the 'Long March' to the rural northwest of the country. Indeed, it has been argued that the association between the CPC and rural China was one forged through necessity – 'We should not lose sight of the fact that the Chinese Communist movement did not abandon its city bases out of choice, but was forced from them at the point of a bayonet. From the moment they lost the cities, the Communists harboured ambitions to return' (Kirkby 1985, p. 8).

This return was in part achieved through Mao's tactic of 'using the countryside to encircle the city' (Visser 2010, p. 1), building power bases in the rural parts of China from which to attack the 'parasitic' cities. After gaining power in 1949, Mao set about reconfiguring Chinese cities to 'serve the people and the economic objectives of "New China"' (p. 14) through a heavily prescribed process of industrialization. Visser (p. 16) points out a contradiction between this modernization, which required that 'most PRC leaders and cadres moved to the cities', and the fact that 'ideological identity was planted firmly in the countryside, its cultural values fundamentally informed by the customs of rural society'. Indeed, Mao 'formalized the primacy of rural literature and other cultural arts for the next four decades', by requiring intellectuals to 'go down to the countryside'.

Staggeringly, this '"back to the villages" (*huixiang*) movement of the early 1960s resulted in the ejection of over 20 million people' (Kirkby 1985, p. 10). Some have argued that this forced migration was necessary to counteract a similar scale of rural-to-urban migration during the 'Great Leap Forward', the disastrous collectivization of Chinese agriculture which caused massive grain shortages and consequent famine and death.

From this period until the recent economic reforms in China, there was a strong physical divide between urban and rural areas. The function of the countryside, right up to the edge of Chinese cities, was seen purely in productivist terms – its role was to provide food for the population. There remain fundamental differences in how urban and rural lands are owned – the former is owned by the state, whilst the latter is owned collectively by farmers. In addition, the hukou acted to sharpen the distinction between cities and the countryside which surrounds them. It has been argued that immediately before the reform era, 'China was a typical dichotomous society in terms of rural-urban relations' (Zhu 2004, p. 208), in no small part due to the operation of the hukou, the household registration system that, as discussed above, allocates people (at birth) as agricultural or nonagricultural. Pre-reform, 'As most of the nonagricultural population lived in the urban areas, the agricultural-nonagricultural dichotomy was identical to the rural-urban dichotomy' (Zhu 2004, p. 208). It was very difficult to transfer hukou status, something that Zhu argues has become easier since the reforms, which in some respects blurs the urban-rural dichotomy in China – paralleling the shift in many other countries observed by Champion and Hugo (2004, p. 3) – 'There is no longer any clear dividing line between town and countryside for individual settlements or their inhabitants: indeed many people reside in one but work in the other'.

Today

The huge scale of recent urbanization in China, facilitated to no small degree by economic reforms, have fundamentally changed how the Chinese people perceive urban and rural, and the relationship between them. 'Urbanization is now dominant in China, both demographically and ideologically' and China's 'culture was characterized by an "attachment to the soil"', but cities are now how the Chinese define themselves (Visser 2010, p. 1).

There is a clear age dimension to changing attitudes towards the countryside in China – whilst 'Older Chinese … have lived most of their lives dominated by a "native soil" (*xiangtu*) mentality' (Visser 2010, p. 9), the phrase 'You're so village' is used by younger people in contemporary China to mock their friends for their naivety. This contrasts with Mote's comment in 1977 that 'Chinese civilization may be unique in that its word for "peasant" has not been a term of contempt' (Mote 1977, p. 103).

This desire for modernization in the form of the city has contributed to the large levels of rural-urban migration which are characteristic of China today. Chinese city governments are selectively loosening the hukou requirements in order to accommodate those migrants whom they consider to be 'desirable', whilst excluding others, who are often forced to live in informal and/or low quality housing in the rural-urban fringe. This selective acceptance of in-migration has been portrayed as China 'reorganizing as a class system based on wealth, rather than maintaining its "caste system" composed of urban and rural residents' (Visser 2010, pp. 18–19).

This wealth-based class system is, we argue, likely to complicate further the constructions of the Chinese countryside – this is the focus of the next section of this chapter.

The Construction of the New Chinese Countryside

Murdoch *et al.* summarize the trend of counter-urbanization in England – 'the quest on the part of many individuals and families for the rural, both as an experience (in the form of countryside tourism) and as a "refuge" from modernity (in the form of a house in the country)' (Murdoch *et al.* 2003, p. 152). As China urbanizes at a similar rate (though clearly at a larger scale) to England in the eighteenth and nineteenth centuries, it may follow a similar path in terms of changing attitudes to the countryside. It seems to us that the two drivers identified by Murdoch *et al.* (2003) as key to perceptions of the English countryside can now be seen in China – modernism and pastoralism. The former is reflected in the 'Chinese slogan, "leave the fields without leaving the countryside" (*li tu bu li xiang*), in which we see an attempt to conceive of modernity without mobility or, in other words, an immobile modernity. This linguistic sleight of hand suggests that rural people ought to move "away" from the un-modern (the fields) but nevertheless reinforces the idea that rural people are best left un-moving (not leaving the countryside)' (Chio 2011, p. 554). At the same time, pastoralism is reflected in the desire to preserve the way of life in rural villages so that they can be visited by tourists. These so-called 'theme park' villages are part of 'a model of tourism called "Peasant Family Happiness" (*nong jia le*), which typically includes the establishment of guesthouses and

Figure 3.5   A Chinese theme park village, Jiangsu Province

The Rising Chinese Middle Class and the 'Construction' of a New Countryside   49

small-scale restaurants within residents' existing homes' (Chio 2011, p. 559), and require that villages are maintained in an image of the 'rural idyll' which we can immediately recognize as pastoralism (see Figure 3.5).

These *nong jia le* are often located in the urban fringe around China's cities, including Beijing, and are increasingly popular with the middle classes who appear to be nostalgic for the "simple life", echoing the behaviour of earlier urbanizers in the UK (Murdoch *et al.* 2003). Oakes (2006), in reflecting on this type of tourism, noted that 'the idea of preservation perhaps offered villagers a more problematic path towards modernization and national integration; many of them complained about being unable to "modernize" the village with newer-looking structures, or reap greater tourism revenues by building some souvenir shops or a large guesthouse because such changes would violate the terms of Langde's status as an officially recognized "preserved cultural relic" (*wenwu baohu danwei*)' (pp. 186–7). So in that case villagers were constrained in the changes they could make to their own community, in order that the rural China experienced by tourists was not tarnished. This privileging of wealthy tourists over the needs of local communities could be seen as reflecting the move to 'a class system based on wealth' (Visser 2010, p. 19), foreseen by others and discussed above.

Chapter 5 of this book focuses in some detail on a particular case study of rural tourism in the Yangtze River Delta so we will not dwell further on it here, but it is possible to see the popularity of theme park villages as a kind of 'refuge from modernity'. As Chinese families become wealthier and Chinese cities bigger and more polluted, it seems eminently possible that short visits to tourist sites will be sufficient, and there may be a desire to actually live in the rural areas surrounding the cities. There is a wealth of writing on the existing trend towards suburbanization in Chinese cities, which 'is driven by change in both residential preferences and government policies. In the past, the constraints of public transport and underdeveloped service facilities created a strong preference for the inner cities ... Now, with rising incomes and much improved services in the suburbs, residents, especially those looking for a lower-density environment and private car ownership, began to accept the concept of suburban living' (Wu *et al.* 2007, p. 280). To market these suburban homes, 'the real-estate developer is beginning to promote a new "healthier" and "greener" life [to sell suburban living to] a rising middle class' (Wu *et al.* 2007, p. 296). This latter form of marketing echoes to a great extent the methods used to sell suburban living to aspiring home-owners in countries such as the UK and USA – London's 'Metroland' being a prime example (see Jackson 2006 for others).

It is certainly the case that the new Chinese middle class represents both an opportunity to make money for property developers and a new and unpredictable force in terms of development patterns in China. The thirst of this new middle class for new ways to spend their money could manifest itself in a desire for a return to a pastoral way of living – or, at least, the sort of 'chocolate box' pastoralism which defines areas such as the Cotswolds in England. So as middle-class English people moved first to the suburbs and then beyond, as the suburbs became engulfed by the expanding city, so might the new Chinese middle classes eventually tire of the sort of ersatz-Western-influenced developments offered in the suburban areas of, for example, Shanghai.

In what follows, we will now draw on a few key examples that might point to new kinds of Chinese 'chocolate box' pastoralism; however, as we shall caution, given that pastoralism or peasant living in China is still considered pretty unfashionable, particularly amongst younger people – with its backward and traditional 'boring socialist' associations – it is the argument here that new kinds of countryside living might rise in the future that not merely draw upon ideas of 'peasant subjects'; rather they might also draw upon traditional ideas of the Chinese past. To make these claims, the final part of this section looks at the emergence of new nostalgic trends in contemporary China and claims that as well as pastoralism, new forms of rural escapism might emerged through 'dynastically themed' housing.

'Traditional' Pastoralism and 'Dynastic-modern' Housing in China

In the section on class above, we discussed the popularity of niche urban housing on the outskirts of cities; but evidence of new, more traditional housing is certainly evident in contemporary Chinese cities and suburban-scapes; thus interestingly in

Figure 3.6   The 'new-old' water-town, September 2010

Figure 3.7   Another perspective on the new-old water-town, September 2010

Shanghai amongst the nine niche towns of Songjiang new city (discussed above), it is noticeable that there is also a traditional 'Chinese town', which is located near the water-town of Zhujiajiao (located in the Qingpu district of Shanghai) (see Figures 3.6 and 3.7).

Interestingly then, whilst the town is of course made up of new-modernist architecture – of clean lines and smooth forms – nevertheless the town is replete with little bridges and rivers which gives the place a certain 'traditional quality', or an imaginary of an ancient water-town lifestyle reminiscent of Zhujiajiao nearby (Zhujiajiao is estimated to be 1,700 years old, and is composed of 36 stone bridges said to be built in the Ming and Qing dynasties and complex river-lines).

Moreover, new suburban spaces and high-rise suburban spaces that exist on the outskirts of traditional cities like Xi'an are also pointing towards the emergence of new-old traditional spaces that draw upon the area's local heritage and identity to sell the developments.

As observed, in a housing EXPO in 2009 in Xi'an (which was held at the Qujiang International Exhibition Centre), the houses for sale were ultimately the same new Westernized niche architectures and suburban spaces we have discussed above in the section on class; the groups attending the Qujiang International Conference EXPO included many very large Chinese developers in the Xi'an area (an expanded list of some of the companies explored can be seen in Table 3.1).

Table 3.1   Exhibitors at the Xi'an EXPO

Investor/ developer	Public/private/ joint company	Name of brochure
Boee Group/Hongji group/ Xi'an Mingdu Real Estate	Joint owned public-private enterprise	Royal Landscape
Jintai-Silugarden Company	Unknown	Mature life, drunken America West Ham
Saint-Cannat Company	Unknown	Saint-Cannat
Shanxi Yihe Real Estate Co., Ltd	Private	Yihe Blue Diamond
Shanxi Teyi Real Estate Development Co., Ltd.	Private	Taupo
Xi'an Real Estate Development No. 4 Co., Ltd./Xi'an Zhong'an Real Estate Co., Ltd.	Joint owned public-private enterprise	Xingqing Palace
Zhongdeng Group/Xi'an Zhongdeng Real Estate Development Co., Ltd www.zhongdeng.com	Private owned enterprises	Hongden Wenjing Dynasty

However, interestingly, whilst the majority of the exhibits favoured Westernized ersatz housing, one development company seemed to be taking an interest in local heritage themes and particularly dynastic imaginaries. Specifically then, the Xi'an Real Estate Development Company had produced an exhibition entitled 'Xingqing Palace'.

Rather than a brochure marketing an 'American'-style Manhattan apartment or a French-themed condominium, what was advertised in the pages of the pamphlet was apartments that were said to be reminiscent of the local 'Tang Dynasty', 'Xingqing Palace', which is an actual palace located on the Eastern outskirts of the City of Xi'an; as sources suggest, the original palace was the home of the Crown Prince Li Lonji who later became the Tang-Dynasty Emperor Xuan Zong in 712 AD. Of course, the real estate company which is building a series of modern high-rise flats (to be finished in August 2013) has only employed the name of the palace to give the estate an air of elegance.

But despite the tokenism here, nevertheless the company insists that their new flats will contain a 'spirit ... inherited from Royal Palaces'; the brochure reads thus:

> The unique advantage of Xingqing Palace is not only the 'form' that it has inherited from Royal Palaces, but more importantly, the 'spirit' it has inherited from Royal Palaces. The details of Xingqing Palace have shown the hidden but

The Rising Chinese Middle Class and the 'Construction' of a New Countryside   53

'respectable' elegant and luxurious. What Xingqing Palace has demonstrated is a sense of [a] wealthy family as everything makes you feel you are living as if you were in [a] wealthy family at that time (Xi'an Real Estate Development Company no 4 2009).

Therefore, it is not only ideas of class and taste being that are being sold here; indeed, as this text demonstrates with its allusions to the real Xingqing Palace and the Tang dynasty, more generally an escapist 'moment in time' is also being offered to the customer. Indeed, the quote above is also drawing the customer back into an imaginary of the 'Tang past' and an associated age of affluence, wealth and style. Thus, later in the text, the brochure suggests

The reason why every diamond is precious is that every piece of [a] diamond has its own distinctive and beautiful story. The reason why a land is invaluable is because that there is glorious history written on that land. Xingqing Palace, top one among the top three Royal Palaces, was the home of royal family. This land is not only a witness of the glory of Tang Dynasty but also a witness of how China walk towards [the] world and merged with the world (Xi'an Real Estate Development Company no 4 2009).

Indeed, with reference to the glory of the Tang Dynasty and the idea of an age that walked 'towards the world' (particularly through the Silk Road, which started in Xi'an), what is also being sold here in these words is a new language of nationalism and pride. Indeed, since the real estate itself is situated in Xi'an, originally called Chang'an in the Tang period, and the starting place of the Silk Road, what is also being sold in this brochure is a new-old language of cosmopolitanism; indeed the text with its allusions to walking to the world recalls the age of Chang'an and an ancient city (and an ancient age), where cosmopolitanism and exchange of goods and culture between West and East was more common; what is being offered to the consumer of this real estate, then, is not simply a Palace of Elegance, status and class, but a time capsule which encourages the Chinese subject to realize his/her glorious, cosmopolitan and prosperous roots; in an age when China is asserting its civilized culture on the world stage, what is being offered by the Xi'an Real Estate Development Company is not simply a language of elegance and status, but a new site of Chinese glory and indeed a new-found confidence.

Green Urbanisms

Finally, it is also noteworthy that as well as nostalgia some new urban real estate development companies are also trying to market and sell new forms of urban living which are based on the idea of what is understood as 'European garden life'. For example, Wuhan Tiandi, an interesting real estate development which consisted of a series of high-rise towers near an urban heritage site called Wuhan Xintiandi, was said to have a 'creative space' within the complex (see Figure 3.8),

Figure 3.8 'The creative space' connected to the Tiandi real estate development in Wuhan, May 2013

which turned out to be a site of tilled land for residents who wished to grow their own vegetables.

Moreover, a series of information pertaining to the harvesting of different crops during different seasons was exhibited at the entrance of the space. Whilst this small example of green urbanism might not be understood as nostalgia for peasant life, nevertheless this small site of green urbanism was certainly being sold as an 'alternative' form of consumer middle-class lifestyle by the developers.[4]

Conclusion – A 'New-Old' Future in the Countryside?

So what might be the longer-term physical and social implications of a changing dynamic in housing demand? We now move further into the realm of speculation, given the differences between China and the Western countries which have blazed the trail of suburbanization and counter-urbanization and, indeed, the difference between those countries themselves.

In the UK, for example, the use of Green Belts to constrain the growth of urban areas has led to development attempting to 'leapfrog' the Green Belt to nearby towns and villages, often accompanied by strident opposition from those living

---

4   Direct observations in Xi'an and Wuhan were conducted by Law, one of the current authors, in 2009.

in existing housing in these areas. This has been characterized as, sometimes successful, attempts by people living in rural areas to exercise power to prevent new development (Sturzaker 2010). But despite these attempts the rural population of the UK has in recent years grown more rapidly than the urban population – indeed, in terms of internal migration, the rural population has grown as the urban population declines (DEFRA 2012). So in the long term, the proportion of the Chinese characterized as urban may eventually peak and decline, though it seems there is some way to go yet before any such peak is reached.

Conversely, the USA has never embraced counter-urbanization to the same extent, perhaps due to the differences in scale. In the UK, one can reach comparatively 'deep' rural areas quite quickly, given the relatively compact nature of British urban form, whereas the substantially greater size of US cities and the concomitant potential commuting time might explain the lack of the same degree of counter-urbanization. So, whilst the people of the USA have embraced suburbia like no other society, there is less of a tendency to live in the countryside and commute back into the cities. At this stage there is no way to be certain about which path China will follow.

Reflecting on the discussion in the previous section, rather than new kinds of chocolate box pastoralism as found in rural imaginaries in the UK, it is possible that what might emerge in China (as an alternative to the clichéd Western suburbs and inner city high rises) are a series of new suburbs and countryside residences that draw upon local or even national themes. Importantly, as Gries (2004), Broudehoux (2004), Callahan (2010) and Wang (2012) have all noted, since the Tiananmen crackdown, China has been hit by new contemporary waves of nationalism that have been implicitly critical of the West (and Japan) and its historical relation to the motherland; as observers have noted then, whilst Westernized consumerism has been popular, many Chinese subjects have also been fairly critical of what they see as an overly Westernized Chinese culture.

Indeed, with regard to new ersatz Westernized suburbs, Zhang (2010) has noted that the new small-town discourse, as espoused by developers and growth coalitions, has not escaped criticism from contemporary Chinese people. Thus, Zhang notes that in 2005, on responding to growing public criticism of the Westernization of Chinese urban space, a Kunming official stated that the 'practice [of urban Westernization] signifies the degeneration and loss of decent Chinese urban culture. Kunming must immediately correct such blind worshiping of Western things and fawning over foreign powers' (Zhang 2010, p. 87).

Moreover, as well as nationalist reactions to Westernization, more generally observers have also noted that since the late 1990s and early 2000s there has been a resurgence of interest in heritage culture and historical nostalgia (see Horner 2009; Law 2012; Law *et al.* 2014); here, then, as opposed to simple nationalism alone, scholars have commented that with the reform era and an increasing academic relaxation to China's feudal past, new forms of nostalgia and dynastic revivalisms are emerging in the contemporary moment.

What these emerging discourses of nostalgia might mean, then, is that new forms of traditional culture including ideas of the 'peasant-imaginary' might resurface: indeed, with protests against contemporary neo-liberal conditions in contemporary China, as Pickowicz (2007) has argued, some traditional peasants have actively constructed a very selective nostalgia for pre-PRC and post-PRC China (between 1943 and 1953), where it is said that a mixture of semi-capitalist and semi-socialist voluntary [agricultural] cooperatives were successful (see Pickowicz 2007).

Whilst Pickowicz's work and indeed the writings of Lee and Yang (who have explored nostalgia for the Chinese Revolution) do not point to any particular or straightforward peasant nostalgia, nevertheless certain kinds of agricultural sentiment are emerging in the present – especially in today's turbulent neo-liberal times (see Lee and Yang 2007). Moreover, as we have seen in the example regarding the real estate settlement in Wuhan and the vegetable patch, it is certainly possible that new forms of green urban living and green agricultural imaginaries could form.

Whether the future brings back a 'new-old' imaginary of pastoral living in China remains uncertain; nevertheless, with a growing culture of nostalgia, and a cultural logic of selective memory, it is very likely that in times to come, new-old houses on the edge and even in the countryside itself are likely to emerge; moreover, like the nostalgic architectures of the West, it is also likely that these new nostalgic spaces (whether they be small towns and/or individual architectures) will also operate as key sites of refuge from modernity.

Indeed, as we have seen in relation to the Xingqing Palace, a place which encourages the Chinese home-owner to realize their connection to an elegant, civilized, wealthy and cosmopolitan past, it is also very likely that these new pastoral spaces will be imbued with nationalistic and statist discourses of the Chinese citizen-subject (see Ren 2013).

We have mentioned only in passing the issues causing and being caused by large-scale rural-urban migration in China. The promotion of tourism as a form of rural diversification has been seen by some as a way of attempting to stem this tide – 'At its base, expectations that rural peasants are "rooted" in the land certainly influence programs to promote rural tourism, even as state governments use tourism development as a means of social, economic, and cultural modernization with one aim, in China particularly, of stemming rural-to-urban internal migration' (Chio 2011, p. 567). This is, however, an extremely delicate balance, as 'Rural tourism relies upon the juxtaposition between the urban and the rural to succeed' (Chio 2011, p. 568), so increasing the scale of tourism, and hence the scale of any associated infrastructure, might damage this market. Another contradiction is the 'the sociocultural milieu of contemporary China in which the modernization of rural regions is a government priority, but socio-economic changes are increasing the need and desire of rural people to seek greater wage-earning opportunities in cities' (Chio 2011). A big question then is whether rural 'peasants' will remain content to act as what are in effect operators of theme park attractions, and miss

The Rising Chinese Middle Class and the 'Construction' of a New Countryside   57

out on the perceived 'promised land' of urban China? It seems unlikely – the scale of migration in China is unlike anything seen before; it is estimated that 'In 2010, 221 million Chinese migrated between urban and rural regions' (Eggleston *et al.* 2013, p. 506), and this level of migration shows no sign of declining. As discussed above, many rural-urban migrants are not granted an urban hukou, leading to a degree of dissatisfaction amongst some (Chen *et al.* 2013) which may lead to increasing conflicts between different groups.

The possibility for conflict, whether between migrants and 'host' communities, or between the suburbanizing middle class and others, seems very real, as discussed in Chapter 1 of this book, and is increasingly a focus for scholars (see for example He and Wu 2009). Indeed, Eggleston *et al.* (2013) speculate that the processes of urbanization could make conflict more likely, as the 'safety net' of rural China for the 'millions of migrant workers, who would return to their rural homes during economic downturns' (p. 513), is reduced in size through the expansion of towns and cities. How this conflict reveals itself and is managed, in a state which continues to discourage open criticism of its policies, will be a critical factor in the future development of China.

Acknowledgements

Thank you to our colleagues and friends Qin Qianqian, Chen Yitang, Shang Shunzi and Song Siqi for their help in gathering some of the information for this writing.

References

Ballantyne, A. and Law, A. 2011. Genealogy of the Singaporean black-and-white house. *Singapore Journal of Tropical Geography*, 32 (3), 301–13.

Bourdieu, P. 1989. *Distinction: A Social Critique of the Judgement of Taste.* London: Routledge and Kegan Paul.

Broudehoux, A.M. 2004. *The Making and Selling of Post-Mao Beijing.* London: Routledge.

Callahan, W.A. 2010. *China, the Pessoptimist Nation.* Oxford: Oxford University Press.

Champion, A. and Hugo, G. 2004. Introduction: Moving Beyond the Urban-Rural Dichotomy, in *New Forms of Urbanization – Beyond the Urban-Rural Dichotomy*, edited by A. Champion and G. Hugo, Aldershot and Burlington: Ashgate, 3–24.

Chen, Z., Liu, X. and Lu, M. 2013. Beyond Lewis: Rural-to-urban migration with endogenous policy change. *China Agricultural Economic Review*, 5 (2), 213–30.

Chio, J. 2011. Leave the Fields without Leaving the Countryside: Modernity and Mobility in Rural, Ethnic China. *Identities: Global Studies in Culture and Power*, 18 (6), 551–75.

DEFRA 2012. *Statistical Digest of Rural England 2012* [Online]. Available at: http://www.defra.gov.uk/publications/files/pb13642-rural-digest-2012.pdf [Accessed: 14 February 2012].

den Hartog, H. 2010. Urbanization of the Countryside, in *Shanghai New Towns*, edited by H. den Hartog, Rotterdam: 010 Publishers, 7–42.

Donald, S.H. and Zheng, Y. 2008. Richer than Before: The Cultivation of Middle-Class Taste: Reading, Tourism and Education Choices in Urban China, in *The New Rich in China: Future Rulers, Present Lives*, edited by D.S.G. Goodman, London: Routledge.

Donald, S.H. and Zheng, Y. 2009a. Introduction: Post-Mao, Post-Bourdieu: Class and Taste in Contemporary China. *Portal Journal of Multidisciplinary International Studies*, 6 (22).

Donald, S.H. and Zheng, Y. 2009b. A taste of class: manuals for becoming woman. *Positions: East Asia Cultures Critique*, 17 (3).

Eggleston, K., Oi, J.C., Rozelle, S., Sun, A., Walder, A. and Zhou, X. 2013. Will demographic change slow China's rise? *Journal of Asian Studies*, 72 (3), 505–18.

Friedmann, J. 2005. *China's Urban Transition*. Minneapolis: University of Minnesota Press.

Gries, P.H. 2004. *China's New Nationalism, Pride, Politics and Diplomacy*. Berkeley: University of California Press.

He, S. and Wu, F. 2009. China's emerging neoliberal urbanism: perspectives from urban redevelopment. *Antipode*, 41, 282–304.

Horner, C. 2009. *Rising China and Its Postmodern Fate: Memories of Empire in a New Global Context*. Athens, FA: University of Georgia Press.

Jackson, A. 2006. *London's Metroland*. London: Capital Transport Publishing.

Kirkby, R.J.R. 1985. *Urbanisation in China: Town and Country in a Developing Economy, 1949–2000 AD*. London and Sydney: Croom Helm.

Law, A. 2012. Post-colonial Shanghai: An Urban Discourse of Prosperity and Futureority, in *Colonial Frames, Nationalist Histories*, edited by M. Desai and M. Rajagopalan, London: Ashgate, 285–304.

Law, A., Bonnett, A., Yang, Y. and Chen, Y. 2014. Creative nostalgia's for the cosmopolitan city of tomorrow: Han and Tang imaginaries in China's Ancient Capital. *Unpublished paper in process*.

Lee, C.K. and Yang, G. (eds) 2007. *Re-envisioning the Chinese Revolution: The Politics and Poetics of Collective Memory in Reform China*. Stanford: Stanford University Press.

Meisner, M. 1982. *Marxism, Maoism and Utopianism*. Madison: University of Wisconsin Press.

Motc, F.W. 1977. The Transformation of Nanking, 1350–1400, in *The City in Late Imperial China*, edited by G.W. Skinner, Stanford: Stanford University Press, 101–54.

Murdoch, J., Lowe, P., Ward, N. and Marsden, T. 2003. *The Differentiated Countryside*. New York: Routledge.

Newby, H. 1985. *Green and Pleasant Land?: Social Change in Rural England*. London: Wildwood House.

Nieuwenhuis, M. 2010. Tracing the Politics of Space in One City & Nine Towns, in *Shanghai New Towns*, edited by H. den Hartog, Rotterdam: 010 Publishers, 291–304.

Oakes, T. 2006. The Village as Theme Park: Mimesis and Authenticity in Chinese Tourism, in *Translocal China: Linkages, Identities and the Reimagining of Space*, edited by T. Oakes and L. Schein, London: Routledge, 166–92.

Pickowicz, P.G. 2007. Rural Protest letters: Local Perspectives on the State's Revolutionary War on Tillers, 1960–1990, in *Re-envisioning the Chinese Revolution*, edited by C. Lee and K. Yang, Washington, DC: Woodrow Wilson Centre Press.

Pow, C.-P. 2007. Securing the 'Civilised' Enclaves: Gated Communities and the Moral Geographies of Exclusion in (Post-)socialist Shanghai. *Urban Studies*, 44 (8), 1539–58.

Ren, H. 2013. *The Middle Classes in Neo-Liberal China, Governing Risk, Life-Building and Themed Spaces*. London: New York: Routledge.

Ren, X. 2008. Forward to the past: Historical Preservation in Globalizing Shanghai. *City & Community*, 7 (1).

Ren, Y. 2008. Migration, changes of city-region structure and implications for planning practices and regional development policies in the Yangtze River Delta area in China. *International Planning Studies*, 13 (4), 415–29.

Shen, J. and Wu, F. 2011. Restless urban landscapes in China: A case study of three projects in Shanghai. *Journal of Urban Affairs*, 00 (0), 1–22.

Sturzaker, J. 2010. The exercise of power to limit the development of new housing in the English countryside. *Environment and Planning A*, 42 (4), 1001–16.

United Nations, D.o.E.a.S.A., Population Division. 2012. *World Urbanization Prospects: The 2011 Revision* [Online]. Available at: http://esa.un.org/unup/CD-ROM/Urban-Rural-Population.htm [Accessed: 8 February 2012].

Visser, R. 2010. *Cities Surround the Countryside: Urban Aesthetics in Postsocialist China*. Durham, NC: Duke University Press.

Wang, H.H. 2010. *The Chinese Dream: The Rise of the World's Largest Middle Class and What It Means to You*. Bestseller Press.

Wang, J. and Siu Lu Lau, S. 2009. Gentrification and Shanghai's new middle-class: Another reflection on the cultural consumption thesis. *Cities*, 26 (1), 57–66.

Wang, Z. 2012. *Never Forget National Humiliation*. Columbia: Columbia University Press.

Wu, F. 2004. Transplanting cityscapes: the use of imagined globalization in housing commodification in Beijing. *Area*, 36 (3).

Wu, F. 2009. Neo-urbanism in the making under China's market transition. *City*, 13 (4).

Wu, F. 2010. Gated and Packaged Suburbia: Packaging and branding Chinese suburban residential development. *Cities*, 27, 385–96.

Wu, F., Xu, J. and Gar-On Yeh, A. 2007. *Urban Development in Post-Reform China – State, Market and Space*. Abingdon: Routledge.

Xi'an Real Estate Development Company no 4 2009. *Xingqing Palace*. Xi'an: Xi'an Real Estate Development Company no. 4.

Xiatong, F. 1947. *From the Soil: The Foundations of Chinese Society*. Shanghai: Shanghai guanchashe.

Yan, H. 2008. *New Masters, New Servants: Migration, Development and Women Workers in China*. Durham, NC: Duke University Press.

Zhang, L. 2010. *In Search of Paradise: Middle Class Living in a Chinese Metropolis*. Ithaca and London: Cornell University Press.

Zhao, P., Lu, B. and De Roo, G. 2010. Performances and dilemmas of urban containment strategies in the transformation context of Beijing. *Journal of Environmental Planning and Management*, 53 (2), 143–61.

Zhou, X. 2005. *Zhongguo, Zhongchan, jiceng, diaochai (Survey of the Chinese Middle Classes)*. Beijing: Social Sciences Academic Press.

Zhu, Y. 2004. Changing Urbanization Processes and *In Situ* Rural-Urban Transformation: Reflections on China's Settlement Definitions, in *New Forms of Urbanization – Beyond the Urban-Rural Dichotomy*, edited by A. Champion and G. Hugo, Aldershot and Burlington: Ashgate, 207–28.

Chapter 4

The Intermediate Role of Medium-Sized Cities in China Between Ultra-Dense Rural Areas and Ultra-Large Cities

Abigaïl-Laure Kern, Marlène Leroux and Jean-Claude Bolay

Introduction

Contrary to a generally accepted myth, the majority of urban populations do not live in megalopolises of more than one million inhabitants. Indeed, despite their visibility and dynamism, they account for a small though increasing proportion of the world urban population: 9.9 per cent in 2011 and 13.6 per cent in 2025. Even if these cities have grown exponentially in the last decades, from 72 in 1950 to 400 in 2000, and from 450 today to 554 in 2015, at the same time, over half of the urban population lives and will continue to live in small and medium-sized cities of less than 500,000 inhabitants according to the United Nations (UN 2012).

In China, the number of people living in small and medium-sized cities is still quite high, despite the phenomenon of rural emigration that has become so notable in the country and which has exacerbated the agglomeration dynamics in major urban areas. Although the population of megalopolises (cities with more than five million inhabitants) has continued to increase, such as in Shanghai, Beijing and Guanzhou, in 2010, less than 20 per cent of Chinese were living in megalopolises (Zhou *et al.* 2013). Despite this evident readjustment, there is still little research that focuses on the subject of medium-sized cities, which is complicated by a lack of definition, and the need to mobilize a number of different disciplines to define its role, the challenges it faces and its evolution over the short to medium term. In fact, there is a real lack of international statistics concerning these cities capable of defining said cities according to the number of their inhabitants. Yet this rapid demographic and spatial transformation proves to be especially difficult for small and medium-sized cities, where capacity is typically inadequate to cope with major urban challenges. The main shortcomings include: inefficiency of local government; insufficient revenues and lack of institutional power to implement centrally managed programs governed from above; persistent corruption; and the failure of local authorities to incorporate urban institutions into local urban planning and decision-making. Small to medium-sized cities must, therefore, be redefined outside of simple demographic criteria, in particular in the People's

Republic of China (PRC), which was nearly 50 per cent urbanized in 2011 and is expected to reach 70 per cent within the next 20 years (Sueur 2011).

China's territorial network of medium-sized cities is currently both too weak and too complex to play the role of being an incubator for both the economy and an urban way of life. In 1955, the central government announced its intention to encourage the development of small cities, mainly to reduce the gap between cities and rural areas: 2006 marked the beginning of the reform entitled the 'modernization of the socialist countryside' (*jiansheshe hui zhuyixinnongcun*), whose principal goal was to foster the development of rural areas in order to limit the countryside-city migration. This goal is being achieved by large-scale urbanization, which in turn reinforces the role of small and medium-sized cities. It is demonstrated by the urbanization of cities' peripheral zones and the creation of new cities:

> The policy of the government encouraged the demolition of entire villages in favour of moving them to new, denser areas, sometimes by uniting several villages, and by providing them with supermarkets, libraries, etc., reflecting urban life. All of these new forms of urbanisation have rapidly fashioned a new rural China, transforming its countryside, its culture and its social structures (Hillman and Unger 2013).

Current research on small and medium-sized cities, especially in China, will help to improve the understanding of the effectiveness of such policies in reducing rural disparities. Moreover, it will help in defining which functional role – but also economic and social – such urban formations are playing today in the context of urbanizing China. Some preliminary thoughts regarding the scope and role of small and medium-sized cities in the urban Chinese landscape will be outlined in the second part of this chapter. In fact a summary of field studies about two archetypical medium-sized cities will be reported: Dengfeng and Dujiangyan, respectively situated in the Henan and Sichuan provinces.

The research carried forward in the two mentioned cities is placed in the third part of this chapter, investigating particularly the challenges they are facing due to the increasing competition between cities of similar size. Moreover it explores how the city government in both cases is tackling the issue of densification vs suburbanization, being this point of strategic interest in the current debate on sustainable development issues. In order to manage better the risks inherent in dealing with this complex research subject, these cities are conceptualized as intermediate urban formations. Their territorial nature 'in between' determines a spatial uncertainty in clearly defining the boundaries between the city and the countryside. However, the research results suggest that these two medium-sized cities function as the keystones connecting two disparate systems: the mega-cities and the dense rural networks.

Based on previously defined parameters, as will be shown later, the concept of intermediate cities is one of the ways to establish a diagnosis of such medium-sized urban formations so as to better identify their current issues and challenges and, later on, the potential responses in terms of public policy.

Definition of a Medium-sized City

The Return of Medium-sized Cities; a Consequence of Urban Development

In contrast to the great volume of research being undertaken on Global Cities (Sassen 2001), research into smaller urban centres, or 'Worlding Cities' (Roy and Ong 2011), is limited by the inherent difficulty in researching the subject. Nevertheless, it has continued to attract the attention of several researchers from different disciplines. There has also been renewed interest in these types of urban centres since urban populations have overtaken rural populations across the globe over the last decade.

While by no means suggesting that large cities be entirely neglected in the future, there are good reasons for putting smaller cities more centrally on the development agenda (Cohen and Vilar 2005). Although their total population is demographically very significant, they are starting by definition from a smaller base so they typically grow faster than large cities. Moreover, residents of smaller settlements in developing countries are extensively underserved with respect to basic services. Indeed, residents of medium-sized cities suffer a marked disadvantage in the provision of piped water, waste disposal, electricity and schools than residents of larger cities (Cohen 2006).

Evidence further suggests that rates of poverty are higher in smaller cities and in many countries; levels of infant and child mortality are negatively proportional to city size (National Research Council, 2003). Many of these small and medium-sized cities lack the necessary institutional capacity to manage their rapidly growing population. As cities grow and evolve, the task of managing them becomes ever more complex. The nature and tasks of urban management and governance are also undergoing fundamental change because national governments have decentralized service delivery and revenue-raising to the lower tiers of government (UN Habitat 2009). At the same time, there are advantages to being small.

Medium-sized cities have time to address residents' basic infrastructure and service needs before the magnitude of the service gap becomes too overwhelming. As they are growing rapidly, they offer critical opportunities to bypass old technologies and to implement efficient, ecologically sound practices that can contribute to shaping a more sustainable future (Cohen 2006) with an impact not only at local level but also in their rural hinterland (Bolay and Rabinovich 2004).

Small and Medium-sized Cities: a Tool to Fight Urban Poverty?

It is increasingly important to recognize that, on a global level, the most extreme poverty is not, in fact, found in the biggest cities (WB 2013). New analytical tools that use data from both censuses and household studies have allowed researchers to formulate a 'poverty-city size gradient', which shows the link between poverty and city size (Elbers *et al.* 2002). The latest research clearly shows that urban poverty is less apparent in the biggest cities (Ferré *et al.* 2012):

> In a fairly large number of developing countries, not only is the incidence of poverty higher in small cities and towns than in the large urban areas, but these smaller urban centers also account for a larger share of the urban poor. In such countries as Brazil and Thailand, with well-known megacities such as São Paulo, Rio de Janeiro, and Bangkok, the share of the urban poor residing in small and medium-size towns exceeds that in the largest cities (WB, 2013).

Recent studies undertaken in developing countries also show that if the urban population in certain countries is concentrated in big cities, urban poverty is spread across the continuum of medium-sized cities, small cities and very small cities (WB 2013). The fact that the most significant cities have lower levels of poverty is strongly linked to hypotheses about the positive externalities of urbanization.

Small and medium-sized cities therefore have an important role to play in reducing urban poverty, provided public policies can encourage economic growth at the same time as providing people with better access to basic public services. According to studies on the 'poverty-city size gradient', implementing these types of public policies in small and medium-sized cities can not only help improve access to public services but also create employment that is not linked to agriculture, therefore providing rural migrants with a better quality of life and reducing poverty in urban as well as rural areas.

Using an Interdisciplinary Approach to Improve Understanding?

In order to better understand small and medium-sized cities in the context of research, an interdisciplinary approach is often required. This might include borrowing from the field of geography, and in particular the concept of an urban hierarchy (Goodrich 1926; Pumain 1994) which can help improve understanding of the spatial dimension of these cities; or from sociology, to explain the impact of the social dimension on human representation and behaviour; or from political science, to investigate how political processes create power plays in these cities; or, indeed, from architecture and urbanism, to understand issues related to their development.

Because medium-sized cities are often, for researchers, an 'unidentified real object' (Brunet 1997), a number of distinctions can be made, depending on their geographic position, their history or even certain social and economic characteristics, which make them more or less specialized, vulnerable or resilient (Demazière *et al.* 2013). Moreover, the definition of medium-sized cities and their sub-categories, small cities, changes, depending on the country and the institution (Maturana and Terra 2010). Demographic data generally provides a means of establishing an initial assessment but there are almost as many methods as there are researchers and national and international bodies that are responsible for collecting and processing data on these cities (Taulelle 2010).

An interdisciplinary approach is therefore often required, in particular when studying these cities in the context of rapid urbanization and a significant population size, as is the case in China.

Medium-sized Cities in China

The Government's Intention Over the Decades

The Chinese Government has long had an interest in medium-sized cities, beginning at the time the People's Republic of China was established in 1949. From 1955 onwards, the government announced its intention to encourage development in smaller cities in order to minimize the load on urban infrastructure as well as to reduce the gap between cities and rural areas (Xu 2008). At the Third National Urban Conference in 1978, the government reaffirmed the importance of medium-sized cities, to help counterbalance the expansion of large cities. Overall the government has expressed, since the 1980s, the intention to control the size of big cities, so to avoid the formation of mega-cities such as the development of medium-sized cities into large cities (Xu 2008). This was the same year of the great agricultural reform that helped liberate farmers from their land while, importantly, keeping them in their regions to avoid large concentrations of migrants in coastal regions at the detriment of inland regions. The Chinese Government's stated intention to restrict the size of cities can also be found in the 'urban planning law' that was adopted in 1990. It responds to two key objectives: 'to strictly restrict the size of large cities, and to sensibly develop small and medium-sized cities'. Overall, up until the 2000s, China's urban development has reflected the government's goal of encouraging the development of medium-sized cities.

On the one hand, the majority of Chinese cities are small and medium-sized; on the other hand, the distribution of the population of cities reveals a strong concentration in large cities. In 2004, 497 cities of China's 661 cities had a population of less than 500,000 people. These small and medium-sized cities represented 75.2 per cent of all Chinese cities, but only 29.6 per cent of the total urban population. At the other extremity of the urban hierarchy, the 28 cities that had more than two million inhabitants each represented 34.3 per cent of the population of all cities, and, amongst these, the seven largest had more than 5 million inhabitants each and accounted for 16.2 per cent of the population in all Chinese cities (Xu 2008).

Another important step is the controversial policy released in 2006 and titled 'building the new socialist countryside' for achieving the reduction of the gap between rural and urban areas. Although the policy takes into account some of the major urbanization side-effects of China, reaffirming the government's historical

66   *Urban China's Rural Fringe*

goal of strengthening small and medium-sized cities, some risks of the upgrading have been described in Wang's contribution in the present volume.

The Majority of the Chinese Population Lives Today in Urban Areas

In 2011, the majority of the country was urban, with more than 50 per cent of the population living in cities; a level which, according to different projections, could grow to 70 per cent within the next 20 years (Ishii and Muzones 2013). So what is the distribution of medium-sized cities in China's urban landscape today?

The principal urban body in China is the city (*shi*), which has an average of 517,000 inhabitants, but there also exists another urban entity in China: the town (*zhen*), which has an average of 10,000 inhabitants.

Cities are administratively classified according to four levels: the province (which includes the municipalities and the autonomous regions that depend on central government), the prefectures, the districts and the counties. The latest available data categorizes 658 Chinese cities according to their size. They are classified as 'super large-sized cities' (with a population over 2,000,000 inhabitants), like Beijing, Shanghai, Guangzhou and so on; 'extra-large-sized cities' (with a population between 1,000,000–2,0000,000 people); 'large-sized cities' (with a population between 500,000–1,000,000 people); 'medium-sized cities' (with a population between 200,000–500,000 people), which are generally at the district level; and finally, 'small-sized cities' at the county level (with a population of between 200,000–500,000 people) (NBSPRC 2011):

> Compared with megacities, Small and Medium Sized Cities SMCs grow faster in terms of economy, demography, and size. In the PRC, out of a total of 658 cities, 533 or 81% are classified as SMCs. The most dynamic changes occur in SMCs and even in the smaller 33,270 towns and townships, as they interface with rural areas geographically, socially and economically. Considering the current growth rate, many smaller towns and townships will join the classification of SMCs, tripling their number in 2030 when the urbanization rate exceeds 70%. (Ishii and Muzones 2013)

Along with the two cities presented as case studies – Dengfeng and Dujiangyan – the number of medium-sized cities in China is steadily growing and so are the challenges they face.

Dengfeng (Henan) and Dujiangyan (Sichuan): Archetypes of Medium-sized Chinese Cities

Dengfeng and Dujiangyan are two medium-sized cities that are facing significant territorial transformations supported by the massive urbanization of rural areas. These two examples, respectively situated in the west and centre of China, illustrate the straightforward and representative application of the national guidelines of the 'building the new socialist countryside': namely the territorial and environmental impact of these national policies on medium-sized cities. In addition to this, these cities both have heritage sites and particular landscapes that give them great potentialities for embracing qualitative strategies of development, although in China today this is not often accounted as an asset in the modernization process.

Dengfeng is a country-level city that falls under the jurisdiction of Zhengzhou, the capital of Henan. Dengfeng is situated at the foot of Mount Song, a sacred Chinese mountain of Sichuan. The relics from the temple of the famous Shaolin monks are kept in the city and, in 2010, Dengfeng was included on UNESCO's world heritage site list. Because of these factors, the city was recently proclaimed the 'capital' of Chinese kung fu, a title it hopes will help benefit local tourism and education related to the national sport. Previously supported by ore mining and intensive cereal agriculture, Dengfeng's current primary source of income comes from the commodification of land as it does from the changes in land use (Miller 2012). Indeed, the value of land increases substantially when it shifts from agricultural to urban purposes, as witnessed almost everywhere in this phase of the China's urbanization process.

Spread over 1220 km², the city has a population of about 650,000. The city's urban development strategy involves the construction of two new cities in the east and west flanks of the city. The new city planned in the east will rehouse farmers who have recently been dispossessed of their agricultural land; while in the west, the new city will consolidate all the activities related to tourism and recreation. These two new towns covering over about 2,000 km² are designed for 820,000 inhabitants. While the local government is still awaiting approval of its project to build the twin cities, it began tearing down six million square metres of housing in the old town and in the rural areas under its jurisdiction in 2012[1] (see Figure 4.1).

Dujiangyan is a country-level city under the jurisdiction of Chengdu, the capital of the Sichuan. Now extending over 1,208 km², the city has a population of about 611,830. The city is located adjacent to the site of Li Bing's famous dam, built in the 3rd century BC, an exceptional irrigation system to which the Chengdu Plain owes its prosperity and fertility. This monument, also included on the list of UNESCO world heritage sites (2000), provides Dujiangyan with a prodigious reputation and real assets for its future development. The city's urban transformation was accelerated by the massive destruction sustained after the May 2008 earthquake, which measured 7.8 on the Richter scale. An urgent need for safe urban and rural housing prompted the construction of numerous new developments in a new city situated midway between Dujiangyan and Chengdu (see Figure 4.2).

---

1   Interview with the Director of the Dengfeng Office of Urbanism (Oct. 2013).

Figure 4.1 Typical Mount Song scenery

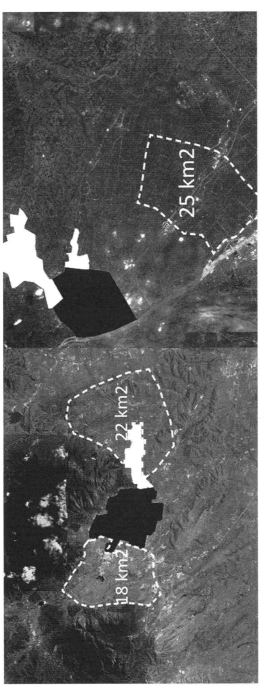

Figure 4.2 Left: Dengfeng city (black). Right: Dujiangyan city (black). Existing new cities (white), planned new cities (dashed)

The Challenges Facing the Medium-sized Chinese Cities of Dengfeng and Dujiangyan

Competition Between Cities, Population Density and Sustainability

The current institutional structure of Chinese small cities allows some to flourish at the cost of the decline of others (Sainjuan 2014). This duality expresses the significant competition that currently exists between cities that engenders both positive externalities – which have developed as a result of the dynamism of local governments – and negative externalities, principally where there has been mismanagement of public investments. This can be observed in these cities, where construction in central business districts (CBD) has stopped, Olympic stadiums have been abandoned and bridges left unfinished. Like all great urban centres in China, each city plans its CBD in the image of Pudong in Shanghai or an entirely rebuilt 'old city' in the hope that it will obtain the same success as the Xintiandi District in Shanghai. However, a series of malfunctions and financial failures have blocked a number of these projects, leaving some neighbourhoods half-destroyed and half-constructed. As a result, in Dengfeng, the destruction largely outweighs the reconstruction, leading to the question of the feasibility of its ambitions for becoming a centre for tourism (see Figure 4.3).

Figure 4.3   District being destroyed, South Dengfeng

The Intermediate Role of Medium-Sized Cities in China 71

Figure 4.4 New residential area, East Dengfeng

The current guidelines for the transformation of villages into arable land and the regrouping of villages into certain dedicated zones can lead to an increase in population density and therefore a form of sustainable land development (Mostafavi and Doherty 2011). However, the excessive sprawl of hamlets and villages in the rural areas around Dengfeng means that these requirements cannot be easily met. One may equally wonder about the massive destruction of the homes of traditional farmers, as the authorities seek to destroy a large proportion of these villages in order to gain 'credits' for changing the surrounding land into urban areas. These efforts are not in keeping with the work being undertaken to depollute the earth for future agriculture and construct housing for those expelled from their land.[2]

The principal purpose of the focus on urbanization has been to streamline and simplify the management of the land by grouping different administrations around urban centres (Bray 2013). However, the risk is that, in leaving all the functions of governance to the cities, these rural spaces won't have the same visibility and they could fall out of step with the social reality of the greater region (Thireau and Linshan 2007) (see Figure 4.4).

Dengfeng and Dujiangyan also exhibit two other strong characteristics of medium-sized cities: poor financial resources and a lack of competency in the urban planning offices and amongst the urban designers who participate in urban projects, as the majority of skills are always concentrated on the mega-cities on the coast (Hsing 2010). However, the national visibility that these cities have gained because of their tourism development potential, and the opportunities they have to attract important investments, has focused the attention of eminent planning institutes, such as the Tongji Design Institute, and has enabled the new city south of Dujiangyan to win the national prize for the best land planning strategy in 2011 (Yu and Yan 2011).

The Scale of Analysis: the Scale of Intervention and the Value of a Study on Territorial Reality

The scale of a country like China, which is almost a continent in itself, lends itself to studies on contemporary urban phenomena or analyses of large-sized cities, while the impact of the multitude of small and medium-sized cities that span the country and which could play a leading role in the urban Chinese landscape are largely overlooked. Studies conducted on a provincial level can ensure better analyses that include the specificities of local governance. This scale of analysis, however, remains very abstract because it is uniquely based on the administrative boundaries while, in considering the physical and temporal nature of the landscape, it appears that development is dynamic and occurring much faster than the decisions made by officials. This 'in situ' urbanization

---

2 Interview with the Director of the Dengfeng Office of Urbanism, Oct. 2012.

(Zhu *et al.* 2013) shows an incompatibility between territorial planning and endogenous urbanization (Friedmann 2005).

In order to test the real impact of the development of medium-sized cities, an analysis of the territory was conducted using an 'imbrication map'.[3] It is primarily a process of observing and transposing the reality of a territory. Indeed, the very hierarchal system of management of the territory, a system referred to as 'Russian dolls', can blur the boundaries between cities and the countryside, thus making it very difficult to make a clear distinction, from a strictly administrative and governance point of view: 'A city is, above all, a powerhouse that controls a territory' (Sanjuan 2014). What is the spatial configuration of this control of cities over neighbouring territories? In other words, what is the relationship between Zhengdou and Dengfeng or Chengsu and Dujiangyan? Thus, representing the territory from a different perspective leads us to produce new knowledge (Vigano 2012). Faced with the difficulty of appraising the value of quantitative information and given the complexity of the administrative boundaries of Chinese cities, the process of representing the reality of a territory with satellite photographs instead of via urban projects uses rather the presence and typology of built forms to tell us about the physical state of an area's development. Using a sample size of 250 km, it is possible to observe that a multitude of small to medium-sized cities is concentrated around large cities, such as Chengdu and Zhengzhou. These cities have around 200,000 to two million inhabitants. Superimposed over this network of very dense urban centres are the towns, villages and hamlets, observable uniquely using a sample size of 50 km, which reveals considerable density. Through this kind of observation with its use of different scales, it appears that the common denominator, aside from the greater landscape (mountains, rivers), is the medium-sized urban settlement in question, which connects the province and the ruralopolis. Although Dengfeng and Dujiangyan are respectively managed by Zhengzhou and Chengdu, can the main cities really exert their influence over hundreds of surrounding villages and hamlets? In spite of the considerable endeavours of local governments to reinforce and legitimize their authority on rural territories, an overview of the density of the built environment and therefore of the activity of surrounding territories suggests the difficulty of carrying out such tasks. Thus, as medium-sized cities have a strong relationship with their rural territories, they should be able to play their role as intermediaries (see Figures 4.5, 4.6, 4.7, 4.8).

---

3 In the first instance, we can observe the urban portrait by using a radius of 250 km around the city being studied or a surface area of 200,000 km² (20 million ha), then undertake the same analysis of an area with a radius of 50 km or a surface area of 7850 km² (Note: Switzerland has a surface area of 41,285 km² while the United Kingdom has a surface area of 242,900 km²).

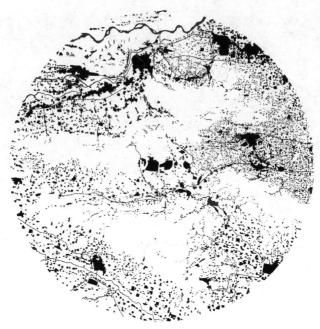

Figure 4.5   50 km around Dengfeng: existing built area and water system

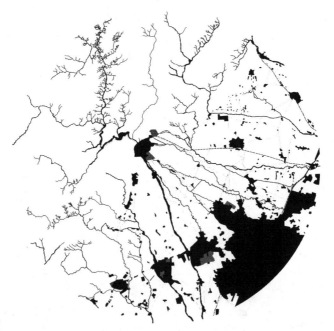

Figure 4.6   50 km around Dujiangyan: existing built area and water system

The Intermediate Role of Medium-Sized Cities in China 75

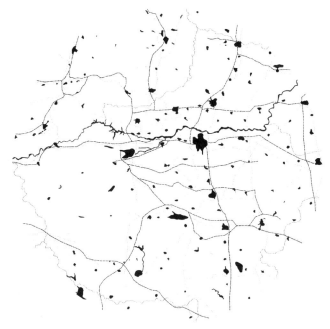

Figure 4.7 250 km around Dengfeng: existing built area and water system

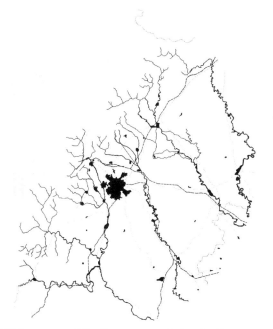

Figure 4.8 250 km around Dujiangyan: existing built area and water system

76   *Urban China's Rural Fringe*

The Concept of Intermediation: a Relevant Diagnosis Tool for Medium-sized Cities

Although research into small and medium-sized cities is fundamental, there is a current lack of methodology, specifically in the context of China's urban centres. In effect, as these case studies have revealed, the diagnostic tools currently available do not take into account the diversity and complexity of the subject. Taking a functional approach, however, such as that developed for other contexts like Latin America, could lead to the development of a useful research tool that allows a better understanding of the challenges that these cities must face. To date, these cities have been defined by their intermediary role in the urban hierarchy, positioned between rural areas and large cities. This role can be better understood by looking at the concept of intermediation, based on an interdisciplinary approach which is instrumental to understanding these cities.

Eight aspects related to intermediation have been developed (Bolay and Rabinovich 2004). First, the demographic dimension which is related to urban growth and the impact of migratory movements. This is followed by the economic, political and institutional aspects, with the identification of the productive and trade sectors feeding local and external goods and services markets and analyses of public institutions serving the local population, in line with their nature, function and territorial scope. The question of the available services and equipment also needs to be put in perspective, in order to know if it is sufficiently specialized and sophisticated to offer services. The environmental key dimension will admit the identification of natural and built resources that facilitate collective life, stigmatizing the depth and extent of contamination by urban activities. The territorial management dimension focuses on planning and organizing the built environment and its consequences on human settlements and its populations. And finally, the social and cultural aspects, these two last dimensions, enquire not only the reflecting behavioural changes and mingling within family and social networks, but also the new forms of expression synthesizing local cultures and outside influences arising from exchange between urban populations and their external contacts.

As it satisfies the requirement of interdisciplinarity for studying medium-sized cities, the concept of intermediation could be particularly useful to measure the intensity of such functions for each city and therefore enable meeting the planning challenges with which they are confronted.

Conclusion

In China, it appears that the scale of medium-sized cities is very pertinent – it is the keystone to improving coordination between an ultra-dense rural area and ultra-large cities. It is under this premise that the central government's current objective would be to reinforce the network of small and medium-sized cities in order to strengthen the intermediary links between these two networks of territorial organization systems, which overlap but do not currently interrelate. In conclusion, studying small and medium-sized cities by way of their role and function could allow the creation of a diagnostic tool that takes the broader context into account – including the concept of intermediation – and allows a better understanding of the complexities of the challenges that these cities must face, therefore helping establish recommendations for urban planning that is adapted to their needs.

References

Bolay, J.C. and Rabinovich A. 2004. Intermediate Cities in Latin America Risk and Opportunities of Coherent Urban Development. *Cities* 21 (5), 407–21.

Bray, D. 2013. Urban Planning Goes Rural: Conceptualising the 'New Village'. *China Perspective* 2013(3), 53–62.

Brunet, R. 1997. *Territoires de France et d'Europe. Raisons de géographe*. Paris: Belin.

Cohen, B. 2006. Urbanization in developing countries: Current trends, future projections, and key challenges for sustainability. *Technology in Society* 28(1–2), 63–80.

Cohen, B. and Vilar, K. 2005. Small cities, big agenda. *Development and Cooperation* 6, 244–7.

Demazière, C., Banovac, K. and Hamdouch, A. 2013. The Socio-Economic Development of Small and Medium-Sized Towns (SMSTs): Factors, Dominant Profiles and Evolution Patterns. TOWN Interim report – Annex 4,, Luxembourg: ESPON. Available at: http://www.espon.eu/export/sites/default/ Documents/Projects/AppliedResearch/TOWN/InterimReport/Annex_4_-_ Socio-Economic_overview.pdf [accessed: 2 October 2014].

Elbers, C., Lanjouw, J.O. and Lanjouw, P. 2002. Micro-Level Estimation of Welfare Policy, Research Working Paper 2911, Development Research Group, Washington DC: World Bank.

Ferré, C., Ferreira, F.H.G. and Lanjouw, P. 2012. Is There a Metropolitan Bias? The Relationship between Poverty and City Size in a Selection of Developing Countries. *World Bank Economic Review* 26 (3), 351–82.

Friedmann, J. 2005. *China's Urban Transition*. Minneapolis: University of Minnesota Press.

Goodrich, E.P. 1926. The statistical relationship between population and the city plan, in *The Urban Community*, edited by E.N. Burgess. Chicago: University of Chicago Press, 144–50.

Hillman, B. and Unger, J. 2013. Editorial. *China Perspective* 2013(3), 3.

Hsing, Y.T. 2010. *The Great Urban Transformation: Politics of Land and Property in China*. New York: Oxford University Press.

Ishii, S. and Muzones, M. 2013. *Low-Carbon Development in Small and Medium-Sized Cities in the People's Republic of China: Challenges and Opportunities.* ADB Briefs, n. 14.

Maturana, F. and Terra, P. 2010. La notion de ville moyenne au Chili, entre la fonctionnalité et la taille de population. Paper presented at the Colloque International Villes petites et moyennes, un regard renouvelé, Tours (France), 9–10 December.

Miller, T. 2012. *China's Urban Billion: The Story Behind the Biggest Migration in Human History.* New York: Zed Books.

Mostafavi, M. and Doherty, G. 2011. *Ecological Urbanism.* Baden (Switzerland): Lars Müller Publishers.

National Research Council 2003. *Cities transformed: demographic change and its implications in the developing world.* Washington, DC: National Academies Press.

NBSPRC (National Bureau of Statistics, People's Republic of China) 2011. China Statistical Year Book 2012. Beijing, PRC.

Pumain, D. 1994. *Hiérarchie urbaine, in Encyclopédie d'Economie spatiale,* edited by J.P. Auray et al. Paris: Éditions Economica, 333–341.

Roy, A. and Ong, A. 2011. *Worlding Cities: Asian Experiments and the Art of Being Global.* Malden, MA: Wiley-Blackwell.

Sanjuan, T. 2014. La ville chinoise est un espace de pouvoir. Urbanités, 30 July. Available at: http://www.revue-urbanites.fr/entretien-thierry-sanjuan-la-ville-chinoise-est-un-espace-de-pouvoir/ [accessed: 2 October 2014].

Sassen, S. 2001. *The Global City: New York, London, Tokyo.* Princeton: Princeton University Press.

Sueur, J.P. 2011. Rapport d'information de la délégation sénatorial à la prospective sur les villes du futur. Paris: Sénat. Available at : http://www.senat.fr/rap/r10–594–3/r10–594–31.pdf [accessed: 2 October 2014].

Taulelle, F. 2010. La France des villes petites et moyennes, in *La France une géographie urbaine,* edited by L. Cailly and M. Vanie. Paris: Armand Colin, 149–68.

Thireau, I. and Linshan, H. 2007. *D'une illégitimité à l'autre dans la chine rurale contemporaine. Études rurales, 179.* Paris: Éditions de l'EHESS.

UN-Habitat (The United Nations Human Settlements Programme) 2009. *Planning sustainable cities. Global report on human settlements 2009.* London: Earthscan.

UN (The United Nations), 2012. *World Urbanization Prospects. The 2011 Revision.* New York: United Nations Department of Economic and Social Affairs, Population Division.

Vigano, P. 2012. *Les Territoires de l'urbanisme.* Genève: Métispresses.

WB (The World Bank) 2013. *Rural-Urban Dynamics and the Millennium Development Goals. Global Monitoring Report 2013.* Washington, DC: The World Bank.

Xu, Z. 2008. Urbanisation et croissance des villes en Chine. PhD Thesis in Sciences Economiques, Institut de Recherches sur l'Economie Chinoise (IDREC),

Université d'Auvergne, Clermont I, France. Available at: https://www.google.ch/#q=URBANISATION+ET+CROISSANCE+DES+VILLES+EN+CHINE [accessed : 2 October 2014]

Yu, J. and Yan, S.J. 2011. *Post-disaster Plan of Dujiangyan*. Shanghai: Tongji University Press.

Zhou, S., Dai, J. and Bu, J. 2013. City size distribution in China 1949 to 2010 and the impacts of government policies. *Cities*, 32(1), 51–7.

Zhu, Y., Lin, M., Lin, L.Y. and Chen, J.M.2013. The Extent of In Situ Urbanisation in China's County Areas. *China Perspectives* 2013(3), 43–52.

Chapter 5

Rural Regeneration in the Yangtze River Delta: The Challenge and Potential for Rural Heritage Tourism Development

Yiwen Wang

Introduction

The diversification of the functional uses of agricultural land has grown in importance since the concept of sustainable development became a matter of global concern before the turn of the new century. Multi-functionality of agricultural land often refers to the production of other goods, services or values in addition to crop and livestock, such as food security, leisure activities, recreational opportunities and cultural tourism (Daugstad *et al.* 2006). Arguably, rural tourism has been one of the most effective tools for diversifying economic activities and generating additional income for the rural community. It has played an important role in regenerating the declining economy of the countryside as a result of intensive global food trading (Sharpley and Vass 2006). While the term 'rural tourism' has been perceived and interpreted in various ways, ranging from general leisure activities to hands-on farming practice, it is the role of 'cultural heritage' in the current trend of rural tourism development that this research was set to explore.

Whereas the focus of rural development initiatives in the 1990s appeared to be on agricultural reform and economic growth, the first decade of the twenty-first century has witnessed a growing interest in the heritage values of rural landscape and the employment of heritage tourism as a key strategy for rural regeneration. The idea of 'heritage-led rural regeneration' has gained rising popularity in Western Europe and North America in recent years (English Heritage 2008; Lincoln *et al.* 2010; Mayes *et al.* 2010). While heritage-led rural regeneration appears to be a new trend and attracts more and more attention in practice, appreciation for the heritage value of agricultural landscape can hardly be seen in China, and the recognition of its tourism potential is yet to be developed.

Certainly, the evolution of discourses on rural regeneration in relation to heritage tourism and the recent pioneering initiatives undertaken in developed countries may afford remedies for the problems of tourism development in China (Y.W. Wang and Verdini 2011). The examination of Chinese rural planning policies and the current socio-cultural and economic circumstances of deprived rural areas, however, are indispensable for identifying the range of issues before then promoting heritage-based approaches towards rural regeneration in China.

This chapter identifies the issues of rural heritage management in the Yangtze River Delta, China, and explores its potential for rural heritage tourism development. A major aim of this research is to unlock the heritage value of existing agricultural villages and their characteristic landscape on the urban fringe.

In China, as a result of its relentless pursuit of economic growth, agricultural land on the urban fringe often bears the brunt of rapid urbanization and is quickly disappearing. The rural landscape of China we see today is the result of various communist rural reform initiatives of the twentieth century, being stratified on top of the traditional rural landscape of pre-modern China. This unique landscape, which exhibits a historic layering of cultural values and natural characteristics, is under threat of destructive development and irreversible transformation. The perceived threats towards rural heritage are mainly posed by the decline of the rural population, peri-urbanization expansion and, above all perhaps, the national government's recent policy on rural development, 'Building a New Countryside', due to which traditional countryside houses are either demolished or modernized at the cost of original morphological and architectural character.

While examining the general issues concerning rural tourism and heritage management in the Yangtze River Delta on a macro scale, this research takes the form of a case study on the countryside around Suzhou City in Jiangsu Province. The city has often been dubbed 'Venice of the East', and its rural areas are also characterized by canal-scape and features clusters of vernacular buildings and agricultural structures. Drawing on field survey, this research examines how rapid urbanization and the government's initiative encroach on arable farming land and threaten the continued existence of rural heritage and evaluates the potential for rural heritage tourism development.

It may be worth noting that the term 'rural heritage' employed in this chapter refers to the tangible agricultural structures, their surrounding open spaces and the intangible traditional skills and cultural expressions historically associated with agricultural practice. The tangible built heritage focussed on in this research is the unassuming, low-visibility heritage that is modest in appearance, mundane in function and often, although not always, made up of structures of the recent past and not statutorily protected. A basic position taken in this research is that places like these are of lesser significance, so have greater flexibility in making changes to their physical structures to meet contemporary needs. Hence, they have a greater potential to stimulate local economies and promote sustainable tourism with the involvement of local communities. Another assumption of this research is that – compared with impressive architectural monuments and archaeological sites – unassuming agricultural structures and vernacular buildings can better reflect the lives of ordinary people in the past. Therefore, they may better communicate with people in the present and facilitate their understanding of the past.

Challenge and Potential for Rural Heritage Tourism Development

Rural Tourism Development in China

While rural farmers still constitute about three-quarters of the country's total population, China remains the largest agricultural society in the world. It is not surprising that it began to venture into rural tourism development fairly late by comparison with other economically advanced countries. However, due to its large rural population, the country's modernization programme has largely depended on the socio-economic aspects of regeneration (Su 2011). The highlighted need to alleviate poverty in the countryside has often been linked to the diversification of farming activities as well as the promotion of the tourism industry (Gao *et al.* 2009; Zeng and Ryan 2012). Similarly, on the more ideological level, the connection between rural tourism development and the 'building the new countryside' policy is also accentuated (Chen 2006; Peng and Li 2008; Ahlers and Schubert 2009; Bray 2013).

Since the early 1990s, the role of rural tourism has taken on an increasingly important role in the socio-economic regeneration of China's countryside. Beginning in 1998, the China National Tourism Admiration (CNTA) launched a series of initiatives to promote rural tourism development, including the introduction of 'China Rural Tourism Year 1998' and 'China Eco-tourism Year 1999' (Su 2011). Another important factor contributing to the current proliferation of the rural tourism industry in China is the launch of 'Golden Week' policy (May Day, National Day, Spring Festival) in 1999 (Shao 2007). The policy has noticeably boosted the domestic demand for various forms of leisure industries, among which rural tourism is a popular choice for the majority of people, mainly because of its affordability in term of cost. This shows that the Chinese government was, at that point, perfectly aware of the enormous range of cultural and natural resources in its vast countryside and began to focus its attention to exploit these.

Following the rise of interests in the recreational value of the countryside and a series of government initiatives to exploit the potential of rural tourism development in the late 1990s, the China government in the following decade recognized the paramount need for extending the scope of statutory protection for cultural heritage to the rural hinterland. The 2002 amendment to the *Law of the People's Republic of China on Protection of Cultural Relics* formalized the 'Historic Village' as a new heritage category in the country's heritage legislation (Li 2014). Since 2003, the national heritage authority has subsequently designated six batches of 'Historic Villages of National Importance' and, by 2014, a total of 347 villages are accorded with this heritage status.

Such top-down government initiatives in China are, as always, effectively implemented and have a marked effect on the society. By 2006, in response to the newly introduced national policy 'building the new countryside', which corresponds to one of the key objectives of the Eleventh Five-Year Plan, the CNTA readopted 'rural tourism' as the main theme of development for that year and directed much of its administrative and financial supports in improving the tourism infrastructure of rural areas. In the same year, the CNTA signed an agreement with the Ministry of Agriculture to work collaboratively to regenerate rural areas by promoting tourism development. The two government bodies established an explicit goal to transform 100 counties, 1,000 townships and 10,000 villages into national exemplary sites of rural tourism in a period of five years (2006–10). Gao *et al.* (2009) estimate that, just in 2006 alone, more than 20,000 villages were developed into tourist destinations, and over 6 million rural residents had benefited from being involved in the fast-growing tourism industry. From 2004 to 2007, the CNTA designated a total of 474 rural tourism destinations as 'National Demonstration Sites for Rural Tourism' in three batches and further assisted the tourism development in these exemplary sites.

Geographical Distribution of Rural Tourism Development

With the exceptionally large territory of rural land in China, rural tourism developments have been taking place across the country. Yet it is discernible that rural tourism development has mainly concentrated on some regions, namely the Pearl River Delta, Yangtze River Delta, Beijing Capital Region and Sichuan Province. The existing body of literature on the subject has also verified such concentration (Chen 2006; Guo *et al.* 2008; He 2008; Wu 2008; Arlt and Feng 2009; Deng 2009; Prideaux *et al.* 2009; Y. Wang and Yin 2010; Z. Yang *et al.* 2010). The regional distribution of rural tourism development is clearly structured: Sichuan Province representing the western area, Beijing Capital situated in the northern region and, to the east and south, there are the Yangzi River and Pearl River Delta.

Historically, the regions of Yangzi River Delta and Pearl River Delta thrived because of fertile farming land and abundant agricultural produce, and Beijing flourished for reasons of being a political centre. Sichuan Province, on the other hand, enjoys the growth in tourist trade in the countryside because of the recent governmental initiatives and grants that deliberately facilitate economic development in the inland region (Jackson 2006; Su 2011). Zhang *et al.* (2011) note that the rapid tourism boom in these regions stems from their high economic growth rate and the clustering effect of historic cities in these regions. Certainly, the tourism boom in the regions is mainly fuelled by the high concentration of heritage assets in the historic urban cores of these cities. However, for the Pearl River and Yangtze River Delta, it can be argued that the rich cultural heritage in the rural areas is easily comparable to that in the urban centres. As mentioned previously, the two regions thrived because of their wealth of natural resource for agricultural produce. On this account, man-made structures, cultivated land and natural surroundings in the two regions have been the long-lasting receptacles of agricultural practice that chronicle the history of mankind.

Rural Tourism Activities and the Role of Cultural Heritage

Generally speaking, rural tourism activities in China can be classified into four broad themes: agriculture, folk culture, natural resources and holiday resorts (Guo *et al.* 2008; Peng and Li 2008). Among the four, agricultural tourism is the most popular, and it is often known as 'Nong Jia Le', meaning 'joy of farmer home'. As Su (2011) and Guo *et al.* (2008) note, the joy-of-farmer-home tourism originated in the 1980s when individual farmers tried to generate additional income by providing authentic countryside cuisine and overnight accommodation in the farmer's home or a place to camp in the farm. In a sense, it was a type of full board and lodging targeted at customers who were often individual urban residents coming from the nearby cities and liked to spend a weekend away from the hustle and bustle of city life. In other words, the early form of rural tourism in China was an embodiment of 'green' or 'eco' tourism that is completely at odds with the mass, one-off, theme-park-like tourism that is currently dominant in the domestic tourism industry. The profit that these individual economic activities could generate was modest. It is not surprising that, two decades later, it has turned into a tourism product capable of providing lodging and service to masses of tourists at the same time – typically on Labour Day, National Day and the Spring Festival holiday. To attract repeat visits and also visitors from other regions and even abroad, it has also evolved into a comprehensive holiday package, encompassing a variety of leisure activities or hands-on experiences, such as hiking, rowing, fruit-picking, fishing, cooking, knitting, pottery and so on. A wide variety of hand-made products or traditional craft works are sold in the theme-park-like farms.

What role does 'heritage' play in the joy of farmer home or, generally, rural tourism? The wide range of activities taking place in the joy-of-farmer-home tourism has involved both natural and cultural heritage. While natural heritage is referred to as the agricultural landscape that is seamlessly blended into the climatic and typological profile of the locality, cultural heritage encompasses both tangible built environments and intangible folk customs and skills. Specifically about historical settlements and houses, they serve as both the scenery and the scene of rural tourism activities. While the statutorily protected 'Heritage', such as ancient water towns, often serves as the scenery for rural tourism, it is usually the non-statutorily protected 'heritage' like farmer's houses or barns that provide authentic rural scenes for leisure activities to take place (Malpass 2009). It is this 'heritage' – in lower case – that has the potential to promote eco-tourism in the Suzhou countryside, and to provide a stage for the joy-of-farmer-home tourism in an authentic rural setting.

Rural Tourism Development in Yangtze River Delta

The Yangzi River Delta is predicted to be the sixth largest urban agglomeration in the world (Wu 2008). A set of highly urbanized cities has generated a great deal of

86   *Urban China's Rural Fringe*

tourism businesses as well as economic prosperity in the region. In recent years, rural tourism has attracted much attention from the government, and tourists too. Conversely, what ensures the future and sustains the development in the region is the continuous economic growth in rural areas.

It is impossible to ignore the potential of tourism development in the Yangzi River Delta since it owns 25 of China's outstanding tourism cities and 48 National AAAA level tourist attractions. Jiangsu Province, Zhejiang Province and Shanghai Municipality are the three major areas in the lower part of the Yangzi River that enjoy the boom of rural tourism development. However, rural tourism thrives in these three areas for various reasons. Deng (2009) and Véron (2013) argue that the rise of rural tourism activities in the outskirts of Shanghai mainly stem from urban citizens' demand for different types of leisure in the countryside for a day-trip activity. While rural tourism in Jiangsu Province features more historic gardens, ancient villages and agriculture-related activities, Zhejiang Province takes the advantage of its natural landscape. In other words, the three regions have special features of tourism, which complement each other.

The list of the national exemplary sites for rural tourism development published by the CNTA shows the obvious advantages of rural tourism development in the Yangzi River Delta, particularly, Jiangsu Province. The first batch of designation in 2004 includes 203 sites nationwide, among which 25 are located in the Yangzi River Delta and 16 sites are in Jiangsu Province. In the next year, another 156 sites were designated. While 37 sites are in the Yangzi River Delta, 27 out of 37 designations were situated in Jiangsu Province (see Table 5.1). Accordingly, a large volume of funds has been invested in the Yangzi River Delta, and Jiangsu Province is arguably the largest beneficiary (Deng 2009). Such official designation serves as an effective tool for campaigning for a rural tourism that not only contributes to economic growth in the tourism industry, but also the agricultural sector.

Table 5.1   National exemplary sites for rural tourism development

	Nationwide	Yangtze Delta	Jiangsu Province	Zhejiang Province	Shanghai
Year 2004	203 sites	**25**	16	6	3
Year 2005	156 sites	**37**	27	8	2

These public campaigns, although being effective in generating publicity and attracting more visitors to the countryside, have limited impact in the operational aspect of tourism development and management. He (2008) argues that, as the local government does not manage and integrate the existing tourism resources and trade, the current tourism market that features small-scale businesses is hardly attractive to investors, and many tourist attractions share a high degree of similarity in tourist activists therein. She also criticizes the lack of public participation in the current development process and points out that rural residents have little right to have a say on decisions made for their homeland.

External Threats to Rural Heritage in Yangtze River Delta

While the growth of demand and interest in rural tourism may entail the protection of cultural heritage in rural areas, there are still several external factors threatening the existence of rural heritage. Arguably, the major threat is posed by two causes: the rapid peri-urbanization expansion and the government initiative launched in recent years: 'building the new countryside'.

Urbanization of Agricultural Land

The main driving forces of peri-urbanization – that is, the inward migration of low-income labourers or the gradual encroachment of greenfield development on the urban fringe – are essentially situational. Yet this phenomenon has become rather typical of cities in China considering that nearly half of the country's growth in the next quarter century will be in peri-urban areas. This continuing expansion of built-up areas consequently results in the incorporation of former rural villages and agricultural land into 'cities' (Long *et al.* 2007, 2009). Whereas the urbanization of agricultural land is clearly observed everywhere in China, it can be argued that it has brought about a catastrophic effect on the existence of rural heritage, particularly in the Pearl River Delta and the Yangtze River Delta.

These two regions currently experience the highest rate of economic growth but, historically, they flourished because of the fertile arable land in the region, which had considerable natural resources and produced abundant crops. This means that there is a relative wealth of cultural heritage that is closely associated with agricultural practice as well as the inland waterways in the regions. The research conducted by Bosselmann *et al.* (2010) exemplifies the threat of urbanization towards the cultural landscape of the water villages surrounding Foshan City in the Pearl River Delta. A similar episode of 'countryside urbanization' can now be observed in the Yangtze River Delta, which experienced economic reform about half a decade later than the Pearl River Delta (see Figure 5.1).

The irreversible transformation of the rural landscape brought about by rapid urbanization and industrialization of the countryside in the Yangtze River Delta has caused concerns (Liu *et al.* 2010; Verdini and Wang 2011; K. Yang and Huang 2011a, 2011b).The acute problems emerging from this widespread occurrence of peri-urbanization include the depletion of arable land, the disruption of ecological balance and, above all, the loss of rural heritage and character.

Figure 5.1 The Yangtze River Delta generally refers to Shanghai, southern Jiangsu Province and northern Zhejiang Province of China

Rural Policy: 'building the new countryside'

Another insidious threat to the continued existence of rural heritage is posed by a series of rural planning policies and initiatives that are proposed to accelerate the modernization and development in rural areas. This is best exemplified by the government's recent campaign, 'building the new countryside'. The idea of building a 'new' countryside is derivative of the overarching and highlighted theme of planning policy – the integration of urban and rural development (Ahlers and Schubert 2009; Bray 2013). The campaign was launched against the backdrop of the widening gap in income and livelihood between the urban and rural population. Long *et al.* (2010, p. 459) summarize the salient features of the government's 'new countryside' campaign into five aspects: 'advanced production, improved livelihood, clean and tidy villages, a civilized social atmosphere and efficient management'.

One point that is particularly relevant to this research is 'advanced production', which is concerned with the optimization of production and circulation of agricultural produce. To optimize the farming system, land consolidation becomes the primary means to resolve rural land-use issues, especially in the urbanizing fringe areas as elaborated by Guo and Zhong in this edited volume. At the same time, many rural villages rent the farming land to a contractor if the community committee agrees.

The other relevant point is to break the traditional stereotype of the countryside as poor and dirty and to transform it into 'clean and tidy villages'. While this brings a substantial amount of financial incentive and support to regenerate rural villages, it also has a destructive impact on the character of rural landscapes. The problem stems from, on the one hand, the mistaken belief that rural areas should be 'developed', instead of 'regenerated', into something similar to those in urban areas in order to provide rural residents with a reasonable standard of modern amenities. On the other hand, the problem relates to the approaches adopted to implement the initiative. Modernization of the countryside is often associated with re-cladding or rebuilding existing houses. Admittedly, upgrading the domestic comfort of existing dwellings should be essential to the initiative. Far too often, however, rural villages and agricultural structures are modernized at the cost of losing the original morphological and architectural character. Instead of adopting modest refurbishment or conservation approaches, radical transformation and destruction of historical structures has become the norm for the 'new' countryside (see Figure 5.2).

Case Study: Suzhou, Jiangsu Province

To better understand the current physical and socio-economic conditions of the countryside in the Yangtze River Delta, this research takes the form of a case study

Figure 5.2   Examples of recently refurbished and new-build houses in the countryside

on the outskirts of Suzhou City, Jiangsu Province. In fact, the name 'Jiangsu' consists of two Chinese characters: river and abundance. The second word 'su' is a compound word, consisting of three sub-characters: rice, fish and grass, which symbolize fertility. It is a region that perfectly represents the identity of the Chinese civilization and the close relationship between agricultural activities and natural landscape, in particular, watercourses.

Likewise, the Suzhou countryside, similar to its historic city centre, is also characterized by canal-scape and features clusters of agricultural structures. Suzhou is one of the historic cities that have long-lasting links with traditional agricultural practice. Whereas it enjoys overwhelming superiority in developing rural tourism (Chen 2006; Wu 2008), it is rarely addressed in the existing body of literature if compared to Beijing and Chengdu.

Field Survey

As part of a research project and undergraduate teaching activities,[1] several field trips, face-to-face questionnaires and semi-structured interviews were conducted between July 2011 and March 2012. With its focus on rural heritage and its tourism development potential, this chapter mainly reports findings on the physical environment of rural villages in Suzhou and partly addresses the socio-economic conditions. A more detailed study on the socio-economic transformation induced by rural land-use conversion and its social cost has been published elsewhere (Verdini 2014).

During the period between July and October 2011, the research group undertook four field surveys across the urban-rural fringe of Suzhou and eight case studies were selected and analysed (Figure 5.3 and Table 5.2) (Verdini *et al.* 2011). The routes of the field trips mainly crossed the southern part of the Suzhou prefecture, including Suzhou Industrial Park, Suzhou New District, Xiancheng and Wuzhong District and the Kunshan and Wujiang counties (Figure 5.4). This is because the southern part of Suzhou is less urbanized and industrialized as it is farther away from Shanghai. In addition, this region has a greater natural resource for tourism development because of its close proximity to Tai Lake. For the above reasons, southern Suzhou was considered strategically important to this research.

Internal Deterioration of the Suzhou Countryside

In addition to the perceived external threats previously explained, another major threat to rural heritage is the demographic decline that has directly or indirectly resulted in the dereliction and dilapidation of tangible heritage in rural areas.

---

1 This research project is supported by the Suzhou Social Science Programme 2011 (11-B-08) and forms part of the undergraduate teaching programme of Xi'an Jiaotong-Liverpool University in Suzhou.

Rural Regeneration in the Yangtze River Delta 91

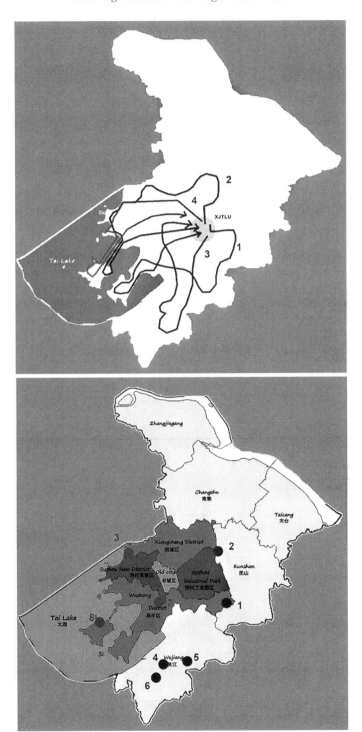

Figure 5.3 The routes of four field surveys and the locations of eight case studies

Table 5.2   The list of eight case studies

Case study		Location	Notes
1	**Xitang Village**	Kunshan County	Edging a new development area in Wuzhong District.
2	**Chuodunshan Village**	Kunshan County	Around Yangcheng Lake; regenerated as part of Building a New Countryside initiative.
3	**Jinchi Village**	Suzhou New District	Featuring a historical commercial street close to Tai Lake.
4	**Village cluster near Pingwang**	Wujiang County	Exhibiting the interwoven relationship between waterways, residences and agricultural practices.
5	**Nankun Village**	Wujiang County	Located in an industrialized area for silk production.
6	**Village cluster in the peninsula of Beimayang Lake**	Wujiang County	Located in an area of high ecological value but suffering from decline.
7	**Wangshan Village Scenic Area**	Wuzhong District	A hillside village; part of Building a New Countryside initiative; a national exemplary site.
8	**Dongcun Ancient Village and the system of island**	Wuzhong District	Located in the Tai Lake, possessing high ecological values and historical interest.

Source: (Verdini *et al.* 2011)

Despite the fact that the official census is conducted periodically, it is difficult to ascertain the actual number of rural residents and unoccupied houses in any given rural area. This is mainly because the rigid household registration system, set up to prevent unauthorized rural-to-urban migration in the 1960s, has nowadays adversely resulted in an enormous 'floating population' – namely migrants from rural areas living in cities. While the actual figure for the rural population loss is unclear, it is certain that there has been a significant increase in the aging population in China's countryside, which has been the case in many other countries in the world. However rural migrants, being generally not entitled to join the urban social welfare, might retain a strong attachment to their land, often contributing to the village subsistence through remittances. This means that a substantial number of historical houses and agricultural structures are left abandoned, such as a large group of elderly people, some of whom may have mastered traditional skills and handicrafts. On the other hand the dual system of household registration might favour a return of migrants to the countryside and possibly their investment in

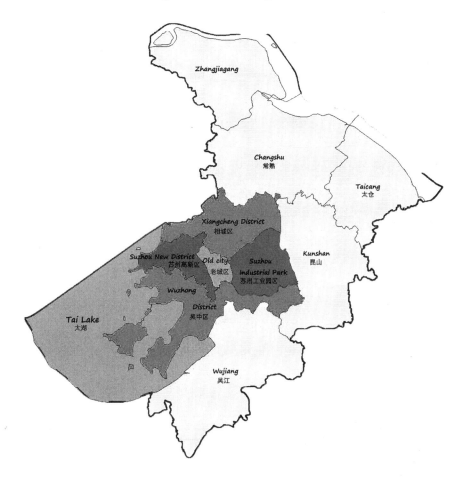

Figure 5.4   The districts and counties in the Suzhou prefecture

retail activities or services, after some years spent in the industrial or construction sector of fast-growing cities.

However, the legacy of countryside industrialization has scattered industrial developments, now often allocated in a disorderly and anarchic fashion in the survey areas. This problem mainly stems from the development of township and village enterprises that the government has promoted and supported since the 1980s (Friedmann 2005; Long *et al.* 2009), making appreciation of the aesthetic value of the traditional rural landscape a complex issue. Modern factories were built, sometimes adjacent to or mixed up with residential buildings and, sometimes, in the middle of farming land or nearby rural villages. In part, because of the phenomenal growth of rural enterprises, yet also because of the decline of the agricultural economy and the rise of secondary industry, many old houses in former agricultural villages were abandoned and became derelict.

Figure 5.5 Aerial photo of the historical high street of Jinshi Village (Case Study 3)

The degree of dereliction in the water villages in Suzhou perhaps can be exemplified by Jinshi Village (Case Study 3), a linear settlement located to the east bank of Tai Lake. Jinshi Village consists of many clusters of commercial and residential buildings erected in different time periods and lying along a canal connecting to the lake. The centre of the village features a continuous row of shop-houses built in the nineteenth century (see Figure 5.5). Not having undergone sweeping redevelopment, the village retains many of its original typo-morphological features as well as its townscape character.

Currently, there are about 500 households and 1,700 people living in the village. Around 35 houses are located in the historical high street area, one-third of which are unoccupied and only one of which retains its original commercial use – as a retail shop selling snacks, processed foods and daily products. Regardless of whether they are occupied or not, most of the houses are in a state of dilapidation, and some are practically uninhabitable (Figures 5.6 and 5.7). The village did not undergo redevelopment because the residents were dissatisfied with the compensation policy and refused to sign the relocation agreement. The historic structures in the high street area are left largely intact mainly because the residents hold the view that the government will resolve the disagreement in compensation

Figure 5.6   Unoccupied shop-houses in the high street and detached house

costs at some time in the future and developers will bulldoze the area and develop it into a holiday resort or an upscale neighbourhood.

Morphological features of these rural villages are often of special interest. Whereas most of the historical buildings in the Jinshi Village cluster together in the centre, the old houses in Nankun Village (Case Study 5) scatter over the settlement. Nankun Village is located in the Wujiang County, which was one of the major silk production centres in China in the past and remains so nowadays too. As silk production is a highly profitable enterprise, most households there have accumulated wealth from the silk-related industries, and some former farmers have become entrepreneurs embarking on new ventures in other types of industrial manufacturing. Undoubtedly, the local government has also contributed greatly to this economic and physical transformation by converting farm land into industrial use. As a result, industrial developments have encroached extensively on the farm land, and a vast area of agricultural landscape was wiped out to make way for profitable manufacturing industries. Nankun Village is one of the few villages in the county to retain much of the original rural morphology and character because of its remote location.

Houses in the village sit across the bay and form a crescent shape (Figure 5.8). With different heights, sizes, styles and locations, the residential structures erected in different time periods reveal the track of historical development in the village. Short rows of houses form a right angle with the crescent-shape bay. Standing in

Figure 5.7   Dilapidated and abandoned houses in the Jinshi Village

Rural Regeneration in the Yangtze River Delta 97

Figure 5.8 Aerial photo of Nankun Village (Case Study 5)

Figure 5.9 View towards the bay and the interlocking arrangement between the old and new houses in the area

Figure 5.10 Dilapidated and abandoned houses in the Nankun Village

between the nineteenth-century houses are the twentieth-century structures that, in most cases, were built in the open space of existing old houses to accommodate new members of the extended family. As the new two-storey structures are higher than the old one-storey ones, the view towards the bay is dominated by the new (Figure 5.9). Although the old houses are being sandwiched by the new and not highly noticeable in the bay view, they have a fairly strong presence in people's spatial perception when walking on the access road. All of the old houses, however, appear to be unoccupied and used as sheds to store crops or stack firewood (Figure 5.10). They are left derelict simply because the cost of modernization and refurbishment is high and there is no growing pressure for space as before. Due to the decline of the agricultural industry, the younger generations tend to leave the countryside to seek better employment.

A Possible Stimulus to Rural Economy: Rural Tourism Development in Suzhou

Although the Suzhou countryside is facing the renewed external threat from urbanization and rural policy and, internally, economic decline, demographic change and physical deterioration of agricultural villages, the rural Suzhou – with some external stimuli – still holds great potential for self-rejuvenation.

'Ubiquitous' Heritage Assets

A question that has to be asked is whether the existing cultural heritage assets and the local communities can support and sustain responsive rural tourism. Mundane and unassuming they may be, but farm houses, animal shelters and storage sheds, together with rice paddies, fish ponds, vegetable patches, fruit orchards and canals characterize the rural landscape of Suzhou. The ubiquitous rural 'heritage' and agricultural landscape of Suzhou provides picturesque and tranquil settings that are as idyllic as the renowned water towns in the region (Ruan *et al.* 2002; Zhou

Figure 5.11   View of Xitang Village (Case Study 1)

Figure 5.12   View of Jinshi Village (Case Study 3)

and Ma 2007; Ruan and Yuan 2011). Rural villages in Suzhou often exhibit a well-thought-out spatial arrangement, in which the man-made built environment seamlessly blends into its natural surroundings. They can provide places and host events for the joy-of-farmer-home tourism in a more authentic fashion (see Figure 5.11 and Figure 5.12).

Chuodunshan Village (Case Study 2) is an illustrative example of ubiquitous rural 'heritage' being capable of staging eco-tourism. Instead of allocating the money from the 'building the new countryside' project to individual households for renovating private houses, the community committee used the government subsidy to improve the public spaces in the village. The local government consequently chose the village to be the site to pilot an environmentally friendly water purification system. The overall quality of the public realm was significantly improved, although the spatial configuration of the village was slightly altered to enhance accessibility and convenience (see Figures 5.13, 5.14 and 5.15).

Most of the buildings in the villages were rebuilt in the 1980s. Some of them are in fact quite contemporary. In other words, no buildings in the village are of heritage value or 'historical' interest. Despite lacking the attraction of historic buildings, a local restaurant makes the most of the rural setting in the village and runs their business in an ingenious way. The restaurant draws customers from some tourist sites or train stations and attracts them by offering a free cruise along the waterway by motor yacht (see Figure 5.16). Customers do sightseeing within and around the village when the restaurant is preparing meals. Most of the ingredients used are sourced locally. There is a large tract of land to the south-east of the village, and many small patches in front of houses too, where the local residents grow various kinds of seasonal vegetables or breed livestock. The amount of local produce not only proves sufficient for local residents' consumption but also provides the restaurant with local ingredients. The restaurant seems to do good business in the area as many customers also come to the restaurant by private car in addition to those drawn from tourist sites. The restaurant gives a fascinating example of how to use the picturesque settings and agricultural landscape of rural villages to brand its countryside cuisine.

Community Involvement in Rural Tourism

To promote eco-tourism in the countryside, it is essential to support and sustain the rural communities. The policy of 'building the new countryside' is a double-edged sword for rural communities. Under the policy, the implementation of land consolidation optimizes agricultural production but many farmers were, in a sense, made redundant. Also, under this policy, China's countryside has gradually been transformed from an agriculture-based society into one with a mix of different industries. The promotion of rural tourism is beneficial to a smooth transition from primary industry to the tertiary. Dispossessed farmers can take part in the development of rural tourism. Certainly, the existing theme-park-like tourism models also help resolve the surplus of rural labourers. However, as Su

Rural Regeneration in the Yangtze River Delta 101

Figure 5.13 Aerial photos of Chuodunshan Village (Case Study 2) taken before and after the improvement of the public realm. The outer service road and the footpath on the south bank of the east-west canal were added

102   Urban China's Rural Fringe

Figure 5.14 The public spaces in Chuodunshan Village

Figure 5.15 Canals and footpaths. Many daily activities of local residents, such as cleaning and chopping vegetables and washing up take place along the canal

Figure 5.16 The restaurant provides customers a free cruise along the canal to the village by motor yacht

(2011) points out, if the rural tourism industry is intended to expand its market and move towards high-quality, personalized services, the government and competent authorities should provide training, finance and marketing support. It is also noted that some younger generations of former rural residents are beginning to move back to the countryside and start up small-scaled enterprises related to rural tourism development.

On the other hand, the older generations may potentially have an important role to play. Traditional crafts, customs, cuisines and farming techniques, for instance, are the intangible assets that suffer from decline. Much of the traditional handicraft products in Suzhou, such as embroidery and bamboo weaving, are produced in rural areas as home-based enterprises. Whereas the term 'rural heritage' denotes an attractive combination of natural and cultural heritage, the term 'cultural heritage' also encompasses both tangible and intangible assets. The importance of intangible rural heritage should be equal to the tangible (Zheng and Zhong 2004).

Discussion

Over the past two decades or so, rural tourism has been actively promoted by the Chinese government agencies to restore socio-economic vitality in the countryside. Although a cursory glance at the various government initiatives and campaigns for rural tourism development may suggest a corresponding rise of interests in protecting rural heritage, such a link appears to be tenuous in actuality.

Cultural heritage – in its both tangible and intangible forms – has been considered as a valuable asset for rural tourism development. From historical architecture and morphology, to traditional dress and handicraft, all have been or potentially will be transformed into a sort of 'product' for consumption in the tourism industry. Nonetheless, the extent to which urban demand for rural tourism can warrant the retention of ubiquitous cultural heritage that is not statutorily protected remains arguable and, perhaps, rather limited.

In the case of Suzhou City, which processes a greater number of cultural heritage properties, area-based statutory protection is accorded to only some historic water towns or ancient villages that are of exceptional historical interest, and could hardly be extended to a larger range. For instance, the shop-houses on the high street of Jingshi Village and the traditional residences scattering across Nankun Village, although being of some historical values, would not be awarded heritage status on the merit of their physical structure: neither would they be appreciated and retained to form the backdrop for rural tourism activities, due to the laissez-faire industrial development in their proximity and, also, owing to their geographical location that is far from the major rural tourism areas of the region. On the other hand, Chuodunshan Village, despite having no historical structures, can be successfully transformed into a place that is capable of hosting and entertaining urban visitors, mainly for the reasons of its advantageous location – which is close to Yangchen Lake, a major rural tourism area – and, in part, the natural scenery, agricultural landscape and morphological character of the village. Likewise, the extent to which rural communities can benefit from tourism development is also purely circumstantial – that is, depending on location and existing natural and cultural resources.

It should also be noted that Jiangsu Province, or the Yangtze River Delta, is located on the coastal area of China and possesses a vast natural resource and economic wealth. Urban citizens in the region have a relatively high demand for leisure and a high level of consumption, which may not be found, or be comparable with those, in the inland provinces. This is to say that the success of regenerating rural villages by promoting rural tourism is not necessarily transferrable to other regions in China. Another unanswered question would then be to what extent can tourism development alleviate rural poverty in other regions?

Conclusion

This chapter has illustrated the challenges and potential for protecting ubiquitous rural heritage through promoting tourism development. While the external threat to rural heritage is mainly posed by the rapid peri-urbanization expansion and the government's 'building the new countryside' policy, the internal demographic decline has also caused the desertion of tangible heritage and the disappearance of intangible heritage in the countryside. Rural tourism can serve as a possible stimulus to reform the economy of the countries and, to some extent, facilitate rural communities a smoother transition from the primary industry to the tertiary. Admittedly, however, it is not a one-for-all solution, or panacea, for communities in the rural land of China.

In conclusion, it is argued that the truly rural heritage is the everyday setting in the countryside that provides local communities with a stage on which to develop responsive tourism in the countryside. The ubiquitous rural heritage better reflects the lives in the past and communicates the present generation. It also has greater flexibility in making changes and greater potential to stimulate local economies and promote sustainable tourism. However, it is evident that today the main driver of rural regeneration is the growing demand for quality countryside coming from the new Chinese urban elite, especially in areas like the Yangtze River Delta, with little involvement of local communities. The role and the effectiveness of community-based rural regeneration could be a future research direction to further explore.

References

Ahlers, A.L. and Schubert, G. 2009. 'Building a New Socialist Countryside': Only a Political Slogan?, *Journal of Pediatric, Maternal & Family Health-Chiropractic*, 38 (4), 35–62.

Arlt, W.G. and Feng, G. 2009. 'The Yangzi River Tourism Zone', in *River Tourism*, edited by B. Prideaux and M. Cooper. Wallingford, Oxfordshire, UK: CABI, 117–30.

Bosselmann, P.C., Kondolf, G.M., Jiang, F., Geping, B., Zhimin, Z. and Mingxin, L. 2010. The Future of a Chinese Water Village: Alternative Design Practices Aimed to Provide New Life for Traditional Water Villages in the Pearl River Delta, *Journal of Urban Design*, 15 (2), 243–67.

Bray, D. 2013. Urban Planning Goes Rural: Conceptualising the 'New Village', *China Perspectives*, 2013 (3), 53–62.

Chen, J. 2006. The Exploration of the Rural Tourism Development Potential of Yangtze River Delta *Special Zone Economy*, 2006 (12), 198–200 (Chinese).

Daugstad, K., Rønningen, K. and Skar, B. 2006. Agriculture as an Upholder of Cultural Heritage? Conceptualizations and Value Judgements. A Norwegian Perspective in International Context, *Journal of Rural Studies*, 22 (1), 67–81.

Deng, J. 2009. 'Devlopment Model of Rural Tourism in Yangzi River Delta', MA Dissertation, Tongji University, Shanghai (Chinese).

English Heritage. 2008. *Leader and the Historic Environment*, English Heritage, London. Available at: http://www.english-heritage.org.uk/publications/leader/ [accessed: 29/04/2011].

Friedmann, J. 2005. *China's Urban Transition*, Minneapolis: University of Minnesota Press.

Gao, S., Huang, S. and Huang, Y. 2009. Rural Tourism Development in China, *International Journal of Tourism Research*, 11 (5), 439–50.

Guo, H., Sun, Y., Ren, G. and Lu, M. 2008. Study on the Development of Leisure Agriculture and Rural Tourism in Beijing, *Geo-Information Science*, 10 (4), 453–461 (Chinese).

He, K. 2008. Discussion on Improving the Disertification of Rural Employment through Rural Rourism Development – Based on the Data of Rural Tourism in Yangzi River Delta, *Journal of Changzhou Institute of Technology (Social Science Edition)*, 26 (4), 96–9 (Chinese).

Jackson, J. 2006. Developing Regional Tourism in China: The Potential for Activating Business Clusters in a Socialist Market Economy, *Tourism Management*, 27 (4), 695–706.

Li, Y. 2014. 'Introduction to Policies on Protection of Villages in China', *WHITRAP Newsletter* [online] (27), 30–31. Available at: http://www.whitr-ap.org/index. php?classid=1487&id=86&action=download.

Lincoln, B., Lindberg, J. and Follett, J.A. 2010. *Heritage-Based Rural Development – Forum Journal, Winter 2010*, Washington, DC: National Trust for Historic Preservation.

Liu, Y.S., Wang, J.Y. and Long, H.L. 2010. Analysis of Arable Land Loss and Its Impact on Rural Sustainability in Southern Jiangsu Province of China, *Journal of Environmental Management*, 646–53. Available at: http://www.sciencedirect.com/science/article/pii/S0301479709003326.

Long, H., Heilig, G.K., Li, X. and Zhang, M. 2007. Socio-Economic Development and Land-Use Change: Analysis of Rural Housing Land Transition in the Transect of the Yangtse River, China, *Land Use Policy*, 24 (1), 141–53.

Long, H., Liu, Y., Li, X. and Chen, Y. 2010. Building New Countryside in China: A Geographical Perspective, *Land Use Policy*, 27 (2), 457–70.

Long, H., Liu, Y., Wu, X. and Dong, G. 2009. Spatio-Temporal Dynamic Patterns of Farmland and Rural Settlements in Su-Xi-Chang Region: Implications for Building a New Countryside in Coastal China, *Land Use Policy*, 26 (2), 322–33.

Malpass, P. 2009. 'Whose Housing Heritage?', edited by, *Valuing Historic Environments*, Farnham: Ashgate, 201–14.

Mayes, T., Meeks, S.K., Bradford, R.M. and Talmage, V. 2010. *Bridging Land Conservation and Historic Preservation – Forum Journal, Fall 2010*, Washington DC: National Trust for Historic Preservation.

Peng, H. and Li, J. 2008. On Rural Tourism Exploration & New Socialist Countryside Construction, *Journal of Pingxiang College*, 25 (1), 49–52 (Chinese).

Prideaux, B., Cooper, M. and Ebrary, I. 2009. *River Tourism*, Wallingford, Oxfordshire, UK: CABI.

Ruan, Y., Shao, Y. and Lin, L. 2002. The Characteristics, Values and the Preservation Planning of the Towns in Jiangnan Water Region, *Urban Planning Forum*, 2002 (1) (Chinese).

Ruan, Y. and Yuan, F. 2011. On Historic Towns Conservation: Conservation and Development of Historic Water Towns South of the Yangtze River, *Urban Planning Forum*, 2011 (5), 95–101 (Chinese).

Shao, Q. 2007. Developing Rural Tourism and Promoting the Construction of New Countryside, *Qiushi Magazine*, 42–44. Available at: http://cnki.sdll.cn:85/KNS50/detail.aspx?QueryID=62&CurRec=17.

Sharpley, R. and Vass, A. 2006. Tourism, Farming and Diversification: An Attitudinal Study, *Tourism Management*, 27 (5), 1040–52.

Su, B. 2011. Rural Tourism in China, *Tourism Management*, 32 (6), 1438–41.

Verdini, G. 2014. The Costs of Urban Growth at the Fringe of a Chinese City: Evidence from Jinshi Village in Suzhou, *International Planning Development Review*, 36 (4).

Verdini, G. and Wang, Y.W. 2011. 'Planning the Urban Fringe: Theoretical Perspectives and Practical Limits in China', paper presented to *The 8th IALE World Congress: Landscape Ecology for Sustainable Environment and Culture*, Beijing, 18–23 August 2011.

Verdini, G., Wang, Y.W., Huang, F., Yang, X. and Li, Q. 2011. *2011 Suzhou Social Science Research Programme: Assigning Open Space Non-Market Values as a Tool for Planning the Urban-Rural Fringe in Suzhou*, Department of Urban Planning and Design, XJTLU, Suzhou.

Véron, E. 2013. 'Les Espaces Ruraux Touristiques Dans Le Delta Du Yangzi, Entre Intégration Ville-Campagne Et Développement Rural', *EchoGéo* [online] (26). (French) Available at:<http://echogeo.revues.org/13607> [accessed: 8/4/2014].

Wang, Y. and Yin, M. 2010. Research on Improving the Quality of Rural Tourism Service in Beijing, *Journal of Green Science and Technology*, 2010 (12), 128–30 (Chinese).

Wang, Y.W. and Verdini, G. 2011. 'Heritage-Led Rural Regeneration: A New Dawn in China?', paper presented to *The 8th IALE World Congress: Landscape Ecology for Sustainable Environment and Culture*, Beijing, 18–23 August 2011.

Wu, G. 2008. Study on Regional Tourism Urbanization and Urban Tourism Regionalization: A Case Study of the Interaction in the Process of Regional Integration of Yangtse River Delta, *Areal Research and Development*, 27 (1), 51–5 (Chinese).

Yang, K. and Huang, Y. 2011a. Protection and Transmission of Rural Spatial Structure, *Development of Small Cities & Towns*, 2011 (3), 65–9 (Chinese).

Yang, K. and Huang, Y. 2011b. Protection and Transmission of Rural Spatial Structure: The Case Study of the Coastal Plain of Jiangsu Province, *Jiangsu Urban Planning*, 2011 (5), 37–41 (Chinese).

Yang, Z., Cai, J. and Sliuzas, R. 2010. Agro-Tourism Enterprises as a Form of Multi-Functional Urban Agriculture for Peri-Urban Development in China, *Habitat International*, 34 (4), 374–85.

Zeng, B. and Ryan, C. 2012. Assisting the Poor in China through Tourism Development: A Review of Research, *Tourism Management*, 33 (2), 239–48.

Zhang, Y., Xu, J.-H. and Zhuang, P.-J. 2011. The Spatial Relationship of Tourist Distribution in Chinese Cities, *Tourism Geographies*, 13 (1), 75–90.

Zheng, Q. and Zhong, L. 2004. A Discussion of Developing Model of Community-Involved Rural Tourism, *Tourism Tribune*, 19 (4), 33–7 (Chinese).

Zhou, X. and Ma, X. 2007. Protection of Architectural Culture Heritage of Water Rural Area in South of Yangzi River, *Huazhong Architecture*, 2007 (1), 214–8 (Chinese).

Chapter 6

Rural-Urban Edge: A Review of Spatial Planning Representation and Policy Discourse in the Pearl River Delta

Francesca Frassoldati and Dongjin Qi

Introduction

Rural and urban adjectives qualify in general wisdom as well as in spatial planning regulation separate and independent realms. This dichotomy presumes the existence of neat demarcation between urban and rural spheres. Rural-urban overlapping is generally contrasted by urban planning either implementing urban containment policies to safeguard an independent countryside or expanding city boundaries in order to include within the urban realm those areas that have been exposed to urban development. More recent urban theories that highlight rural-urban interconnection seldom apply to conventional regulatory efforts.

However, the emergence of subjective practices to reconfigure traditional paradigms in the use of rural places is rather common. In rapidly urbanizing China, functional mixing of rural and urban features occurs frequently in the outskirts of cities, but even in remote places as the chapter by Sturzaker and Law illustrates in this volume.

This chapter reviews the current conceptualizations of the rural-urban edge in contemporary urban-driven Chinese society and attempts to determine whether demarcation or merging between 'rural' and 'urban' address spatial planning in an emerging urbanized megaregion such as the Pearl River Delta.[1] The chapter refers to the term 'rural-urban edge' in a critical sense. A binary differentiation applies to definitions such as urban or rural administrative boundary, urban or rural population according to a socio-demographic threshold and urban or rural land use regulation. Although the three indicators may have interconnections, indeed they make up three imperfectly overlapping definitions of rural and urban spheres. For various reasons, in China the referent of the terms 'rural' and 'urban' has shifted at

---

1 This study is part of a long-term research project supported by the State Key Laboratory of Subtropical Building Science at the South China University of Technology (grant 2012ZC31) and by the National Natural Science Foundation of China (grant 50950110350).

different paces in the administrative, social and economic fields, which resulted in rural-urban edge being seen as a replaceable political construct.

It has to be questioned the objectivity of such an edge as a spatial descriptor. In China the rural-urban edge represents an institutional boundary between local and central powers, or collective and state organizations. Rural institutions and locales in the more wealthy regions do not necessarily reflect an actual marginality or characterize remote and sparsely inhabited areas. The proximity to urban lifestyle introduced with modern technologies and the integration of primary, secondary and tertiary sectors have furthermore expanded urbanity far beyond built-up areas of cities, even when institutional differences remain in place. If spatial planning has to coordinate multiple development strategies, unbiased understanding is crucial. Yet the urban growth discourse simplifies the potential conflict between different regulatory systems in a conflict over land use.

The study contrasts this myopic view by exploring the undervalued role of local institutions that self-adapted to urbanization. We argue that in Chinese emerging urban regions the conceptualization of the urban fringe as a third space for spatial planning, neither urban nor rural, is not itself a solution to oversimplification. The rural and urban planning profession bears the responsibility for being a technical means for the misrepresentation of regulatory conflict in the first place. Spatial planning in China universally adopts city-design paradigms and conveys city-centred decisions into fixed asset investment, thus subverting its function of relational coordination of spaces and institutions.

The aim of this chapter is, therefore, twofold. First, we briefly review the recent transformation of rural and urban separated governance, arguing that so far the purpose of rural and urban planning policies in China have remained to materialize political and non-spatial decisions (Liu and Stapleton 2006). Notwithstanding dramatic changes, the 'local sphere' activism is an unlikely implication of spatial decisions in formal urban institutions (Huang 2012). Second, and following on from this, the chapter attempts to illustrate the interactions of rural institutions with the urban sphere as a form of social compromise between local and centralized powers. The reference is to concepts such as 'nexus' (Duara 1988: 25) or 'bundle' (Haila 2007) of relational praxes, or in other words a conduct order based on reciprocal roles that substitutes exclusive jurisdiction of the legal state (Hamilton 2006: 69): rural and urban institutions coexist on opposite sides and with differentiated roles because none of them have exclusive power on decisions.

The study draws from experiences in the Pearl River Delta (PRD) in Guangdong Province, one of the coastal Special Economic Zones, in which rural-urban integration tackles multidimensional dynamics that will neither be controlled nor directed by means of homogeneous zoning. In a number of situations, rural institutions did efficaciously transform space based on the coexistence of rural-urban diversity. We wish to emphasize the relational character of decision-making about space in the PRD. This contrasts the rigid foundation of the national urban planning discipline and the ambiguous rural-urban integration policy which is mostly based on that urban planning tradition (an ambiguity that is further explained below). Scholarship's concern about China's rural space is frequently centred on structural incoherence of rural and urban land-ownership, divergence of local objectives vs. national targets, and fragility of superimposed urban models in rural areas. However, a different question overcomes these concerns in the PRD case: is the interaction revolving around the rural-urban edge really the short-lived occurrence which will easily dissolve into a simplified urban paradigm?

The Representation of the Rural-Urban Edge in China's Spatial Planning

The ambiguous rural-urban hybridization has been scrutinized since the 1960s in mature industrialized societies. Pahl (1966) firstly invited us to observe urbanity as the gradient of a rural-urban continuum that encompasses social behaviour, functional organization and to a lesser extent the attitude towards spatial differentiations (more recently on the same issue, see for example Brandt 2003; Isserman 2005; Ward and Brown 2009). In different regions and times the focus has shifted to urban sprawl in North America (Peiser 1989; Angel *et al.* 2010), post-urban and counter-urbanization agglomeration in Europe and the US (Garreau 1991; Soja 2000) or disputed idealization of the countryside (Satsangi *et al.* 2010). Another strand has unfolded that concerns rural idyll accompanying the weakening of the socio-economic role of agriculture in rural areas (Ward and Brown 2009, among others[2]) and the implications for both rural and urban governance of the prevailing appreciation of local milieus (Mardsen *et al.* 1993; Goodman *et al.* 2011).

From this review, emerging urban societies appear to characterize, mostly, undisputed rural-urban transition. In these contexts, urban economy and trade are assumed to guide spatial planning and local policy, not concerns for the rural realm (Logan 2001; a more critical perspective in Agergaard *et al.* 2010). Urbanization, therefore, is broadly seen as a denial of traditional rurality and a period when the main national and local concerns go to GDP growth, social mobility of individuals and new regional agglomerations dominated by industrialization (Gugler 1996; Scott 2002). However, as Tacoli (1998 and 2003) puts it, these societies do indeed have practices in which rurality transforms thanks to, and to the advantage of, urban growth.

Undeniably, China's socio-economic dynamism during the last three decades lead to a shrinkage in the volume of rural administrations and people's dependence on rural livelihoods. However, few conceptualizations depend on political representation as much as rural and urban definitions in coastal China,

---

2 A more comprehensive overview of debated issues is in the conference output collected by Brandt, Tress and Tress (eds) 2000. Multifunctional Landscapes: Interdisciplinary Approaches to Landscape Research and Management. Conference material for the International Conference on Multifunctional Landscapes: Roskilde: Centre for Landscape Research-University of Roskilde.

where the significant rural proto-industrialization dating back to the late Empire and Republican eras was negated and neglected for geopolitical reasons in the 1950s (Bramall 2007: 8). Modern plants for the processing of agricultural products (such as sugar refinery, mechanized weavers and so on) built by local landlords outside the city boundary in South-Eastern China (Hamilton 2006) were frequently stigmatized for their capitalistic exploitation and diverging tasks were strategically assigned to promote non-commercial agricultural production and basic industrialization (Bramall 2007). Since the land reform in 1952, the sharp divide between rural and urban administrative systems was a reliable representation of the economic spaces of city and countryside.

However, since the late 1960s and more clearly in the 1970s the rural governments have had the possibility of developing local industries for local needs (Bramall 2007), which later became the reign of commune and brigade-level enterprises. The organized presence of an industrial policy in rural areas, one that promoted local initiatives opposite to the city's vertical regulation, made the rural-urban edge more permeable and undermined the codified conceptualization of the rural space as the supplier of sole agricultural production. The effects were so great in institutional terms that, according to Lynn (1998), this rural industrialization was the beginning of the end of the communist planning system. It surely was the end of static, self-contained rural settlements in the coastal regions where industrialization was started a century before.

The implementation of Special Economic Zones in selected coastal regions since 1978, which included four cities in Guangdong Province and since 1994 the whole PRD, resulted in even more remarkable effects in terms of industrial and urban growth, which promoted the conventional wisdom that the rural realm is simply a city-to-be. Rural settlements in the PRD have the characteristic of medium-sized towns, and inhabitants are likely to work for industries or retail and services instead of retaining farming as the prospect for their entire life.

With Lin's (2001a, 2001b) seminal work on rural-urban interaction in the PRD, it emerged clearly that the nearby urban market had acted as a forerunner of development in rural places during the initial stages of economic reforms in China, due to the different regulation of land uses. By the end of the 1990s, also in other Chinese regions rural development was simply equated with urbanization by policymakers and urban planning tools were urged to regulate land use changes (Lin 2001b). Yet, and as we will discuss in more detail below, the relation between urban and rural interests has been fragmented into multiple intra-rural and intra-urban frictions and synergies of interests (Solinger 1999).

All these matters reflect the general challenge of 'how to govern' urban megaregions where rural and urban activities, spaces and inhabitants coexist and 'how to plan' functional spaces that do not fit with conventional city and countryside boundaries. It is frequently the spatial proximity and convenient mix of interspersed intensive agriculture, cottage industry, residential compounds and urban centres that attract daily commuters, short-term migrants and new settlers (Chung and Zhou 2011). Most of the contributions regarding China's disordered urban growth, however, revolve around city growth management (Wu 2002; Logan 2001), social polarization (Lin 2009) or resource misuse (Ding and Lichtenberg 2011), with few studies concentrating on regional rural-urban interaction in spatial or institutional terms (Ho 2005; Chung and Zhou 2011; Huang 2010).

To some extent, there is the suspicion of a prejudice in the understanding of praxis to be examined (as denounced in Haila 2007), in which ideological positions may develop based on implicit judgements of the Chinese urbanization. Such prejudice intersects indifferently Chinese and international studies. On one hand, it is regarded as 'underdeveloped' and a process that will go through known stages, while on the other, as a collection of exclusive and specific paths that do not allow for any generalization (Lin 2001b, p. 385). Neither the generalizing nor particularism view is satisfying. Beyond China's governance of the rural-urban edge, the question is whether the spatial planning standard that is applied universally for providing a 'better' space through rationalized actions in all contexts can encompass both city and non-city spaces (see on this latter point Gallent *et al.* 2008). The judgement of 'better' is clearly embedded within a cultural system, which in China has been traditionally dominated by the paradigm of a regular inhabited environment to rationalize and domesticate natural resources (Hoa 1981).

Biases of Conventional Rural-Urban Planning in the PRD Horizon

The 'better' mentioned above is frequently framed by scholars into three dimensions that might summarize the advantages borne by urban formalization: namely, land-ownership, decision-making and the urban design power in rationalizing urbanization. It will be argued that conventional illustration of these three characteristics does not necessarily fit with regional development paths highlighted in the PRD. On the contrary, the discrete and not continuous regulative planning frame of differentiated ownership, localized decision-making and non-formalized spatial layouts have indeed supported rural-urban interactions more than arbitrary divide.

Despite formal changes, the Chinese post-reform period has retained traditional structures of property rights and institutional arrangements for decision-making that radically differ between rural and urban administration, which can be summarized as: rural, locally rooted collective ownership, the collective capacity to make decision vs. centralized ownership and the capacity to make decisions in urban areas. This distinction has polarized criticisms for the mixed and uneven nature of property rights and some centre-local conflict on the entitlement to make decisions. In fact Haila (2007) convincingly calls for the acknowledgement of a bundle of rights in both urban and rural realms which reflects in a nexus of regulatory forces, some of which prevail without excluding others. Rural, flexible arrangement in land use regulation indeed has proved instrumental to the PRD trajectories of urbanization. As far as peculiar socio-economic rural agglomerations pre-existed, the opportunity to mobilize local and shared decision-making in

114 *Urban China's Rural Fringe*

a fashion that is distant from the institutional centralism of urban policies has promoted intermediate poles of urbanity.

The absence of individual land-ownership or, alternatively, the lack of centralized regulation is generally stigmatized as an element of uncertainty. However, cases such as the urban redevelopment of villages in the city of Guangzhou led by the collective institution and negotiated with the government (Chung and Zhou 2011), or various cases in which the village committees invest in logistic services, hotels, restaurants and property development around the major PRD cities, question the ownership issue as an element that hampers structural transformation. These collective poles absorb rural-urban dichotomies and drive the rural-urban edge away from the city border (Lin 2001; Ho 2005). Moreover, the answers given to land-ownership concerns contain misleading conclusions, as they generally support *a priori* the concept that unequivocal individual property rights would grant fair decision-making (Haila 2007).

Beside ownership, several authors highlight the anarchy of rural areas as opposed to the vertical transmission of orders from the centre that characterize city planning with reference to the formal regulation of spatial uses (Wu 2002). In fact, many Chinese authors explain the construction of hierarchies of power as an overlapping of competencies instead of neatly separated roles (Shue 2008), which extend far beyond rural-urban edges. Each governmental level sets and transmits targets, according to its own role, that guide the relation with others' decisions and praxis. This relational conduct may manifest in some imperfect correspondence between the stated narrative of facts and actual practice, but both are meaningful components of decision-making (Huang 2008). The imperfect coexistence implies the exercise of relativized responsibility, summarizes Huang (2008), including eventually a calculated reticence of ruling exercised by formal institutions that crafts a flexible sphere for action by subordinates and a pragmatic open-ended process. In synthesis, targets of central and local institutions or the ones expressed by society and individuals may be very distant, but their coexistence is nevertheless acceptable as far as open antithesis does not emerge.[3]

Even in the frequent event of annexation of subordinated administrations, considered below, pre-existing locally rooted institutions may retain some organizational relevance in the new hierarchy of decision-making because of their strategic capacity to mobilize resources. Particularly in Guangzhou, the main city of the PRD, rural villages that have been incorporated into urban districts were rescinded as administrative units and urban Street Committees attained administration of local affairs, but *de facto* the ruling group of the village renovated its influence in economic and practical decisions (Chung and Zhou 2011). In fact, with decentralization reforms, the regulatory power of the central

---

3 It is only in these terms that the famous saying to act 'like a man crossing the river who has to feel for the stepping stones' attested to Deng Xiaoping during his visit to Shenzhen acquires practical significance. There is (or there has been) the possibility to try, although without any safeguard.

state can hardly modify the roots of existing local regimes, for better or worse (Huang 2010; White 1998). These pragmatic adjustments enrich with unexpected nuances of disenchantment the central government discourse of 'big stability and small adjustments' (da wending xiao tiaozhen).

Finally, the blame on weak, formalized spatial planning in rural settlements undermines the acknowledgement of clear social and spatial conventions that have been regulating PRD rural spaces for centuries (Siu 2007). The introduction of regulatory market forces in this relational world – whatever the nature of that market (Haila 2007) – has stimulated regulatory urban control by zoning tools (Lin 2009). In the Chinese context of decision-making, spatial planning offers the objectivity of both a target (the overall view of the future) and fixed boundaries to exercise power within. Chinese modernist planning has applied physical design as a zoning control since the establishment of the Republic of China; at the time of collectivization, the state unequivocally allocated city land uses whilst collectives oversaw flexible land use redistributions in the countryside. Late 1970s reforms increased the size of the urban economy with the backing of planning disciplines. Finally, since the 1990s spatial planning has expanded its control over urbanizing rural settlements (Leaf and Hou 2006). The function of planning-by-design is not any coordinated implementation, but is the reference for operational arrangements that are relatively unpredictable in detail. However, physical design makes urbanity appear predictable and certainly persuasive. The multitude of 'development zones' established in the PRD as prospective investments to drive collective land requisition is a possible example of the way formal urban development planning can prove *de facto* unrealistic (Wong and Tang 2005). Figure 6.1 illustrates the actual condition of Zhaoqing city and surrounding farmland, located in the north-western side of the PRD; at its back, the Urban Planning Bureau expects to develop a new business and cultural centre, which will multiply threefold the current urban area, as Figure 6.2 illustrates. The predictable expansion of the urban edge does not guarantee any feasibility of realistic urban decisions.

Figure 6.1   Present rural-urban edge of Zhaoqing, one of the nine cities of the PRD

Figure 6.2   The urban future of Zhaoqing, as displayed at the local Urban Planning Bureau

Evolving Rural-Urban Relations

The multi-faceted complexity of rural urbanization is better understood if investigations focus on the tensions in the non-city-space. It is fundamental to remark that in historic China 'urban' qualified the city-space[4] as an administrative sphere of rulers in direct relationship with the central state (so-called statutory cities) beyond physical differentiation. City-making had been, in the past, a powerful enacting of central rules. Flourishing market-towns, like Foshan in the PRD, were to a great extent urban according to commerce and trade functionality, social life and organizational complexity, and even considering their physical structure. However, they were not included in the Imperial urban realm, as for a long time they have not been administrative seats (Rowe 1984; Liu and Stapleton 2006). For a lengthy period, Chinese cities have had the peculiar role of administrative structures of the state more than the offspring of local resources of autonomy and entrepreneurship (Rowe 1984, p. 38).

Chinese urbanization, and to a great extent the boundary between urban and rural realms, might be interpreted as the gradual integration of settlements within the urban-ruled sphere, whatever their productive base and grade of economic complexity was, for better centralized control. At least in governing matters, the argument may be that the edge between rural and urban is variable according to conveniences. This contingency has to be considered when the initial phase of the 1980s industrialization of the two main Deltas of China, Pearl River and Yangtze, is regarded as a process based on non-urban areas to accommodate transformations of the state-lead economy, reducing at the time the dramatic inconvenience of

---

    4   We use here the term city-space as intended by Soja (2000: 8): a phenomenon which embodies the 'configuration of social relations, built forms, and human activity'.

rural abundance of underemployed manpower and migration towards major urban centres (Lin 2001; Tian and Ge 2011; Tian and Luo 2012).

A key debate revolves around the city boundary as a concept on the move. According to the fortunate definition of different waves of modern Chinese regional urbanization (Yeh *et al.* 2006), there are four stages of the role of city and, consequently, of rural-urban boundary rearrangement. In 1949–78 the extreme control of resources allocation in the city induced a kind of institutional anti-urbanization and counter-urbanization: China's urban population was less than 20 per cent, but massive industrial expansion and agglomerations were invisible as they were hidden within rural administration (Whyte and Parish 1984; Lin 2001). A double system emerged of formally non-urban places, which were, however, territorial centres potentially capable of economic diversification. In the 1950s, the stark differentiation of the rural realm signified diverse land-ownership, labour allocation and resource redistribution (Siu 2007); an effective 'invisible wall', as defined by Parish (1981). Rural space and workers were strategic assets for national security, and were restrained to agricultural production and basic industry.[5] Centralized planning was implemented by imposing productive targets more than peripheral control over local decisions, which through time developed into forms of negotiation (White 1998). Thus some flexibility was retained locally about the use of land and soil (Siu 2007).

A different period for rural-urban relations was the first decade of the open door policy (1978–88), characterized by tentative arrangements to 'control the growth of large cities, rationally develop medium-sized cities and actively develop small cities' (as stated by the National Urban Planning Conference in 1980 and adopted as a national policy by the State Council in the same year; Yeh *et al.* 2006; Whyte and Parish 1984). Basically, legal opportunities to 'leave farmland, not the village; enter the factory, but not the city' (*litu bulixiang, jinchang bujincheng*) fuelled Town and Village Enterprises, land use change and administrative redefinitions (Yue *et al.* 2005): flexible land use decision-making empowered rural localities and rural households, particularly in areas such as the PRD (PRD Open Economic Region has been institutionalized since 1985). The earliest migration reached the clusters of industries that were forming where rural institutions successfully operated the switch from Commune and Brigade Industries (*shedui gongye*, introduced in 1958 and reformed in the early 1970s) to export-oriented Town and Village Enterprises (*xiangzhen qiye*, since 1984). Migrants settled temporarily in factory dormitories where they had scarce contacts with the formal city. Local economic decisions driven by aspiration to an urban lifestyle accelerated in the late 1980s. Although the overall structure of these settlements was not changed, single buildings have been beautified, modified, enlarged and so on to fit with a more urban context. The

---

5   All over China, this was also the time for massive construction of social, economic and physical infrastructure in the countryside, which were later dismissed as inefficient after the de-collectivization (Hoa 1981; Bramall 2007).

local tertiary sector (construction, infrastructure, transportation) thus became a driving force of decentralized trajectories of urbanization.

The third phase from 1988 to 2001 is in fact characterized by structural land use change and administrative reforms to the advantage of the urban sphere.

Figure 6.3   Dwelling makeover and traditional building in a village that is now surrounded by Guangzhou city

However, taking again the example of PRD, rural and urban modes of production and regulation diverged in this period more than socio-economic matters in the previous decade (Yue *et al.* 2005; Tian and Ge 2011). To relieve the disadvantage of rural inhabitants, from 1991 the Villagers' Committees and Community Shareholding Cooperatives were allowed to redistribute to indigenous households net profits from land-leasing to overseas entrepreneurs or locally based successful enterprises, which were thus rather pleased not to leave the rural collective rights system permanently. On the other hand, regulation about *de facto* urbanization did become at that point a threat to the ambition of having an overall control of functional city-space. Beginning in 1987, major administrative reorganization redefined what was urban and what is rural. Local cadres at township and town (*xiangzhen*) level were encouraged to support aggressive investment policies by the allocation of collective land to other uses, thus boosting compulsory land requisition by local governments (Lin 2009). The resulting continuous renegotiation of the regulating power also became explicit, as shown in Table 6.1.

Table 6.1   Rural-urban edge in the institutional bodies

Institution	City (*chengshi*)	County (*xian*)	Township and Town (*xiangzhen*)	Village (*cun*)
Land-ownership	State	Ostensibly rural, without direct control of land use	Mostly non-collective (former communes)	Rural grassroot organizations (collectives)
Land resource governance	By the municipality, through the Urban Planning Bureau	Overall control. Progressively abolished	To promote local urbanization and control farmland	The families of village
Spatial layout	Regulatory plan, strategic plan, sector plans, etc.	Interface between the province and subordinate administrations	Rural and urban plan, sector plans	Village committee, families in the space they are responsible for

China's fourth wave of urbanization is constructing a discourse on the quality of spaces and urban life as an infrastructure for urban competition (Wu 2007). Tertiary industries and urban consumption, which is itself a profitable economic sector, sustain a 'headquarters economy' and project Chinese main urban regions onto a global stage (Liu and Stapleton 2006). Urbanization is regulated according

120   *Urban China's Rural Fringe*

to top-down centralization (so-called 'three concentrations'[6]) to increase land use efficiency, particularly with reference to industrial estates (Wong and Tang 2005; Tian and Ge 2011). Migration has also changed since the late 1990s (Yeh and Wu 1996, Wu 2002, Huang 2010). Today, migrants frequently hold some vocational training diplomas and seek an urban future in both central cities and emerging second tier cities or towns (Siu 2007). Rural-urban interaction, in terms of multi-directional flows and synergies in a space neither conventionally urban nor rural (Tacoli 1998, Rigg 2006), in fact 'squeezes' remoteness. Current planning practice indicates growing tensions over questions of control, both between central and local administrations within the region, and among actors at local levels (Leaf and Hou 2006, Tian and Luo 2012), notwithstanding rural-urban dualism still prevails in decision-making.

The Underlying Distortion of the Rural-urban Integration Discourse

As drafted above, the spatial morphology of coastal China does not fit with the binary of a rural space for traditional subsistence as opposed to urban and modern industrial agglomeration (see, for example, the literature review in Yaping and Min 2009). Centres with different dimensions and a generally urbanized countryside caused the urban economy to penetrate ostensibly rural contexts. At a broad level, McGee's definition of *desakota* patterns in 1980s East Asian regions had the merits of incorporating mixed agricultural and commercial specializations with new cottage industries, and traditional dense rural settlements hybridized with modern lifestyles. It represented an alternative to the extension of the rural-urban dichotomy as in European and North American experiences into a context-appropriate Asian 'whole' (McGee *et al.* 2007).

The push for rural industrialization and strong pro-growth motivations has increased the hybridization of rural-urban and urban-rural functions backed by the government since the 1960s. The rural-urban dichotomy has thus been contradicted by the development of a rather dense, rural-borne urban offspring that intersperses with the relatively lower density of the discontinued urban expansion. Based on that observation, Zhou and Shi (1995) were the first Chinese authors to recommend a redefinition of rural and urban thresholds according to the influence of main centres (see also Tian and Ge 2011; Yuan *et al.* 2006), which aimed at grounding more nuanced and coherent policies.

Other Asian countries have pursued similar rural development paths to diversify the opportunities for work in rural areas, limit rural migration and finally stimulate the domestic demand (Agergaard 2010). For these reasons, Chinese authors currently identify a reiterated differentiation between a natural process

---

6   Namely: concentration of industries, development of large-scale agriculture, rearrangement of scattered villages and farming settlements into town form. The policy has been implemented since the early 2000s.

of expansion of central cities (*chengshihua*), in which the integration of migrants and a former rural population within the city welfare system may prove difficult, and the growth of towns and villages (*chengzhenhua*) where households have the relatively easy possibility to shift in socio-economic terms from rural to urban without facing immediate institutional integration with the city level. The point is that it is misleading to oversimplify the transformation of towns and villages merely in terms of land use change and proximity to the main city core as a process of city growth, as the comprehensive construction of citizenship is an exogenous process to the people involved.[7]

Whatever the public debate, the direction of government policies does seem to be one of differentiation of cities on the one hand and towns and countryside villages on the other. The rural-urban matter, either in terms of an existing divide or as a potential integration, seems to be confined to the latter and implicitly solved in terms of administrative simplification of the countryside (the process named 'townization'), due to the controversial urban-rural integration (*chengxiang yitihua*) (Jing and Zhang 2003; in this volume, Kern *et al.* further develop the issue of intermediate city in Chinese development). The PRD megaregion has been an exemplary test of the process.

The One-way Mechanism of Rural-urban Land Use Change Forged in Shenzhen

One of the main points of frictions in rural-urban integration is land use allocation, spanning from the protection of the status quo to the support to changes. Agricultural policy privileges the preservation of farmland also as an indirect household security system, whereas local governments promote the various shades of integration or transition from rural into urban (Tian and Luo 2012). Since 1985 the Land Administration Bureau, supported by state and provincial authorities, supervises the protection of land-quality, hampering local initiatives of change from farming to construction. However, it is stated by the Land Administration Law (LAL; issued in 1986, amended in 1988, 1998, 2004) that rural land use rights encompass: i) agricultural use through contracts to farmers; ii) rural construction use for local farmers' residences, collectively owned enterprises and rural public facilities; iii) conversion to urban use upon requisition; and iv) state acquisition in the public interest for the necessity of infrastructure construction.

None of the milestones that changed the role of rural institutions into developer-seekers, such as the institutionalization of Special Economic Zones (SEZ) and the dismantling of rural communes, was intended as impacting on land use allocation. However, it was their combined effect with the provisional institution of shares in joint ventures to provide land use rights to foreign industries that urged the reform

---

7 See the issue discussed at length for China Economic Weekly by Li Tie, the director of Centre for Cities and Small Towns Reform and Development of the National Development and Reform Commission (NDRC): http://www.js.china.com.cn/zc/gj/308097.shtml (accessed on 20/04/2013).

of land administrative designation. A grey area expanded in which constructions were admitted and land use change accepted in rural areas, separately from the administrative allocation of land use. In 1987 Shenzhen pioneered the sale of land-use rights in public auction, which facilitated the coexistence of land use markets and administrative control of the pace of urban growth (Dinh *et al.* 2013, p. 199). In 1988, the National People's Congress approved an amendment to the 1982 Constitution of the People's Republic of China that states: 'land use rights can be transferred in accordance with the law'. As reconstructed by Yeh and Wu (1996), in December 1988 LAL was amended accordingly: 'all state-owned and collective-owned land use rights may be transferred by law', and 'the State introduces the system of compensation for the use of State-owned land'. Finally, the State Council released an Interim Regulation in 1990 to direct the sale and transfer of state-owned land use rights. Since then, land use rights have generated distinct pricing systems, but constitute a remarkable system to stimulate urban growth and finance local municipalities (see Table 6.2).

Table 6.2   The mechanisms of land use rights

	Enacted by	Mean
Transfer of land use rights (*zhuanrang*)	Local institutions or individuals upon approval	Payment to the previous right owner
Requisition	State (through local governments)	Collective rights are compensated either by the state or by users
Administrative allocation due to public interests	Local branches of national institutions in the name of the state	Future fee for the public utility use are the guarantee for previous right owners; new right owners have no right to resell use rights
Leasing or conveyance (*churang*)	State guarantee of the negotiation of the right to use the land	Negotiation, tender upon invitation, auction at open bidding, quotation (since 2002), short lease, and other flexible methods

Source: adapted from Wu *et al.* 2007: 37–47.

Besides restrictions in land uses, the successive implementation of the Agricultural Land Protection Law (1994) has introduced the functional obligation for cities (*chengshi*) and town (*xiangzhen*) (Table 6.1) to maintain grain-crop reserves thanks to clearly defined agricultural land use zoning. The praxis in the PRD cites is indeed quite different, as in the last 20 years those approved urban plans do not usually last as long as the approved previsions because of overly vigorous efforts to boost growth. Shenzhen had its first Master Plan for a SEZ approved in 1982, which was quickly substituted by a more comprehensive Master Plan in 1986, with the forecast of reaching 123 square kilometres of urbanized area by 2000. Three years later, the development strategy of Shenzhen augmented the previsions to 160 square kilometres, exceeding the size of land to be allocated to a SEZ. Large-scale speculation also made the second plan obsolete. In 1996 a new Master Plan 1996–2010 was approved, which reshaped the direction of development. By 2006 the Shenzhen government was at work on the Master Plan 2010–20, to drive the redevelopment of the central core and adjust to the different administrative framework, in which the SEZ has less impact on land use management and collective ownership is abolished (Ng 2011). According to provincial data, the revenue from the lease of the use right of state-owned land granted to the Shenzhen government a total value of 3,710 million Yuan in 1997, which made 55 per cent of the total revenue from land use right leasing in the whole PRD for the year (GSTJ 1998). In the following years Shenzhen has always been the first or second city in the PRD for value of revenue from land use right leasing, seeing an increase up to 4,283 million Yuan in 2004 (GSTJ 2005). However, all other PRD cities quickly adopted the mechanism of land use rights to support growth with local resources.

Land Use Change as an Economic Tool: Some Figures of the PRD Urbanization

The city financing system acts frequently as the demand side for rural-urban shift: the extension of the market of construction rights for urban uses is an important asset for local administrations. Since 1994, China's fiscal system transformed slowly to a more decentralized system, divided in centrally levied taxes, local taxes and taxes shared between the state and local governments. The latter include taxation of local business incomes, urban land use and land appreciation that are charged autonomously. Indirectly, this means that the greater number of industries located in a territory, the more can be extracted in taxes from them, therefore encouraging local public investments in infrastructures and industrial or business districts, requisitioning collective-owned land, without any previously declared market interest (Yaping and Min 2009; Wu 2002). Yet 'becoming urban' is a lucrative activity not only because of the immediate fee on land-leasing (which is retained mostly at the local level, but frequently is kept low in order to attract investments), but also as a permanent revenue paid by the final land use rights owner (in some test cases[8]).

This process has, evidently, a regenerative power: potential new business attracts workers; the price of residential and commercial land increases; the government receives more revenue and builds more infrastructures in support of potential businesses, although these are not necessarily committed to market

---

8   A complete reflection on this issue is in Yu-Hung Hong 'Potential Impacts of Real Property Tax Reform on Industries in China: An Input-Output Analysis' IIOA Conference, Beijing 27 June–1 July 2005.

Table 6.3   The lease of state-owned land compared to administrative allocation in the PRD

Nine cities of PRD:	1998	2000	2002	2004
Grant Value of transaction (million Yuan)	5,136	10,489	11,224	21,546
Area (1000 m²)	68,300	50,110	70,640	91,422
Administrative allocation				
Area (1000 m²)	17,320	9,850	33,780	43,793

Note: After 2004 data are not published in the annual Yearbook with the same detail, making any comparison impossible.
Source: GST 1999, 2001, 2003, 2005.

success (Wong and Tang 2005). Contextual to land use change regulation in the 1980s, urban planning rules were redefined. The City Planning Ordinance (1984) and the City Planning Act (1989) settled a framework for planning nationwide, substantially adjusting local regulatory powers to fiscal and administrative decentralization. Vertically, from the central government downwards to local administrations, a different society and economy is formally accommodated into an institutional space. At the same time, the pragmatic application of the new framework does not completely discontinue the relation with previous entities which may act as commercial developers (Chung and Zhou 2011), interfaces with foreign investors or interest groups (Huang 2008; Haila 2007; Lash 2009).

Control is then contested among different administrations, in a characteristic fragmentation that had been named 'state sprawl' (Shue 1995), and is functional to maintain the central-state system through market regulation (Haila 2007; Huang 2008). Among the derived contradictions, revenues derived from lease of land use right are mostly retained locally and contribute to a city's commodification, even if land is nominally owned by the socialist state. The market regulation legitimizes the differentiation of interests, which are eventually incorporated into the institutional system, while the state party retains socialist ideals. Chinese spatial planning rationales can be better understood as centralized 'implementation-without-negation' of individualistic markets (Huang 2008). To some extent, master-plans, detailed plans, district plans and so on in these contexts have the representational function of locating major infrastructures and zoned activities, while planning is, in a nutshell, the bargaining process between central and subordinated organizations, particularly at the edge of the official city-space (Tang 2000). Practical behaviour and plans are usually vaguely related, and therefore – paradoxically – a centrally planned state is one where plans (that is, ruling standards of control and legitimacy) are not the result of planning in the sense of coordination (Leaf and Hou 2006). In other terms, more than adapting the plan and target systems to market forces, the market (that is, demands of consumers) is incorporated in the construction of the planned state.

Annexation: the Administrative Path towards an Urban PRD

Efforts to realign functional reality with its administrative representation invariably extend city rules everywhere. The craze for urban administration in the PRD is merging cities with historic responsibility on the overall prefectures that date back to the early Ming Dynasty with other entities such as county-level cities and counties, which have had a territory defined later and include a mixed situation of settlements and intensive agriculture organized around smaller rural centres (in the PRD, counties have been upgraded or downgraded to fit the hierarchy of cities; counties in Table 6.4 located in the peripheral areas of Guangdong Province). This way urbanization and design will be 'the mediator as well as the outcome of the process of extending state's control over the economy and society' (Tang 2000, p. 354), as rural space tends to elude central control.

Table 6.4   Administrative readjustment in Guangdong Province 1981–2011

Number of:	1981	1991	2001	2011
Prefecture-level city	4	20	21	21
County-level city	10	6	31	23
City district	18	41	48	54
Town under city administration	–	**1301	1529	1132
County and autonomous county	96	72	45	44
Township and ethnic township	*1942	338	40	11
Subdistrict (urban) committee	–	n.a.	351	442
Village (rural) committee	*27067	24706	22881	22189

Note: *Prior to 1986 the county was divided in communes outside the city area, which were later differentiated into town governments and independent townships; **before 1990 read 'town government'.
Source: GSTJ 1992, 2002, 2012; CSSB 1982.

The urbanized region has been reassembled in the 2000s into 'designated urban places': urban districts, towns and administrative villages, all interacting strongly with the urban area of main cities, in some cases economic and social services becoming practically integrated with different administration. That puts pressures on the reallocation of some mandates, structure and functional responsibilities between governments. Some attempts to rationalize the local system of government pursue the conversion of counties into urban districts, therefore transforming suburban towns into more formalized Street Committees. Administrative annexation results obviously in a growing city-built area, but more specifically in formerly independent cities annexed to the main municipality

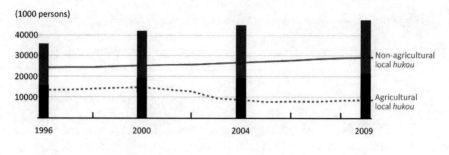

Figure 6.4 Distribution of the population in the PRD according to the *hukou* registration and long-term residents registers

as urban districts. The administrative upgrade of subordinated towns and rural centres may ease great urban projects, but generally accelerates local speculations and uncertain absorption of collectively owned land into state-owned land.[9] In the PRD the most recent wave of administrative annexation reclassified urban and rural functions, places and people's *hukou*[10] to such an extent that the registered non-farming *hukou* stretched from 43 per cent in 1995 and 44 per cent in 2000 to 70 per cent in 2006 (GSTJ 1996–2010; see Figure 6.1 below).

Is There Any PRD Rurality? The Rural-urban Edge as a Policies Trap

As we have illustrated above, the implied opposition of rural and urban characteristics is deeply problematic when applied to Chinese coastal urbanized regions such as the PRD. In the following discussion, we consider the hypothesis that the notion of a rural-urban edge moves parallel to administrative value judgements and their formalization, and that those institutional discourses do not linearly fit or coordinate the actual territory. The traditional rural and urban definitions are found to be emptied of their practical significance in these terms, and correspond to an unclear picture that sometimes hides forms of urbanization within the rural realm and in other cases accepts rural structures within urban formal boundaries. If this is the case, elaborating on the hypothesis formulated by Wilson and Rigg (2003, p. 687), would rural multi-functional commodification represent a solid modernization of the countryside beyond administrative definitions? Universal answers are difficult, but our explorations of the PRD support the idea that the

---

9   The typical by-product is the phenomenon of 'village in the city' (*chengzhongcun*) in PRD (Chung and Zhou 2011, Siu 2007: 330).

10   The *hukou* is the national form of identity registration which is associated with the home place, designated as either farming or non-farming and cannot be easily changed by individuals.

Rural-Urban Edge 127

rural sphere in urbanized regions is to a great extent already multi-functional although this characteristic is invisible in public discourse. Moreover, it can be suggested that even in historic times, before modern conceptualizations of rural-urban divides, there was in the region an attitude that statutory cities should have regular functional interactions with villages and towns (Rowe 1984).

Demographics provide another angle to look at the process of urbanization of the countryside. Although the total population with *hukou* did maintain a regular moderate growth rate, it was redistributed between rural and urban registrations as explained above. Yet the permanent population, an indicator that is calculated since the 2000 National Census to incorporate migrant workers,[11] is indeed quite regular in its yearly growth rate of between 1 and 2 per cent. The permanent population is differentiated into urban and rural residents based on algorithms, which had been adapted several times to evaluate local rates of urbanity (percentage of workers in the primary sector, dimension of the place in terms of population, its fiscal consistency and so on). According to this definition, PRD urban residents are estimated as totalling 60 per cent in 1995, overcoming 70 per cent by the year 2000 and topping 80 per cent in 2006.

There is a significant between the two figures, which can be explained by the fact that a large volume of the long-term urban residents are located in town and village structures: rural communities and integrated urban economies, which add to a clear urban set. It would seem that the administrative designation imperfectly equates the non-rural spaces with city territories, and overlaps town and country administrative integration to a physical and morphological unity. This latter point is fundamental. There is a long tradition of city design in China, and the tentative extension of this know-how to newly designated towns, which were not compelled to any form of zoning until very recently (as part of the system of collective-owned land), may easily generate exaggerated expectations. When differences between the institutional city and the institutional countryside are not acknowledged, the only valuable rurality is the one coinciding with large-scale agriculture, and the existing blending of forms of rurality surviving within an urbanized territory simply become irrelevant as provisional land occupancies. In other terms, although cityspace is growing and purely rural economy is shrinking, a large proportion of the urban growth actually involves towns and villages. What is the spatial and social meaning of that? The general improvement of daily life in rural places[12] suggests a different lifestyle which is relevant in fast-growing

---

11   Permanent population group: the persons who reside in the same place for longer than six months and hold a registered temporary residence permit or work contract; GSTJ registers the permanent population since 2005 and estimates previous years. [Before 2005 permanent population was not accounted for in official statistics, however the Provincial Office provides accurate estimates.]

12   The equation of rurality with poverty in developing countries is another debated issue in geographic and developmental studies (Rigg 2006).

regions such as the PRD, one that does not cut off the links with the countryside and specifically the 'rural' structure of a community (Ho 2005).

There are specific problems of spatial and administrative mismatch in the logic of rural-urban integration:

- The *hukou* definition of agricultural and non-agricultural households is purely administrative;
- The algorithms which define rural and urban statistics are volatile referents;
- In contemporary societies, urban and urbanized regions do not coincide, with the latter that can extend far beyond the conventional urban realm;
- Traditional forms of participation to collective choices at the community level are not acknowledged, even if they may anticipate viable arrangements.

Adding a clear comparative perspective on rural-urban misleading definition, it is worth remarking that in Europe more than 70 per cent of the total population is urban but a majority of the population lives in urban centres with fewer than 50,000 inhabitants (Eurostat 2010). If agriculture has to be considered the typical rural activity (Tacoli 2003; Wilson and Rigg 2003), it is an activity that within a highly urbanized world survives mainly because of forms of subsidy. That has been happening in China too since the mid-2000s. Targeted sector policies have been set, but spatial policies have not been fully developed. In fact, it is not clear if spatial policies may effectively support the rural-urban coexistence of rather differentiated spaces despite being necessarily proximal.

Conclusion

Not only are there the mismatches about definitions of rural and urban, but the institutional context of China – and particularly of her fast-growing regions such as the PRD – offers peculiar distortions. The personnel enrolled in the administrative system are basically appointed and evaluated by superiors in terms of achievements in attracting investments locally. Actually the main aim is often to impress the leadership with prospects of growth, which are meant to be, *ça va sans dire*, marketable urban growth. As far as these adventures are only apparently settled for or by the market, they do not always guarantee market profitability. Indeed, market rationality based on demand is visible in the non-designed transformations: sub-municipal levels which offer housing for migrants, convenient sub-contracting in villages that expand the supply chain of industrial estates, commercial agriculture and so on. Despite their being subsidiaries of (and not necessarily exploited by) urban economies, in the near future planning may refuse to legitimize these market solutions.

In the introduction we indicated three milestones of spatial policies – the ownership regime, the presence of overlapping competencies and objectives and the distortion of universal spatial design – which bias the understanding of rural spaces. Firstly, our analysis of the administrative rural and urban definitions and the movable edge between the two has revealed that under these labels there are multi-functional organizational realities in which rural characteristics cannot be interpreted as weaknesses only because they do not homologize to urban regulation. Secondly, from the previous step derives a fundamental question on the linearity of rural-urban transition for regions such as the PRD, and many other regions in China and elsewhere, in which fast industrialization not concentrated in consolidated cities empowers a plethora of intermediate places, either towns or villages, which benefit from larger urban or regional economies. The conclusion is that only once the mutual interaction and a spatial coexistence of rural and urban realms within a functional region are acknowledged, the definition of multi-directional policies and coherent spatial layouts can proceed without assumptive separations, which have proved ineffective. This suggests that rural and urban are not absolute qualities of space but need to be assessed relatively to the context and most of all reciprocally. As far as the edge between the two is a social and political construction, there is the prospect for rurality to characterize in the PRD urbanized region as the multi-functional and responsive interface to universal urban paradigms.

References

Agergaard, J., Fold, N. and Gough, K.V. 2010. *Rural-Urban Dynamics. Livelihoods, Mobility and Market in African and Asian Frontiers*. Abingdon: Routledge.

Angel, S., Parent, J., Civco, D.L. and Blei, A.M. 2010. *The persistent Decline in Urban Densities: Global and Historical Evidence of 'Sprawl'*. Harvard: Lincoln Institute of Land Policy.

Bramall, C. 2007. *The Industrialization of Rural China*. Oxford: Oxford University Press.

Brandt, J. 2003. Multifunctional landscapes – perspectives for the future. *Journal of Environmental Sciences*, 15(2), 187–92.

Chung, H. and Zhou, S.H. 2011. Planning for plural groups? Villages-in-the-city redevelopment in Guangzhou city, China. *International Planning Studies*, 16(4), 333–53.

CSSB (China State Statistical Bureau) 1982. Zhongguo Tongji Nianjiang. Beijing: China Statistic Press [China Statistical Yearbook].

Ding, C. and Lichtenberg, E. 2011. Land and urban economic growth in China. *Journal of Regional Science*, 51(2), 299–317.

Dinh, H.T., Rawski, T.G., Zafar, A., Wang, L. and Mavroeidi, E. 2013. *Tales from the Development Frontier. How China and Other Countries Harness Light Manufacturing to Create Jobs and Prosperity*. Washington: The World Bank.

Duara, P. 1988. *Culture, Power, and the State. Rural North China, 1900–1942*. Stanford, CA: Stanford University Press.

Eurostat. 2010. A revised urban-rural typology, in: Eurostat Regional Yearbook, edited by Eurostat. Luxembourg: Publications Office of the European Union, 239–53.

Gallent, N., Juntti, M., Kidd, S. and Shaw, D. 2008. *Introduction to Rural Planning*. Abingdon: Routledge.

Garreau, J. 1991. *Edge City: Life on the New Frontier*. New York: Doubleday.

Goodman, D., DuPuis, M. and Goodman, M. 2011. *Alternative Food Networks: Knowledge, Place and Politics*. London: Taylor and Francis.

GSTJ-Guangdong Sheng Tongji Ju, volumes from 1992 to 2010. Guangdong Tongji Nianjian. China Statistic Press, Beijing [Guangdong Statistical Yearbook].

Gugler, J. 1996. *The Urban Transformation of the Developing World*. Oxford: Oxford University Press.

Haila, A. 2007. The market as the new Emperor. *International Journal of Urban and Regional Research*, 31(1), 3–20.

Hamilton, G.G. 2006. *Commerce and Capitalism in Chinese Societies*. Abingdon: Routledge.

Ho, P. 2005. *Developmental Dilemmas. Land Reform and Institutional Change in China*. Abingdon: Routledge.

Hoa, L. 1981. *Reconstruire la Chine: Trente Ans d'Urbanisme (1949–1979)*. Paris: Edition du Moniteur.

Huang, P.C. 2008. Centralized minimalism: Semiformal governance by quasi officials and dispute resolution in China. *Modern China*, 34(9), 9–35.

Huang, P.C. 2010. The theoretical and practical implications of China's development experience: The role of informal economic practices. *Modern China*, 37(3), 3–43.

Isserman, A.M. 2005. In the national interest: defining rural and urban correctly in research and public policy. *International Regional Science Review*, 28(4), 465–99.

Jing, P. and Zhang, F. 2003. Latest development in studies on the urban and rural integration. *City Planning Review*, 27(6), 30–35 (in Chinese).

Lash, S. 2009. Against institutionalism. *International Journal of Urban and Regional Research*, 33(2), 567–71.

Leaf, M. and Hou, L. 2006. The 'Third Spring' of urban planning in China. The resurrection of professional planning in the post-Mao era. *China Information*, 20(3), 553–85.

Lin, G.C.S. 2001a. Evolving spatial form of urban-rural interaction in the Pearl River Delta. *Professional Geographer*, 53(1), 56–70.

Lin, G.C.S. 2001b. Metropolitan development in a transitional socialist economy: Spatial restructuring in the Pearl River Delta, China. *Urban Studies*, 38(3), 383–406.

Lin, G.C.S. 2009. *Developing China. Land, Politics and Social Conditions*. Abingdon: Routledge.

Liu, H. and Stapleton, K. 2006. Chinese Urban History. *China Information*, XX (3), 391–427.

Logan, J. (ed.) 2001. *The New Chinese City: Globalization and Market Reform.* Oxford: Blackwell Publishers.

Mardsen, T., Murdoch, J., Lowe, P., Munton, R. and Flynn, A. 1993. *Constructing the Countryside.* London: UCL Press.

Ng, M.K. 2011. Strategic planning of China's first Special Economic Zone: Shenzhen City Master Plan (2010–20). *Planning Theory and Practice*, 12(4), 638–42.

Pahl, R.E. 1966. The rural-urban continuum. *Sociologia Ruralis*, 6, 299–327.

Parish, W. 1981. Egalitarism in Chinese society. *Problems of Communism*, 1, 37–53.

Peiser, R.B. 1989. Density and urban sprawl. *Land Economics*, 65(3), 193–204.

Rigg, J. 2006. Land, farming, livelihoods and poverty: rethinking the links in the rural South. *World Development*, 34, 180–202.

Rowe, W.T. 1984. *Hankow: Commerce and Society in a Chinese City, 1796–1889.* Stanford, CA: Stanford University Press.

Satsangi, M., Gallent, N. and Bevan, M. 2010. *The Rural Housing Question: Community and Planning in Britain's Countryside.* Bristol: Polity Press.

Scott, A.J. 2002. Regional push: towards a geography of development and growth in low- and middle-income countries. *Third World Quarterly*, 23(1), 137–61.

Shue, V. 1995. State sprawl: The regulatory state and social life in a small Chinese city, in *Urban Spaces in Contemporary China: The Political Economy Potential for Autonomy and Community in Post-Mao China*, edited by D.S. Davis et al.. Cambridge: Cambridge University Press, 90–112.

Shue, V. 2008. Rule as repertory and the compound essence of authority. *Modern China*, 34(1), 141–51.

Siu, H. 2007. Grounding displacement: Uncivil urban spaces in postreform South China. *American Ethnologist*, 34(2), 329–50.

Soja, E.W. 2000. *Postmetropolis. Critical Studies of Cities and Regions.* Malden, MA: Blackwell Pub.

Solinger D.J. 1999. *Contesting Citizenship in Urban China: Peasant Migrants, the State, and the Logic of the Market.* Berkeley, CA: University of California Press.

Tacoli, C. 1998. Rural-urban interaction: a guide to the literature. *Environment and Urbanization*, 10(1), 147–66.

Tacoli, C. 2003. The links between urban and rural development. *Environment and Urbanization*, 15(3), 3–12.

Tian, L. and Luo, C. 2012. Land share-holding system and land use in industrialization of countryside: a case study on Shunde. *City Planning Review*, 36(4), 25–31 (in Chinese).

Tian, L. and Ge, B. 2011. Land use characteristics and driving forces of peri-urban area in the transitional economy. *Urban Planning Forum*, 3, 66–73 (in Chinese).

Wang, J. (ed.) 2005. *Locating China. Space, Place, and Popular Culture.* Abingdon: Routledge.

Ward, N. and Brown, D.L. 2009. Placing the rural in regional development. *Regional Studies*, 43(10), 1237–44.

White, L.T. 1998. *Unstately Power: Local Causes of China's Economic Reforms*. New York: M.E. Sharpe.

Whyte, M.K. and Parish, W.L. 1984. *Urban Life in Contemporary China*. Chicago, IL: The University of Chicago Press.

Wilson, G.A. and Rigg, J. 2003. 'Post-productivist' agricultural regimes and the South: discordant concepts? *Progress in Human Geography*, 27(6), 681–707.

Wong, S.W. and Tang, B.S. 2005. Challenges to the sustainability of 'development zones': a case study of Guangzhou Development District, China. *Cities*, 22(4), 303–16.

Wu, F. 2002. China's changing urban governance in the transition towards a more market-oriented economy. *Urban Studies*, 39(7), 1071–93.

Wu, F. 2007. Re-orientation of the city plan: strategic planning and design competition in China. *Geoforum*, 38, 379–92.

Wu, F., Xu, J. and Yeh, A.G.O. 2007. Urban Development in Post-Reform China: State, Market, and Space. Abingdon, Oxon: Routledge.

Yaping, W. and Min, Z. 2009. Urban spill over vs. local urban sprawl: Entangling land-use regulations in the urban growth of China's megacities. *Land Use Policy*, 26, 1031–45.

Yeh, A.G.O., Xu, J. and Yi, H. 2006. Fourth wave of urbanization in China. *City Planning Review*, 30, 13–18 (in Chinese).

Yeh, A.G.O. and Wu, F. 1995. Internal structure of Chinese cities in the midst of economic reform. *Urban Geography*, 16(6), 521–54.

Yeh, A.G.O. and Wu, F. 1996. The new land development process and urban development in Chinese cities. *International Journal of Urban and Regional Research*, 20, 330–53.

Yuan, J., Zhou, Y. and Huang, W. 2006. Several long-standing mistaken ideas in the theoretical studies and planning practices of Chinese metropolitan regions. *Geographical Research*, 25(1), 112–20 (in Chinese).

Zhou, Y. and Shi, Y. 1995. Toward establishing the concept of physical urban area in China. *Acta Geographica Sinica*, 50(4), 289–301 (in Chinese).

Chapter 7

Preservation and Sustainable Development of Suburban Historical Villages: A Case Study of Dayuwan Village in Wuhan

Shidan Cheng, Yang Yu and Rongbo Hu

The past 30 years of rapid economic growth in China also saw a drastic expansion in the scale of cities, which had a huge impact on historical settlements in the suburban area. The tension between the preservation and development of these settlements has heightened. Based on the case study of Dayuwan Village in Wuhan, the chapter presents challenges and opportunities facing suburban historical villages in their preservation and economic development. The chapter argues that the preservation of these villages, which depends on an increasing demand from urban areas, calls for a wider participation of local stakeholders in the local development process, such as the preservation of intangible heritages, in addition to the physical environment. The lesson drawn from the case study suggests that further efforts should be made on the utilization of historical heritage and the natural environment for cultural tourism in the attempt to integrate historical preservation with the improvement of villagers' livelihood and daily lives.

Introduction

During China's rapid urbanization, historical sites are been often perceived as symbols of backwardness and declination. Many cities aimed to demolish old areas, replacing them with large-scale new developments which were regarded as the drivers of economic development and symbols of modernity. Within this backdrop, the damage or even the wipe-out of urban heritage became a common practice, posing unprecedented threats to the traditional urban texture and even individual historic buildings. In the 1980s, the State Bureau of Cultural Relics began to establish a framework for the preservation of historical and cultural heritage, which gradually expanded from the protection of individual buildings to clusters of buildings, progressing to the protected site alongside its environmental context. A three-tiered preservation scheme comprising relic preservation unit, historical and cultural blocks all the way to historical and cultural cities was established, together with the identification of corresponding principles and approaches in line with the different nature and characteristics of the preservation entities.

134 *Urban China's Rural Fringe*

In the first 20 plus years, the scope of this preservation scheme was limited to the historical heritage inside the urban area without covering, by any means, the rich legacy of the millennial agricultural civilization of China, being comprised of relics, organic villages and unique rural landscapes. Up to 2003, the State Bureau of Cultural Relics, under the Ministry of Culture, and the Ministry of Construction began to implement schemes for the preservation of historical and cultural villages. However, due to the lack of professional staff, financial support and weak administration, the preservation efforts were quite limited and the decline and deterioration of historical villages continued on a downward trend. In the past 10 years in China, the number of villages with historic features still relatively intact sharply decreased from 5,000 to the current 2,000 to 3,000 (Bi 2011). As an integral part of Chinese civilization, traditional villages carry important historical elements. They are comprised not only of historic buildings but also of spaces for rural lives and production, some still active; they are indeed living communities without which Chinese culture would not be entirely understood. Therefore, the preservation of these villages means the preservation of an important component of the memory of Chinese culture.

Paradoxically, poverty and backwardness are the reason why these villages survived. In fact most of the well-preserved ones are located in remote, isolated and purely rural areas. On the other hand, poverty and decline have also led to irreversible demographic decline and the abandonment of rural activities. In contrast, in more prosperous villages, former farmlands and partly formerly built sites have been replaced by industrial developments, new towns and infrastructure projects of various sizes and types. This is the situation faced especially by those villages located in the suburban areas of large cities. Compared to 30 years ago, most cities in China have at least tripled in scale; some have even expanded by 20 times their original size. As a result, many suburban villages were demolished and completely redeveloped due to the rapid urban sprawl. In order to draft a preliminary balance between the reasons for economic development and the reasons for historical preservation, in this specific transitional area between the city and the countryside, the case study of Dayuwan will be introduced. The chapter discusses the challenges and opportunities in the preservation of a typical historical village in suburban Wuhan, drawing lessons from the implementation of a real project. In addition, it will provide suggestions on how to reconcile the preservation and development of similar villages threatened by the rapid urbanization. As with many other traditional villages, Dayuwan also went through a period of decline. Currently, this village has been transformed into an important destination for cultural tourism in the surrounding area of Wuhan. The School of Urban Design of Wuhan University participated in the local development plan for Dayuwan alongside the preservation plan. The chapter presents the results of this experience and the efforts to promote historical preservation and to support the villagers' income. Additional information regarding the major events of the historical preservation and touristic development of Dayuwan Village can be found on the Huangpi District Government and the Cultural Affairs Bureau of Wuhan Municipality websites.

Challenges and Opportunities Facing Historical Villages

Suburban areas, here assimilated to the urban-rural fringes, are transitional areas between the city and the countryside. In China's rapid urbanization, urban boundaries are constantly changing along with urban sprawl. Even if some villages are not included in the city plan or located in the major directions for urban growth, they might still be deeply affected economically, socially and culturally. Apparently, compared to farmers elsewhere, suburban farmers enjoy more economic opportunities, for example job opportunities in urban areas, the sale of local products to urban residents or tourism activities using natural or historical resources, which can all generate relatively high economic returns. However, these activities may also bring negative issues. One the major impact for historical villages, for instance, is the draining of rural labour into cities that may result in a demographic decline of the rural population. The hollowing-out of villages might determine, quite quickly, the decaying of the local environment (Zhou 2013). The newly rich farmers living in the suburbs tend to partly renovate or completely tear down their old residences. In the presence of 'loose' planning control, their aspirations of achieving a modern, urban lifestyle might materialize in, arguably, refurbishment, using urban buildings as the prototype of their desires. By doing so, the historical features of many villages can be altered, if not completely lost. Furthermore, in pursuing economic development, sometimes local governments overdevelop local businesses and tourism activities by demolishing historical sites and replacing them with reproductions. Regardless of whether or not such practices are legitimate or acceptable, they often result in a cheap replica of the past and a general sense of shabbiness, undermining not only the physical historical environment but also the cultural symbols of villages. Unfortunately, these practices have become more and more common under the circumstances of profit-oriented urban development processes.

Dayuwan in Huangpi District Wuhan City is one of the few villages which have survived, although located at the fringe of Wuhan, the biggest city in Central China and 10 km away from downtown Huangpi District. Before becoming a popular destination for local tourism, Dayuwan was rather poor back in the late 1990s, with an annual household income of less than 1,000 RMB Yuan, mainly derived from agricultural production. The village was also lacking in basic infrastructures, being characterized by low living standards and lack of vitality. Then, as in other Chinese cities entering a stage of rapid development, the combination of increasing demand for labour, high salaries and urban life attracted many young villagers to the city, which resulted in an increasing rate of housing vacancies in Dayuwan. On the other hand, those who remained, benefitting from the spillover of Wuhan, gradually renovated their old houses or built new ones in the nearby areas. Fortunately, the overall historical layout of the village and much historical architecture from the late Ming and early Qing dynasties were not directly affected by these trends. Similarly to many remote historical villages, the preservation of Dayuwan can be attributed to its rather secluded geographic location (Wang 2010). Located in a hilly area to the south-east of the renowned Mulan Mountain, in the north part of Wuhan, Dayuwan Village is surrounded by mountains and the Sheshui River, flowing through its western part, creates a natural barrier which cuts it off from the outside world. Besides the morphological features, this area is being included in the ecological tourism zone of north Wuhan, being statutorily protected from heavy urban developments.

A remote geographic location protects historical villages from the impact of urban expansions but also, at the same time, makes financial support from government less readily available. In fact only limited dedicated grants for the preservation of cultural heritages are allocated from the local government, who tend to prioritize urban areas instead of remote, historical villages. The historical buildings in Dayuwan were for a long time deprived of appropriate and effective preservation and maintenance. Even when cultural tourism development was initially supported by the local government, as a component of the overall strategic re-launching of the village, financial support was barely available. More than a decade ago, with the rising popularity of tours to historical towns, the local government attempted to make Dayuwan a hotspot for heritage tourism similar to Zhouzhuang and Tongli in the Yangtze River Delta, by taking advantage of its historical resources. However, due to a lack of financial support and insufficient infrastructure and tourism facilities, the tourism development of Dayuwan was limited. With the economic development of the Huangpi District and Wuhan city, heritage protection schemes have developed rapidly in the past few years and, finally, there has been an increase in financial input allocated by the local government. In the meantime, the tourism of Dayuwan went through a course of gradual development, avoiding the commonly seen over-commercialization of other historic touristic sites located in the more prosperous regions of the coast. In fact, even if the appreciation of local resources has been remarkable, overall market forces have been less extreme. This situation has determined a favourable condition for the local government in engaging in experimentation and, generally speaking, in accepting new ideas and approaches for the preservation and development of the site.

Contrary to what is general practice, especially for certain remote areas, professional support and technical expertise have been mobilized since the very beginning. Experts from major universities, planning and design institutions and government heritage authorities have contributed to surveying, reviewing and evaluating the site and later on planning, branding and designing the future development. The role of local officials and technical staff from the local government in charge of the project has also been valuable. Besides a general openness to more innovative practices, the responsibility for the preservation and development of Dayuwan has been that of the deputy director of Huangpi District, who is also an expert in urban planning.

In addition, more financial resources were gradually provided: from one side, the revenue coming from the urbanization process of underdeveloped land at the fringe has been made available for the redevelopment of suburban historical villages. Meanwhile, investments in heritage tourism projects were also more readily available from the city, with the involvement of some private companies from Wuhan which specialize in tourist development.

Finally, alongside the local development process, the village generated a growing tourism market. Urban tourism to rural areas is constantly on the rise in China. This is due to the higher spending capability of urban households and the increase in car ownership, allowing tourists to reach areas that only few years ago were considered remote. Holidays in rural areas are becoming very popular in China and historical villages can offer a unique charm for resting and enjoying rural heritage. It should be stressed that, no matter what the opportunities and challenges are, the future development of Dayuwan is rooted in its unique natural environment and historical resources. Over the past 20 years, the local government and the population have fully recognized the value of their historical heritage and have progressed from the original architectural protection to a overall, comprehensive perspective of preservation.

The Preservation of Dayuwan Historical Village

History and Characteristics of the Village

The history of Dayuwan can be dated back to the Ming Dynasty around 1369, when the village was established by immigrants from Wuyuan, Jiangxi Province. Since most residents were of the Yu family, it was named Dayuwan, literally meaning the Yu village. As recorded in the family pedigree, the ancestors chose the location of the village because it was deemed a rare and auspicious place in terms of Fengshui (Zhang 2009). Currently, the village has 108 families, more than 300 residents and a total land area of 20 hm. Most buildings in the village were built in the late Qing Dynasty in harmony with the hilly topography. Generally, the village layout, architectural form and decoration all have their unique features.

Clear Layout of Fengshui

Viewed from the top of the Xifeng Moutain on which Dayuwan is built, the Fengshui model is very evident in the village layout (see Figure 7.1): the mountain on the east represents the dragon, the mountain on the west resembles the tiger, while the ridges of Hulu and Xifeng mountains connect with each other, the two turtle-like mountains to the south forming a natural stronghold to the village. Two inlet and outlet creeks meet in the village pond, altogether forming a Taiji pattern (Pan 2006). Set in the north and facing the south, with deep and fertile soil and

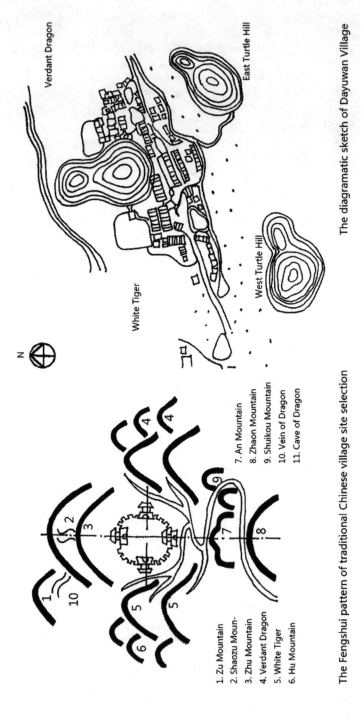

Figure 7.1 The Fengshui pattern of Dayuwan Village's site selection

Figure 7.2   The architectural forms in Dayuwan Village

lush vegetation, the village boasts mountains, woods, farms and waters, whose relatively closed-up spatial composition coincides greatly with the ideal living environment aspired to by the Chinese ancestors (Jin 2002).

Exquisite Architectural Form
The historical residential complexes in Dayuwan are uniquely designed. A typical complex consists of three courtyards with three main houses, two side houses and skylights (see Figure 7.2). The houses are characterized by grey roof tiles, upturned eaves and corridors for rainy days and also boast complete sewage systems with open and covered drains. The overall layout was well arranged with different households sharing connected walls, frames or corridors. The household units are both connected and isolated, forming a self-defense home security system (Chen 2010). The houses use stone slabs and sticky rice grout for structural walls, and rammed earth for interior walls, which are not only strong but also thermally effective.

Artistic Details and Decoration
The built-up environment is also rich in detail and artistic decoration, such as colour paintings under the eaves of houses, which derive from famous folk-tales and express people's aspiration of a happy life. In addition, historical relics such as inscribed boards, cooper lamps, spinning wheels, looms, stone pestles, horse

140 *Urban China's Rural Fringe*

tethers, even stone rollers from the Jiaqing era of Qing Dynasty, have all become integral parts of the folk culture (Cai 2006).

History of Village Preservation

The historical value of Dayuwan was first discovered by relic experts from Wuhan in 1989 who believed that the layout and architectural style of the village embodied the traditional Chinese Fengshui theories and the Confucianist ideal of a happy life and regarded it as a rarely seen historical and cultural heritage. Subsequently, the relic authorities at the provincial and municipal levels demanded preservation efforts from the local Huangpi government and the strict control of new development in the village.

In November 2002, Dayuwan was named a provincial heritage and the Huangpi government initiated an official preservation program which started with the protection of physical elements and then a preservation plan made by the relic experts of Wuhan with a focus on the village layout and architecture of the Ming and Qing dynasties.

In August 2004, the Wuhan municipal government filed an application for Dayuwan to be included in the list of National Historical and Cultural Villages. As a part of this effort, Wuhan Municipal Bureau of Land Resources and Planning entrusted the Hubei Provincial Institute of Urban Planning & Design to make the Historical and Cultural Village Preservation Plan of Dayuwan which went beyond the preservation of physical elements to include intangible cultural heritage such as local customs, handicrafts, festival, agricultural and Fengshui cultures. Also, three scopes of preservation were identified in the plan, namely, the core area, controlled area and coordinating area, with specific preservation guidelines for each area and its architecture. In the core area, the preservation stresses historical authenticity while in the controlled and coordinating areas, harmony with the context is required.

In September 2005, Dayuwan was named a National Historical and Cultural Village by the Ministry of Construction and State Administration of Cultural Heritage. The district government allocated a fund of 20 million Yuan for the repairing of heritage buildings and improving of road infrastructure in accordance with the preservation plan.

In 2007, the district government identified the preservation and development of Dayuwan as a National Historical and Cultural Village as one of the priorities of the year and made a regulatory detailed plan for the core preservation area of the village. In 2009, with the making of preservation and repairing plans for the historical buildings in Dayuwan by the School of Architecture, Wuhan University of Science and Technology, preservation of the village started to become more systematic and effective. Up to November 2011, 40 million Yuan has been invested in the preservation of the village, covering such things as the repairing of historical buildings in the core area and the renovation and updating of 28 decrepit buildings to satisfy the call for safety. At the same time, the village environment has also

Preservation and Sustainable Development of Suburban Historical Villages 141

been improved with the combing of the Sheshui River waterways, the building of the dam, restoring open and covered drains and hardening of the road surface.

Thoughts on Preservation

Dayuwan is the only historical village in Hubei Province which was named a National Historical and Cultural Village by the State Administration of Cultural Heritage. The reason why it has been preserved in its entirety along with its community life lies not only in objective factors such as its geographic location and fine architectural quality, but also for the commitment and the involvement of different subjects over more than 20 years since the discovery of its historical resources. Experience can be taken from its preservation and it can also be a reference point for other historical villages.

Application for Historical Heritage Preservation
For suburban historical villages, it is extremely difficult to secure public funds for the repairing of historical buildings and improving of environments. Usually, only those included in the national, provincial, municipal heritage lists may be eligible for designated funding. After being successfully named as the Provincial Heritage Preservation Unit, a National Historical and Cultural Village and thus becoming a landmark of Huangpi District and Wuhan city, subsequent financial support has evidently increased which has, in turn, helped improve the decrepit buildings and village environment.

Preservation of Both Tangible and Intangible Heritage
Undoubtedly, vernacular buildings are an important element of historical villages to be recognized. This is because the vernacular architectural system, normally still inhabited by local residents, accommodates various activities of village life. When attention is given to the main buildings, the integrated preservation of both the tangible and intangible heritage of historic villages might fail. As a matter of fact, this has meant in several other villages China has ignored the local community and stripped down a historical village to an isolated and soulless shell. Different to many historical village attractions where villages have been relocated and fallen into obscurity, in Dayuwan what is preserved is not only the unique village layout and vernacular buildings, but also the natural environment where the village's roots are, the agricultural environment which generations of residents depend on and the intangible heritage such as the traditional pottery-making crafts, the farming-reading culture, customs and festivals. Here visitors can experience the living traditional rural life by themselves.

Participation of Different Stakeholders
The preservation of Dayuwan began with the evaluation and promotion by architecture and heritage experts and the support of heritage authorities, followed by the strong support of local governments who played a leading role in the

142 *Urban China's Rural Fringe*

program application, funding, repair and infrastructure construction. Nevertheless, preservation of historical villages demands the participation of local residents. With years of promotion, residents now have a high awareness of heritage preservation which is further strengthened by the Code of Conduct of Dayuwan Residents. The code covers various aspects such as the prohibition of unauthorized construction, registration of relics, environmental protection and public sanitation and so on.

The Use and Sustainable Development of Historical Villages

Tourism Development of Historical Villages

The preservation of historical villages does not mean just to keep them intact. Villages evolve with our times and villagers should also enjoy modern civilization and prosperous lives. Under the precondition of ensuring the authenticity of historical villages, a common approach to economic growth is tourism development. As early as 2002, the local government has taken tourism as a strategy to revitalize Dayuwan and the village has been included as a tourist spot in the Mulan scenic and tourism area.

In 2004, the district government entrusted the School of Urban Design Wuhan University to make the Detailed Planning of Daywan Scenic Spot, based on which the Municipal Bureau of Heritage made the Detail Plan on the Preservation Development and Utilization of Dayuwan Scenic Spot. The plans expect to integrate the building complex with its surroundings, and also include the tangible and intangible heritage while highlighting the five major tourism elements: the historical Ming and Qing building complex, a cultural square and a stage for folk opera performances, village museum, handicraft workshop and rural guesthouses.

However, the lack of funding has always stood in the way of Dayuwan tourism development. In the five years after the tourism plan was approved, few development projects were implemented. Later, local tourism department attempted to realize their ultimate objectives by using market forces through the establishment of tourism enterprises and identified a strategy of state ownership, government planning and enterprise operation. In 2009, the Huangpi government promoted the founding of the Dayuwan Tourism Development Company which was operated by a professional team whose objective is to forge a comprehensive tourism area integrating sight-seeing, recreation, catering, fishing and farming activities and so on. To date, tens of millions have been invested in major projects such as the restoration of a traditional Chinese herbal medicine shop, Baizi Hall, the residence of a scholarly family, a folk-art street, a stone-ware district as well as the largest wedding photography centre in Central China (see Figure 7.3).

In October 2012, the new Dayuwan scenic area was officially opened to tourists. On the 18th May the first National Folk Culture Festival was opened in the village with total tourist numbers at roughly 100,000 on the opening day. On the 15th May the top 50 competition for the Miss International Tourism was

Figure 7.3 **Tourism activities in Dayuwan Village**

held in Dayuwan which attracted large numbers of tourists. Driven by a series of cultural tourism programs, Dayuwan thrived with a great improvement in villagers' living standards.

Tourism-oriented Revitalization

To coordinate heritage preservation and economic development, many villages took tourism development as an important approach. However, the introduction of tourism to a historical village is a complicated process which calls for large financial input for the construction of facilities. The funding cannot rely solely on the local government and residents, but also the participation of outside enterprises. When investing in a tourism attraction, companies attach importance to its economic value which is decided by three factors: the uniqueness of the object, accessibility of the tourists and the compatibility between the tourism object and the scenic area (Zhu 2009). Nevertheless, participation of the enterprises may lead to over-commercialization and the deterioration of the original atmosphere of the village – this is becoming a matter of concern even in China (Ruan 2004). The guideline for Dayuwan tourism development, addressing issues such as state ownership, government planning, and enterprise operations, can to a certain degree pave the way to possible over-commercialization. Although it is still too early to deem the Dayuwan practice as a success (or failure), it provides an example on how the sustainable development of peri-urban historical villages is currently addressed in contemporary China. Nevertheless, successful tourism-oriented revitalization of historical villages may include the following:

1. Guiding tourism development with planning. Planning ensures the consistency of tourism development, and it is also the instrument which government can use to regulate enterprise behaviours. Preservation plan is the precondition of all other development plans without which the cultural and social values of historical villages will depreciate. Simple as it sounds, many tourism practices today in China tend to put business planning before preservation planning.
2. Adopting an integral development strategy. Tourism resources cover not only the historical buildings but also the vernacular culture and the natural surroundings. Therefore, to turn a historical village into a tourism product, there is the need to integrate different local resources and to enhance their connections and accessibility.
3. Implementing appropriate sales techniques. To attract tourists, historical villages need proper measures of place marketing in a bid to enhance visibility and people's awareness of the unique resources. Cultural or promotional activities are the major promotional techniques, such as photography competitions, pageants, conferences, festivals and so on. In addition, to be included in the list of National Heritage, or even World Heritage, the tourism product should also show a certain competitive advantage over others.
4. Fully considering residents' interests. The tourism development of historical villages should avoid the risk of main street over-commercialization and, in general terms, of gentrification. The drain of the original residents also means the loss of intangible heritage such as local customs, handicrafts, dialects and thus the real village life. To retain the residents, we need to improve incomes and living standards. Usually, a mature village attraction may generate income from tickets, catering, accommodation and so on. With tourism development in the village, some Dayuwan residents began businesses such as rural restaurants and souvenirs. Many young people find jobs inside of the village and many people returned home from large cities.

Conclusion

The survival of Dayuwan can be attributed to its unique closed-up environment, relatively backward socio-economic development and its assets in architectural layout, structure and design, which can be called passive preservation. More importantly, after the historical value of Dayuwan was recognized, efforts were made by experts, government, residents and enterprises together to implement a multi-tiered preservation for its revitalization. This kind of active preservation is a stance we should take in the preservation of historical villages at urban fringes. In the transition of Dayuwan, various urban resources were fully utilized and a development mode was established which comprised integral preservation, public-private cooperation, gradual development and the inclusion of both tourists and residents. Surely, as every historical village is unique in its own right, no experience can be universally applied. However what was reported here seems to follow a general pattern of development that has been already observed in other parts of the world. Similar concerns regarding the fragility of the local rural environment and the need to balance preservation and development, mostly driven by tourism, has been central in the discussion on how to deal with rural villages and cultural landscapes (UNESCO 2003). The goal of achieving the sustainable development of a village like Dayuwan is a test as to whether the local government, professionals and residents can properly deal with its challenges, considering that what has happened in China, in recent years, detaching itself from a common and internationally accepted minimum standard of preservation.

References

Bi, Z.L. 2011. Preservation of historical villages in China's urbanization. *China Cultural Newspaper*, 1 Aug.

Cai, H. and Li, Y.J. 2006. Historic and cultural village Dayuwan and its conservation planning. Proceedings of the 2006 Conference of the Chinese Urban Planning Society.

Chen, M. 2010. The Value Judgments and Value Protection of Historic and Cultural Village – Taking Huangpi Dayuwan as an example. *Journal of Green Science and Technology*, 11, 114–15 (in Chinese).

Jin, T. and Zhang, X.L. 2002. Analysis on the Construction Thoughts of Tranditional Rural Settlements in China. *Human Geography*, 17 (5), 45–8 (in Chinese).

Pan, H.T. 2006. A Visit to an Historic and Cultural Village – Hubei Wuhan HuangpiDayuwan Village. *Towns and Villages*, 2006 (2), 96–7 (in Chinese).

Ruan, Y.S and Gu, X.W. 2004. An Analysis About the Practical Patterns to Conserve the Historic Districts in China. *Journal of Tongji University*, 15 (5), 1–6 (in Chinese).

UNESCO 2003. Cultural Landscapes: the challenges of conservation. Paper n. 7. Paris: World Heritage Papers.

Wang, P.L and Long, W.J. 2010. The Value and Protection Study of the Historic and Cultural village. Based on the Survey of Dayuwan Village. *China Science and Technology Achievements*, 2010 (9), 17–9 (in Chinese).

Zhang, F.X. and Yu, J. 2009. Rural Homeland Construction and Protection and Utilization of Historic and Cultural Village: Case of Dayuwan Village in Huangpi District Planning. *Huazhong Architecture*, 27 (12), 118–22 (in Chinese).

Zhou, Q.S. 2013. Problems and Countermeasures of the status quo of China's traditional village protection Visit to a National Historic and Cultural Village – Wuhan HuangpiDayuwan. *China Construction*, 29 Jan. (in Chinese).

Zhu, X.X. 2009. Tourism Resource of Historical Chinese Villages and its Evaluation, Kaifeng. Henan University (in Chinese).

Chapter 8

Public Participation in Contested Spatial Planning: Learning from a Failed Urban Development Project

Lei Sun and Xiaonan Zhang

Introduction

Recent work on metropolitan growth in developing countries (see Shaw and Satish 2007; Zhang 2000, 2002) has suggested that changes in governance have a significant influence on urban spatial changes and suburban development. China is taking a decentralization process so the local governments have more power to control public policies, resource allocation and delivery of public goods and services (Zhang 2002). The decentralization of power opens up broad space to multi-scale forms of governance with multi-stakeholder arrangements (Rakodi 2003; Zhao *et al.* 2009). In the multi-stakeholder arrangement system, conflicting interests should be allowed and negotiation between the government and other sectors replaces mere command control from government. As a result, spatial planning is facing much more challenges stemming from the uncertainties of current local developments (Zhao *et al.* 2009).

Rural-urban fringes are the frontier regions in the course of urbanization in China. Besides the environmental problems caused by the rapid urbanization in China (Enserink and Koppenjan 2007), there are also rising social and economic conflicts at the rural-urban fridge (see Chapter 1 and 3). The physical relocation of rural families often leads to economic, social and cultural deterritorialization (Hsing 2010). Whether or not these conflicts and issues can be successfully resolved will significantly determine the course of urbanization as well as the ability to achieve urban and rural sustainable development in China.

The unsatisfactory governance is one of the main reasons for the current tension and conflicts in cities and rural-urban fringes (see Liu and Wong 2012; Dyer 2011; Yep 2004). Another reason are the political and institutional contexts that influence policy-making and development activities. Because of the political and institutional environment, spatial planning is frequently inconsistent with local development facts (Zhao *et al.* 2009). So far economic development is still at the top of the agenda, if not the sole agenda item, for local governments at municipal or lower levels.

Because of unfair treatment, protests launched by aggrieved peasants have been on the rise since the late 1990s. In 2005 alone, the Ministry of Land and Resources recorded 87,000 protests related to land grabs, a 6 per cent increase from 2004 (Hsing 2010). Inner city redevelopment projects caused similar deterritorialization issues to local residents. Like their inner city counterparts, peasants protest against forced eviction, demand fair compensation and request adequate relocation by going through the 'letters and visits' system, and by initiating litigation against government agencies, officials and developers. Despite their grave plight and the large number of aggrieved peasants, these protests remain largely fragmented and localized (Hsing 2010).

Many dispossessed and displaced peasants have resorted to individualized modes of protest, such as physically occupying homes and farms slated for demolition, thus becoming so-called 'nail households' (*dingzihu*) (Hsing 2010). This phenomenon can be perceived as peasants' counterplots against state monopoly of the rural urbanization process wherein peasants lost their farmland, the sole source of their livelihood, and have received little compensation (Liu and Wong 2012). Again, this phenomenon is quite similar to the redevelopment projects in inner cities as disadvantaged local residents take individual action against the local government and developers.

In recent attempts to build a harmonious society amidst the intense atmosphere of social change, the Chinese government made some moves to make this transitional period less conflictual and more accommodating (Liu and Wong 2012). One such move is emphasizing the importance of public participation in spatial planning as it is considered the cornerstone of good governance (Enserink and Koppenjan 2007). For example the China Council for International Cooperation on Environment and Development (CCICED) highlighted that public information and participation for sustainable urbanization is one of their four main policy recommendations (CCIED 2006).

In China, local urban and rural communities have developed a number of participatory and deliberative institutions such as consultative meetings and public hearings that fit in with the socialist tradition of political participation (He 2004; Palmer *et al.* 2011). The country is gaining more experience with public participation. However at the same time the increasing size and frequency of rural and urban protest and labour unrest nationwide points to a situation that calls state governance into serious question (Chung 2004). The urgency and significance of public participation in China's urbanization process prompted us to focus on the reasons behind, up till now, the not-so-successful implementation.

This chapter explores public participation and governance issues in spatial planning using a unique inner city redevelopment case study. The reason for using this case study in the book, which is focusing on rural-urban fringe management and development, is that urban-rural fringes share many common issues with the deprived inner urban area, for example the informal housing marketand the disadvantaged local residents/community. Also as urbanization is a dynamic process rather than a static condition, the three types of place – the inner city, the urban edge and the rural fringe – are not three isolated containers of human activity and politics (Hsing 2010). Therefore the governance of these areas cannot be separated and lessons can be learned from each other. By using a relevant inner city case study in the book we can also bring a new perspective to the common issue shared by both fringe and inner city areas in China.

Unlike other places, the Drum Tower Muslim area has little ambiguity (so it is clear as to who constitutes the local community and who comprises government). In particular, there is a strong Muslim community in the area. In 2006, the expansion of Damaishi-Sajingqiao Street in the west side of the district initiated by the Xi'an municipal government was suspended due to resistance from local residents (Zhai 2009). The typical Chinese-style redevelopment measures, which refer to large-scale demolition and reconstruction, did not work since the local Muslim community was determined to protect its social fabric. This failed project can serve as a good case study for an understanding of what type of participation has or has not been used and why it does not work. It can also provide some insights on how the role of a strong community can, and should, participate in the process of spatial planning.

This chapter examines this failed redevelopment project based on in-depth interviews with people from both the local government and community. The rest of the chapter is divided into six sections: firstly it provides background information on public participation in China; secondly there is an introduction to the case study area and its characteristics; thirdly, the trajectory of the failed urban redevelopment project is presented; fourthly, the research methodology and findings are described and there follows a discussion (in the fifth section) in connection with the findings from other relevant research; and, finally, we draw some conclusions and suggestions for further study.

Public Participation in China

Public participation in spatial planning is widely considered to improve the quality and effectiveness of decision-making as it widens the knowledge base, stimulates creativity and creates social support for policies (Enserink and Koppenjan 2007). More importantly, public participation has the intention to shift the development paradigm, to promote a people-centred approach that prioritizes demand over supply mechanisms (Plummer and Taylor 2004). Public participation, especially starting from an early stage, in the development process could provide a channel for the public to have a say regarding the future development of their place and potentially bring more social sustainable solutions (Zhang 2004).

As distinct from that envisioned in the West, public participation in China must be understood contextually (Palmer *et al.* 2011). Up till now, public participation in China is still in its infancy. This is partly due to the fact that the Chinese civic society is still generally weak (Rowe 2005). Individuals' rights are frequently infringed in the name of the 'public good'. Also because of the dominance of the

150   *Urban China's Rural Fringe*

government's economic rationale, it is usually difficult for local people to defend their property rights, not to mention preventing the disappearance of traditional physical and social fabrics that are of great significance to them. As observed by Plummer and Taylor (2004), a primary difference in the operating context and the background to participatory initiatives is that, unlike most other countries recently embarking on participatory processes, economic reform has preceded socio-political reform in China, and economic rights are prioritized over social and human rights. This places the participatory activity – which is fundamentally concerned with inclusion and social equity – on a different footing.

The main stream of public participation in the last three decades in urban China has been closely connected to the development of urban neighbourhood communities and the transformation of Urban Residents Committees (URCs) (Xu 2007). The URC is a neighbourhood-level, quasi-governmental organization present in all cities and towns across China. According to the PRC Urban Residents Committee Organizing Law (1989), these Committees, whose employees are civil servants, are autonomous, though they often work closely with and carry out the local government's administrative tasks (Derleth and Koldyk 2004), such as monitoring family-planning compliance and maintaining household registry rolls. The public participation programs run by URC were less successful compared with the programs run by well-established, trusted community groups (Lei 2001). Beside through the URC, alternative approaches have frequently been employed by local people individually to resist urban redevelopment projects, for instance refusing to cooperate and acting as a 'Nail Household' or repeatedly submitting petitions. The results of these actions have not proven to be effective and significant.

From the limited number of studies on public participation, Chinese scholars have found that the means of public participation is critical and that different community organizations have yielded different mobilization results (Xu 2007). On another account, Western scholars have a proclivity to link community mobilization and participation in China with local governance (for example Benewick *et al.* 2004; Chen and Zhong 2002; Jennings 1997; Shi 1997): their studies on participatory behaviour frequently characterize grassroots participation in China as atomistic and informal, driven by individual interests and benefits rather than collective goals (Xu 2007).

Given this information, the examination of the interaction between local residents and municipal governments in a redevelopment program would not only contribute to a better understanding of how these social and economic conflicts evolve, but also help to form a basis for articulating practical solutions to mitigate the negative consequences led by the currently prevailing redevelopment model.

Case Study Area

Xi'an is the capital city of Shannxi Province and the regional centre of the Northwest China. The greater Xi'an consists of nine districts and four towns

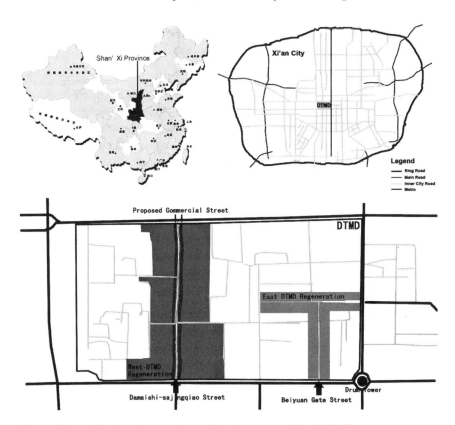

Figure 8.1   The location and spatial structure of the DTMD

covering an area of 10,108 km² and a population of 8.3 million (XCPB2007). In 2006, around 5.4 million people were concentrated in the urban area of 3,600km² (XSB 2007). The city is one of China's Great Ancient Capitals and was designated as a Cultural Renowned City by China's State Council in 1982. With more than 1,000 years of history as being the economic, political and cultural centre of ancient China, it is now a world-renowned tourism destination attracting millions of people every year. Due to its geographical location, the Xi'an city together with its industrial basis was well preserved during World War II. From 1964 to 1978, following Mao's 'Three Line Development Strategy', Xi'an became one of the largest receptors of state investment in industries and ranked the 7th largest city in China in 1982. However, with the opening up of China's east coastline from the 1980s, Xi'an gradually lost its comparative advantage in economic development. In spite of the cultural and political significances, Xi'an is now among the second tier of Chinese cities. With a GDP of 324 billion Yuan, it ranked 28th in 2011.

The Drum Tower Muslim District (DTMD) is located at the centre of Xi'an city, covering an area of around 54 ha with a population of about 60,000 people, of which more than half are Hui people (local Muslims) (XMHDPPO 2003).

The district's eastern, western, northern and southern boundaries are respectively Shehui Road, Zaoci Lane, Hongfu Road and the West Avenue (Figure 8.1). The DTMD is administrated by Lian Hu District government and the whole area is divided into eight neighbourhoods based on the location of the mosques. Over 70 per cent of the properties in the area are privately owned, and the historical buildings and commercial streets are mainly concentrated in the east part of the DTMD.

The Hui nationality was formed in the Yuan dynasty (A.D. 1271–1368) and developed in the Ming dynasty (A.D. 1368–1644). Their daily life is greatly influenced by Islamic norms and dogmas. The mosque plays an important part in Hui people's social and spiritual life. It is the place they go for daily worship and hold various ceremonies such as weddings and funerals. Small food stores run by families absorbed around 70 per cent of the local labour (Zhai and Ng 2013). However, one of the significant characteristics that distinguish the Hui people from other Muslims is that they speak Chinese and in some aspects they are highly Hannized, that is, they comply with the important moral principles of Chinese culture. For instance, Confucianism emphasizes mutual responsibility: within a family, it means the parents are morally obligated to provide material support for their children before their marriage, and for the children, especially the males, it is their obligation to take care of their parents when they are old. It is found that many local Muslims live with a big family consisting of three or even four generations. According to Huang and Wu (2011), 86.6 per cent of the DTMD residents investigated expressed the willingness to remain in the traditional living pattern.

Trajectory of the Urban Development in the DTMD

During the first 30 years after 1949, the development of Chinese cities followed an imbalanced model. Industrial sectors were invested in heavily while other aspects of urban life were neglected. Although Xi'an was one of the largest receptors of national investment during this period, little resources had actually been channelled to regenerate its inner urban areas. Before the 1990s, neither local people nor municipal government were capable of changing the dilapidated physical environment in DTMD and only small-scale refurbishment was occasionally implemented by local residents. Before the 1990s, the majority of the properties in the DTMD were small courtyards with single-storey buildings.

The Xi'an municipal government started regenerating the DTMD in 1991 with a small-scale refurbishment project aiming at beautifying the Beiyuan-Gate Street in the east DTMD. In 1997, a cooperative redevelopment project lured 5 million Yuan from the Norway government and matched this funding from the Chinese state and municipal governments in the east part of the DTMD. The boundaries of the redevelopment project were, respectively: Huaue alley to the south, Guangji Street to the west, Xiyangshi to the north and Beiyuan-Gate Street to the east. The program mainly focused on controlling the Floor-Area Ratio (F.A.R) as well as preserving historical buildings and courtyards. The project has three major achievements: 1. restoring the traditional courtyards and buildings; 2. safeguarding the physical and social environment surrounding the Grate Mosque; and 3. injecting vitality into the local economy. Notably, the flagship project for the second round of redevelopment – the preservation of No. 125 in Huajue Alley – was awarded with the 'Cultural Heritage Protection Prize' by UNESCO in 2002. Commentary from both academics and local residents was mainly positive. It is agreed that the redevelopment projects did not only change the dilapidated image of inner urban areas in Xi'an city, but also successfully preserved both tangible and intangible heritage in the DTMD. Moreover, the redevelopment projects stimulated development of tourism in the area and added many working opportunities.

In 1993, the Xi'an municipal government set an agenda to redevelop the west DTMD and the pilot redevelopment project was implemented in1995. It was a property-led redevelopment project with some old properties in the northwest corner of the DTMD being replaced by tower blocks. In 2002, the Damaishi-Sajinqiao Street redevelopment was initiated in the west DTMD. Being different to the redevelopment practices in the east DTMD, no external funding was available for preservation-related actives. Indeed, the major object of the program was to widen the street by demolishing the properties alongside it so as to mitigate the increasing traffic congestion. The project was listed as one of Xi'an's 'Ten Key Projects of the Year 2005' and was attached with high political priority. It was supervised by one of the vice-governors of the provincial government and directed by the chief executive of Lianhu District government. In 2005, the Lianhu District government conducted a comprehensive survey in the DTMD and a research report was produced. Based on the report and consultations conducted with the government officials and academicians, a redevelopment proposal was produced in 2005 by the Xi'an City Planning and Design Institute (CPDI), a public institution administrated by the Xi'an Planning Bureau. According to the plan, around 1,000 properties needed to be demolished for the expansion and beautification of the Damaishi-Sajingqiao Street. Two pedestrian streets (Figure 8.2) in parallel with the main street were to be built to accommodate small businesses and several flats were also to be erected. When consulted, the majority of the local residents were unsatisfied with the proposal. They believed that the planned commercial area was too small to accommodate the small businesses, which are the main source of income for many local families. Later the Lianhu District government published the relocation and compensation plan, according to which owners of the properties with a registered floor space larger than 20 m² would be moved to several condominiums that were going to be built on No. 64 Xianmiyuan, a piece of land previously owned by a SOE (State Owned Company) and 500 metres away from the redevelopment area. The construction and relocation work was promised to be finished within 18 months. The rest of the relocations with properties smaller than 20 m² were to be accommodated at No. 43 Daxing Road, which is 7 km away from the DTMD. A monetary compensation plan was also in place for those

154   *Urban China's Rural Fringe*

Figure 8.2   Local government-proposed plans in Sajinqiao Street area

Figure 8.3   Run-down houses in the district

Public Participation in Contested Spatial Planning

who wish to purchase a property on the market. For private-owned residential and business properties the compensation prices were respectively 1,680–2,180 Yuan/m^2 and 3,800–4,000 Yuan/m^2, which amounted to only one-third of the market prices (Zhai and Ng 2013) (see Figure 8.3 for the housing conditions in the area).

The district government advocated the local people for cooperation. Local party members and officials were promised higher compensation for taking a lead in signing the expropriate contract. It was hoped that the rest of the local people would follow suit. From 13th March to 20th May 2005, 291 demolition contracts had been signed, covering a floor area of 29,000 m^2, which was less than one-third of the total houses that needed to be demolished. The speed was much slower than the government had expected. For the local people, in spite of the obvious low compensation prices, they also worried about their post-redevelopment life. For some of them, the relocation would deprive them of their only source of income. Constrained by low educational background and Islamic convention, it is difficult for the local Muslims to make a living outside the DTMD. The redevelopment was also thought to have a detrimental impact on the indigenous culture and social life. Some of the interviewees expressed the concern that the relocation would deconstruct the social structure and lead the Islamic convention to be assimilated, as people living outside the DTMD may not necessarily comply with the Islamic doctrine in their daily life. Besides, the local people were also suspicious about the sincerity of the government since the construction of the promised resettlement condominium near the Lianhu District stopped a week after the announcement of the compensation policies.

With mounting pressure to accomplish the planned redevelopment, the executive of the district government had to accelerate the expropriation process. The government decided to tear down all the previously contracted buildings together, aiming at displaying muscle to the local people. In spite of officials from different government departments and policemen, the district government also hired hundreds of temporary workers to maintain the order. The local residents invited some local media to report the incident, but none of them turned up. The bulldozer quickly dismantled many properties and the local people were stunned, as the government had expected. However, the intimidation aroused stronger resistance and the local people became militant. From the beginning, the district government's strategy was to divide the local people and treat them separately. There was an informal rule that officials should be included in every meeting held by the local residents. Any self-organized discussions regarding the demolition and compensation issues without the attendance of officials were regarded as a challenge to the government. After the demolition, local people gathered together and reached an agreement that no one should sign any contract with the government individually before the compensation and rehabilitation conditions are collectively accepted. The Imams from the two mosques in the community were put forward to take the leadership, although two of them initially refused to do so. They started to employ various venues such as the Ethnic Committee and the People's Congress to make their voice heard. Petitions were sent to municipal, provincial

156 *Urban China's Rural Fringe*

and central government. The resistance lasted for three months and eventually the central government sent out a group of inspectors to investigate the redevelopment project. The conclusion was that the relocation project was carried out without proper permission and therefore the whole redevelopment project should cease.

Research Methodology and Findings

This research employed a case study research methodology to obtain micro level data of the failed redevelopment project initiated by the Xi'an municipal government in 2005. Case study as a research methodology is preferable when the focus of the research is on 'how' and 'why' a contemporary phenomenon takes place within some real-life context, when the researcher has little or no control over events and when multiple sources of data are used (Yin 1989). Research methods include a literature review, document search, semi-structured and unstructured interviews and observation. Both quantitative and qualitative data were collected and cross-checked to minimize the bias of data.

The filed work took place in the Xi'an DTMD in April 2012 and November 2013. Fifteen semi-structured interviews were taken with people who were deeply involved in the redevelopment process, including the chief designer of the redevelopment proposal, the deputy secretary of the Xi'an Political Consultative Conference, the director of the Lianhu Residents Committee, relocated families and local activists who were involved in preparing for the petition materials and organizing the resistance. Additionally, 12 unstructured interviews were given to local residents that either witnessed or directly participated in the redevelopment project. The local residents' living conditions and community-oriented activities organized by the Residents' Committee and supported by the volunteers were observed. Second-hand data converted from previous studies and official documents were also used in this research.

There are nine major findings from this case study: 1) the polarized attitudes held by the local residents and the government officials towards the compensation policies originated from their different interpretations of property rights and land ownership; 2) instead of encouraging the public to participate in the regeneration process, the local government, with strong entrepreneurism, followed a market logic and had an inclination to utilize the state apparatus and the institutional set-up to marginalize the local residents and distort the compensation price so as to obtain a higher margin from the redevelopment; 3) in the unfair wrestling between the municipal government and the local people, both sides exhausted their political resources and even became militant to maximize the gains from the redevelopment; 4) although the deeply rooted mutual distrust between the local residents and the government had significantly increased the political and economic cost to regenerate the west DTMD area, for local residents, the government is still thought to be the only candidate who is capable of regenerating the area; 5) the initiation of government-led regeneration is premised on the fact that the municipal government could gain economic benefits from the project, which means, only when the municipal government can secure a full grasp on the rent gap generated from the regeneration project or ensures it is the primary landlord of the redeveloped properties will it devote resources to regenerating an area; 6) in spite of the social and economic successes, the Beiyuanmen Street regeneration in the east part of the DTMD was achieved, widening the inequality among the local residents and raising the local people's expectations on the levels of benefits they can get from the regeneration to a staggering high level; 7) in contrast, living conditions in new buildings provided by the local government for accommodating the relocated families are poor and up to November 2013 only around half of the units are occupied by relocated families and tenants; 8) both the municipal government and the local residents tend to agree that the selection of communicative strategies and the adoption of some compulsory measures may fundamentally alter the development of the whole incident, which suggests the consequences sometimes are unpredictable and highly dependent on the interactions between both sides; 9) although the Resident Committee plays an important role in the governance of local communities, especially in delivering social regeneration programs and enhancing the communication between the local people and the government, it has a limited capacity in influencing the local authority's physical regeneration agenda and speaking for the local residents.

For the local officials and professionals who are working for the government, the inflation of land and property prices in the west DTMD is due to public investment in the infrastructures and thus the government should be one of the major beneficiaries of the redevelopment project. The local residents are thought to be too 'greedy'. If following their requirements on compensation and relocation, the government would not be able to balance the revenue and expenditure without external funding. As the chief designer of the redevelopment proposal put it:

> The government has invested a lot of money in the DTMD for a very long time, you can't expect more. What the local Muslim residents really want is using public money to expand and beautify their street, to modify their houses and to make places to for accommodating their businesses. They themselves refuse to be relocated but want all the Han people to be evacuated.

Similar opinions were also implied in the comments from the director of the local Residents' Committee:

> The compensation policies were fair but some of the residents wanted more and were hard to be convinced. The local residents can really benefit from the redevelopment as they will be able to live in new apartments, which is a great improvement compared with their current living conditions.

For local residents, however, the compensation was far lower than they expected. According to one local resident:

158　　*Urban China's Rural Fringe*

> It is impossible to buy a similar housing unit in the area with the compensation got from the government. If we want to stay here after the redevelopment, we have no choice but to pay extra money by ourselves. Why on earth should we accept the offer?

Further, living in the new apartment provided by the municipal government does not necessarily mean the local residents will see an improvement in their living standards, as one put it:

> The new apartment doesn't have central heating system, which is unusual in the newly built communities in Xi'an, and we have to use coal stove to heat our house like what we did before. However, without a lift, we now have to carry the coal up to six floors.

One thing that has been emphasized by nearly all the local residents and some of the Muslim officials was that moving out of the area would cause great inconvenience. One local activist gave the reasons:

> The mosques are the most important thing for our Muslim people, we cannot live without it as we do our daily worship and hold our ceremonies in it. It is also impossible to find so many Muslim foods in any other places. More importantly, this community is where our ancestors used to live and local people have their family cemeteries here, which is untouchable.

Obviously for the local residents the value of their property does not only consist of the construction costs of the new buildings, but also includes the existing social and cultural elements as well as the convenience brought by the location, which was not mentioned by the officials. Yet not all the local people were against the redevelopment. Some Han people were satisfied with the government's proposal. As one former local resident, a Han, now living in a community outside of the DTMD stated:

> I signed the contract once the government announced the redevelopment plan and we are now living in an apartment with central heating and decent environment. I am quite happy with that as my new neighbours are quite friendly and we no longer get ourselves into frequent disputes with the neighbours as we used to.

The genuine conflict between the municipal government and the local people was who should be the major beneficiaries of the redevelopment. As another local activist put it:

> We were really disappointed about the redevelopment proposal and asked the government to reconsider about it. We hope the Damaishi-sajingqiao Street can be regenerated following the east DTMD pattern and the owners of the

commercial buildings alongside the street are willing to give up part of their property and land rights for the main street expansion, as long as they are allowed to retain the ownership and development rights to the rest part of their land. Yet all our suggestions were rejected by the government as they determined to expropriate all the properties from us and make money from the commercial redevelopment alone.

The current institutional set-up enables the government to manipulate the participation process and to suppress local residents' resistance. As one of the local activists complained:

Our suggestions were neglected by the government and we hardly have any chance to change their mind. The planning bureau, the design institute, the police, the media and even the Residents' Committee are all directly or indirectly controlled by the government and no one (in the government) really speaks for us … when we ask some of the local medias come to cover the demolition conducted by the government, none of them responded … the police only follow the government's order and it is unrealistic to put hope on the court for a solution as well … the officials asked us to include them into every meeting we have at that time … to avoid been discovered that we were preparing for the petition, we rented a house somewhere away from the DTMD and I stayed there for a whole month to write up the materials. I did not go back to home until all the documents were finished and carried to Beijing.

Although the institutions and media within the jurisdiction of the municipal government were firmly controlled by the government, the local residents can still exert political influence using the sensitivity of ethno-politics and their connection with the national religious organizations. One of the activists put it in this way:

We got support from other Muslim group from other provinces such as Shandong, Gansu and Ningxia. We also sent our materials to the national Ethnic and Religious Association and got response from them as well.

Another effective way to resist is rampant construction. As one of the local residents who was rebuilding his house stated:

I have to build my house into a four-storey flat, although I only got the permission from the government for a three-storey building. Since I have two children and each of them will take one floor for their marriage and me and my wife will take one floor as our bedroom … we also plan to use the ground floor for small business. Everyone in our community is doing like this … I know someone who has a close relationship with the officials even build six floors … I wish the government can lent us some money to rebuild our house, as currently I have already borrowed 160,000 Yuan for the construction, it is a heavy burden for ordinary families like us.

Several months later, when the DTMD was visited for the second time, the self-sponsored reconstruction was finished (see Figure 8.4).

The first floor is converted into a tailor's shop for traditional Muslim costumes, as the shop owner put it:

> I don't have any other skills but tailoring traditional Muslim costumes, so I open this small shop once we the reconstruction of my house finished. It (the business) brings me an average income of around 2,000 Yuan per month. Although it is only a fraction of the money made by the shopkeepers on the Beiyuanmen Street, we don't need to pay for the rent.

Indeed the rent of the commercial properties alongside the Beiyuanmen Street, which is less than 600 metres away from the place mentioned above, in the east DTMD was astonishingly high, which makes some of the local residents very rich. As one of the local landlords stated:

> My grandfather was an official in the Nationalist government (1920s-1949) when he bought a three-floor property on the Beiyuanmen Street. Our family suffered a lot during the Cultural Revolution because of his statues and the money he made. The property was confiscated by the government ... it wasn't until the 1990s when the using right of that property was returned to us ... .so we are allowed to use it for 40 years ... the building is rented out for restaurant for an annual rent of 1.2 million Yuan, which will be evenly distributed into 4 shares for me and my three other brothers ... Indeed the majority of the properties alongside the Beiyuanmen Street are owned by government, public institutions or State Owned Enterprises, which either bought or confiscated the properties from local residents in the wave of nationalization private properties during the 1950s and 1960s.

Figure 8.4   The changes brought by the self-sponsored physical regeneration

Public Participation in Contested Spatial Planning   161

Nearly all local families in the DTMD are now rushing to fill their land with three- or four-storey buildings. Apart from the need to match the enlarging family size, an important incentive for the local people to do so is to secure compensation when the compulsory purchase is imposed. They are trying to warrant their violation against the regulations by expressing their suspicions to some of the officials and identifying examples of profiting from breaking the rules within their community. An old couple living in the public house put it in this way:

> We are Han people and the house we are currently living in is social housing allocated by the government ... indeed my husband owned a house in this area many years ago, to avoid being punished during the Culture Revolution, he escaped to other places, when he came back, the previous property had been confiscated by the government, and that is why we are living here ... we share the corridor with our Hui neighbours. Several years ago they demolished their single-storey house and rebuilt it into a 4-storey apartment. They expanded their building area and eroded half of the corridor ... you know they have the relationship with some of the officials.

For the local residents, the government is still more trustworthy compared with private sectors in taking on the responsibility of regenerating the DTMD. When asked who should take the responsibility to regenerate the area, one local person said:

> Of course the government should do it, no one else has the capacity and resources. Additionally, the local people are not allowed to regenerate the area even some of them have the potential to take the leadership. Anyway, it is the centre of the city, and they (the government) can't just let it be like this. It is their responsibility to intervene and improve the environment of this area. We believe sooner or later this area will be redeveloped by them.

However, some of the local people are not that optimistic about the government's sincerity and enthusiasm to retouch the area. One of the activists stated:

> If we were a little bit more coward at that time, we would have been relocated ... it is now difficult to drive the local people away like what they did seven years ago, as the forced eviction is sensitive and has been banned by the central government. The politicians know the local people are tough and they have plenty of other opportunities to make progress and get promoted.

The Urban Residents Committee (URC) plays an important role in delivering social regeneration programs and consolidating social stability at a local level, as the chief executive of the LianHu URC put it:

We are now running several social programs targeting the most vulnerable residents in our community ... we established the help centre for disabled youth, we started up learning centre and inviting retired professionals and scholars to deliver training courses regarding skills and moral principles to residents who are eager to learn, anyone in our community can take the class for free as long as they are interested ... we work closely with the local police to maintain the stability of our community ... .we regularly visit those who had been released from jail and we also have the latest information about the new comers in our community ... although we have only less than ten formal staff, we got around thirty enthusiastic volunteers who also have a strong connection with their neighbours ... that is how we get information and link ourselves with the whole community.

However, the URC is less likely to stand up and speak for the local residents in a bargain (an agreement whereby both sides utilize all their resources in order to maximize gains) when the opponent is the government, as all the formal staff of the URC are registered as officials and their salaries are paid by the government. Moreover, most of the social regeneration initiatives are directly or indirectly funded by the government. Therefore, the URC together with the voluntary public participation it advocated are merely part of a hegemonic project (Laclau and Mouffe 1985, Graf 2011) that is manipulated by the government.

Discussion

The interactions between the municipal government and local residents in land expropriation and compensation processes that happened in both China's urban fringes and inner city areas share a number of similarities. From the very beginning, local government with a strong entrepreneurship would identify the most lucrative areas to regenerate or develop and would secure itself to be the main beneficiary of the project. Local residents would normally be consulted, yet the aim of the consultation is simply to legitimize the disposition process. Participation in such a form does not mean that local people are in a position to bargain with the government on what they can get for what they will lose, and neither does the government intend to engage local residents in decision-making regarding how the original community will be developed or regenerated. Further, the current institutional set-up leaves very few formal channels for Chinese local residents in both inner urban areas and rural fringes to resist the government's actions, and in many cases only informal venues such as petitions and public protests can occupationally cause enough political pressure for the municipal government to abandon their plan. However, local residents usually utilize public protests as the last option, since it could cause great loss for both sides. For individuals, with inadequate protection from the legal system, it could be very risky for their personal safety; while for local politicians, public protesting usually means great political failure and could cause damage to their political career.

The Reason for the Disparity of Redevelopment Policies in the DTMD

The entrepreneurism of the local government is well manifested in the spatial disparity of redevelopment policies adopted in different parts of the DTMD. The nationalization and confiscation of private properties between the 1950s and the mid-1970s enabled the local government and SOEs to take ownership of properties on Beiyuanmen Street, which had long been a commercial street, from local residents at a very low cost. Later in the 1990s, a booming tourism industry motivated the municipal government to invest in preserving the physical and social fabric of the east DTMD. The redevelopment initiatives in the east DTMD were public-funded conservation and beautification projects integrated with the Xi'an city's tourism development strategy while the Damaishi-sajingqiao redevelopment project in 2005 was a property-led redevelopment. The disparity emerged partly due to the fact that 'conservation of historical quarters or preservation of cultural heritage is a luxury that many governments in the developing world could ill afford' (Shin 2010, p. 44). Xi'an municipal government at that time was facing mounting pressure to develop the local economy and improve the city image while constrained by its administrative and fiscal capacity. Public resources need to be allocated to areas such as the east DTMD where high economic and political returns can be generated and collected by the municipal government, being the primary landlord of properties alongside the street; while for areas without such potential, property-led redevelopment accompanied with accumulation by disposition is the primary means for regeneration, as identified by Yeoh and Huang (1996) as the 'politics of selection'.

With limited resources but great pressure to develop the local economy, disposition became one of the important means for the entrepreneurial municipal government to finish their primitive accumulation (Harvey 2005a). The state ownership of urban land written in the Chinese Constitution (1982) and the monopolization of the government in the primitive land market enabled the gap between the market price for transferring the land use rights to the developers and the compensation fees for expropriating land and properties from the citizens to be collected by the municipal government. This is the basic reason that leads to the conflicts not only in inner cities but also the rural-urban fringe. Could public participation help the local people to improve their situation in the planning and development process?

The Institutional Set-up and Public Participation in the Property-led Redevelopment

Angle (2005) divided the redevelopment-related decision-making into 'input', 'policy formulation' and 'adjustment'. Currently in Chinese urban development projects, public participation usually happens in the 'input' and 'adjustment' stage while policy formulation is more than often dominated by the government or the coalition of government and private developers. Since the Chinese planning system is still largely based on a top-down, command-and-control regulatory approach, the input from local residents usually has little impact on the decision-making. The pre-redevelopment survey conducted in the west DTMD in 2005 suggested that over 90 per cent of the interviewees wished their community to be regenerated following the public-funded conservation and beautification pattern in the east DTMD, yet the final proposal was a property-led redevelopment plan supported by the government.

How were local residents been marginalized? Under the one-party-ruling political system, 'Democratic Centralism' is the form of Chinese democracy, as suggested by Tong (2000), which emphasizes an equal weight to the views of all participants at its 'democratic' end while at its 'centralism' end a single outcome is demanded and is expected to be accepted by all the participants. Theoretically, such a political system demands high-level participation in the initial stage of policy formulation, yet from the case study it is found that: 1. local residents had very low-level engagement at the beginning; 2. no functional venue was provided by the current institutional set-up for citizens to influence the decision-making; 3. the rule of law was inadequate to protect the citizens' right to participation.

Local residents had very low-level engagement at the initial stages of the west DTMD redevelopment. Although their opinions were collected in a comprehensive survey before the redevelopment, there was actually no guarantee that the results would necessarily serve as the evidence base for the decision-making. The decisions were in fact made by politicians from the district government, together with officials from the planning bureau, the professionals from the planning and design institute and some local elites such as academics who were inclined to support the physical redevelopment plan. Public participation was symbolic and manipulated by the government, ranking at the lowest level among all the forms of public participation given in Arnstein's (1969) 'ladder theory'.

Superficially, local residents were eliminated from the decision-making process for two reasons: 1. local people are thought to have inadequate professional knowledge required by the decision-making process; 2. since local people had already been consulted in the survey, there is no need to include them in the decision-making process. Yet there are more deep-seated reasons. High-level public participation could seriously affect the local government's economic profits as the lucrative property-led redevelopment projects resented by the local people might be abandoned. Further, so far the Chinese government is still alert to any civil movements demanding more civil rights and democracy. Public participation apparently has the potential to open a 'Pandora's box of grievance' (Johnson 2010) and is only 'acceptable when it is irrelevant to power sharing' (Fan 2013, p. 4).

Within the current institutional set-up, local residents also lack the venue to influence decision-making. Local people are not able to establish the community-controlled organizations that have political strength to bargain with the local government. In China, all the Non-Governmental Organizations (NGOs) need to find themselves an authority as their upper-level administration (Fan 2013). The semi-official statues constrained the NGOs' capacity to act as real civil organizations: they often distance themselves from any confrontations between local people and the coalition between government and private sectors (Johnson 2010). This can be seen clearly from the operation of the URC, which attracts local volunteers from the community and works closely with public institutions in delivering social regeneration projects and maintaining stability but never gets itself involved in disputes between the municipal government and local residents. So far, there is no sign that the Chinese government will loosen its control over the NGOs and let them develop into a strong civil force. Second, within the given institutional set-up, the government is in a dominant position. It does not only control nearly all the institutes which participated in the redevelopment project, such as the planning bureau, the design institute, the demolition offices and even the media, but it also tries to manipulate social groups and their activities.

Theoretically, a democratic political system should be able to provide a legal framework that can protect the people's civic rights to participation (Angle 2005). Yet in China, the 'government-to-legislature' relationship is 'one of division of labour rather than separation of power' (Cho 2002, p. 729), since legislative leaders and law-executers normally subordinate to the government cadres. For local people who seek legal protection against illegal activities conducted by the government, the legislators and law-executers always stand alongside the governors. Against such a background, it is not surprising to see that the petitions sent by the west DTMD residents yielded no response from the Xi'an Planning Bureau, the Xi'an municipal government as well as the Shanxi Provincial Government, while local medium refused to report on the compulsory demolition. Even the local Imams were suffering pressure and were initially unwilling to put themselves forward as the negotiators to bargain with the local government.

The Interaction Between Local People and the Municipal Government

Mobilization

Local people in the west DTMD were not empowered to make decisions on redevelopment projects in their own community. Instead they were mobilized to accept the plans made by the local government before the implementation and were left with very limited flexibility in changing the plans. Historically, mobilization was one of the most important means for the CCP to achieve its aims. Before the 1970s Chinese people were frequently mobilized to participate in neighbourhood-based programs such as community beautification, infrastructure provision or land reclamation. In this case a scenario – in which widening and beautifying the street was viewed as being for the common good – was set and the collective endeavour of the local people was called for. Some people are expected to act as role models for the rest, just like those described by Bakken (2000, p. 423) as 'a structure of simulation'. Here the local party members and officials were required to sign a contract with the local government immediately and they were promised relatively higher compensations as a reward. However, the economic and social transformation since the 1980s has cultivated a growing awareness of individual interests among the Chinese people and an increasing demand for protecting individual interests from being infringed by the fuzzy 'public' interests (Han 2004). The mobilizing strategy was proved to be inefficient in the west DTMD regeneration: as the deadline has passed, only about one-third of the local households signed the contract and most of them have local officials and party members in the households. Interestingly, local people in the west DTMD employed similar tactics to resist the government's infringement on their property rights. They use fairness and the inseparable relationship between local Muslim people and the DTMD as slogans to mobilize local people to stand up and defend their benefits.

The interaction between the local residents and the government

The interaction between the local residents and the municipal government thus falls into a 'passive chain reaction' (Figure 8.5).

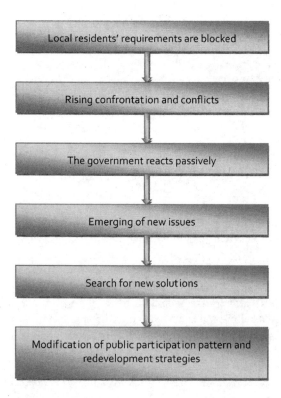

Figure 8.5   Passive chain reaction
Source: modified from Bao and Sun 2007.

Actually, within the current Chinese context, even with the right to petition, it is very difficult for the public to resist state-led physical regeneration and protect their indigenous culture and social fabric. The prevailing rampant construction within the DTMD implies that local residents all have a practical understanding of what is the outcome of the physical fabric within the DTMD. What seems to be practical for them is to maximize the economic benefits they can get from the regeneration by utilizing the given policies. Compensation based on floor space is widely accepted by both government and the public in China and enlarging the floor space before the expropriation thus becomes a rational choice for the local people. Within the Chinese planning system, construction activities in the urban areas are monitored by the Planning and Construction bureau. According to the Town and Country planning Act 2008, if local people want to rebuild their housing, they have to apply for a Building Permit (BP), which gives the parameters regarding the height, floor space and architectural style of the new building. The massive-scale property redevelopment since the 1990s dramatically stimulated self-sponsored reconstruction activities and many local people in the DTMD replaced their traditional single-floor courtyard with multi-floor flats in the hope of getting more compensation from the expropriation that will happen someday. The DTMD was designated as a historical area in the Conservation Regulations on Xi'an Historic City (Zhai and Ng 2013) and the height and elevation of new buildings are required to follow given codes. Yet most of the local residents chose to neglect the regulation after getting their BP. Since over 70 per cent of the properties in the DTMD are privately owned, the prevailing unregulated constructions have profoundly changed the physical environment of the DTMD and downgraded local people's living environments. The rampant constructions were described as 'greedy', yet for the local residents this is a spontaneous reaction to the possible infringement on their property rights conducted by the municipal government.

Local people were intimidated by the demolition of contracted buildings enforced by the district government in 2006. Having realized that their economic interests were possibly to be infringed by the government, the local residents began to react in a militant way. By selecting their own leaders and making rules to be obeyed by all the members, they enhanced their cohesion. They also managed to use their unique identity as the ethnic minority to increase their political influence. However, with limited capacity to resist the powerful municipal government, sending petitions to upper-level government for arbitration became their major means to resist. In the petition, local people gave their own interpretation of the rights to property. Apart from the legal concept of ownership, they also employed the cultural, political and moral concept to oppose the state-sponsored gentrification. They believed that the proposed redevelopment would not only expropriate their properties at an unfair price, but also brutally cut off the majority of the relocated families' connections to their cultural life as well as their means of making a living, which are, of course, crucial to the local families. Moreover, the local Muslim cemetery is also located within the redevelopment area (also see Zhai and Ng 2013) and it is morally unacceptable for them to see it distorted

168   *Urban China's Rural Fringe*

by redevelopment. The local residents' survival strategies significantly raised the economic and political cost of redevelopment projects in the DTMD and made it temporally 'safe' from the property-led redevelopment.

Conclusions

This chapter examines the trajectory of urban redevelopment in the DTMD and interactions between the local residents and the district government in a property-led redevelopment project. It found that the government has strong entrepreneurism and takes advantage of the institutional set-up and the political system to dispose of local residents for accumulation. It has a totally different view compared with the local residents on the issue of who should be the primary beneficiaries of the inner city regeneration project. The government's urban policies were also made after careful evaluation of economic and political costs and benefits. This is a process that local people, whose benefits would be affected, are usually excluded from. The inner city regeneration can easily become property-led redevelopment accompanied by gentrification. Due to the state ownership of urban land and the monopolistic position of the state in the land market, the municipal government became the major collector of the 'rent gap', while the institutional set-up leaves limited venues for the local people to influence decision-making. It is local people who usually bear the greatest economic and social costs of the redevelopment. This setting is quite similar to the development projects at rural-urban fringes.

The Chinese legal framework has proved to be insufficient in protecting people's rights to participation, and the strong state apparatus can easily intensify the tension between both sides and make local people militant. Within such a context, the interaction between the government and the local people falls into a passive chain reaction and survival strategies frequently adopted by the local people are rampant constructions and petitions, which will dramatically increase the economic and political cost of the redevelopment project and eventually make it too risky for local politicians to intervene.

From the case study, we learned that local governments are still considered the main actor in spatial planning and development. However the process needs to be transparent for all stakeholders, including local people/community. Public participation is expected by all in helping to soften and minimize the conflicts in the spatial planning and development process, however a higher level of public participation depends on further changes in the institution and law. The approach of participation is also important. Adopting a low-level participation approach, combined with passive attitudes towards participation, cannot lead to positive results, as shown in the case study.

The case study ultimately shows that strong local communities need to be developed to achieve meaningful public participation which can further lead to more sustainable spatial planning. Under these conditions, a realistic scenario would be the abandonment of a particular development plan, like the case studied in this chapter. This would be a far better result compared to what was happened in many areas in China where households were unfairly treated and forced to be relocated.

References

Abramson, D. 2011. Transitional Property Rights and Local Development History in China. *Urban Studies*, 48(3), 553–68.

Angle, S.C. 2005. Must we choose our leaders? Human rights and political participation in China. *Journal of Global Ethics*, 1(2), 177–96.

Bakken, B. 2000. *The Exemplary Society: Human Improvement, Social Control, and the Dangers of Modernity in China.* Oxford: Oxford University Press.

Bao, J.G. and Sun, L.X. 2007. Differences in Community Participation in Tourism Development Between China and the West. *Chinese Sociology and Anthropology*, 39(3), 9–27.

Barnes, S., Kasse, M. and Allerbeck, K.R. 1979. *Political Action: Mass Participation in Five Western Democracies.* Beverly Hills, CA: Sage.

Benewick, R., Tong, I. and Howell, J. 2004. Self-Governance and Community A Preliminary Comparison between Villagers' Committees and Urban Community Councils. *China Information*, 18 (1), 11–28.

Bray, D. 2005. *Social Space and Governance in Urban China: The Danwei System from Origins to Reform.* Stanford, CA: Stanford University Press.

CCICED, 2006. 'CCID policy recommendations'. CCICED Update, 9(1), The Secretariat of China Council for International Cooperation on Environment and Development, Beijing.

Chen, Y.F. 2012. *City Chinese Logic.* Beijing: SDX Joint Publishing Company.

Chien, S.S. 2010. Economic Freedom and Political Control in Post-Mao China: A perspective of Upward Accountability and Asymmetric Decentralization. *Asian Journal of Political Science*, 18 (1), 69–89.

Cho, Y.N. 2002. From 'rubber stamps' to 'iron stamps': the emergence of Chinese local people's congresses as supervisory powerhouses. *China Quarterly*, 171, 724–40.

Derleth, J. and Koldyk, D.R., 2004, The Shequ experiment: Grassroots political reform in urban China. *Journal of Contemporary China*, 13(41), 747–77.

Deutsche, R. 1996. *Evictions: Art and Spatial Politics.* Cambridge, MA: MIT Press.

Dyer, G. 2011. A democracy is built – on a property boom. *Today*, 10 March, 18–20.

Enserink, B. and Koppenjan, J.F.M. 2007. Public participation in China: sustainable urbanization and governance. *Management of Environmental Quality: An International Journal*, 18(4), 459–74.

Fan, L. 2013. International influence and local response: understanding community involvement in urban heritage conservation in China, *International Journal of Heritage Studies* [Online]. Available at: http://www.tandfonline.com/doi/full/1 0.1080/13527258.2013.834837 [accessed 13 November 2013].

Friedmann, J. 2006. Four these in the study of China's urbanization. *International Journal of Urban and Regional Research*, 30(2), 440–451.

Geovanni, A. 2007. *Adam Smith in Beijing: Linages of the Twenty-First Century*. London: Verso.

Graf, W.D. 1996. Democratization 'for' the Third World-Critique of a Hegemonic Project. *Canadian Journal of Development Studies*, 17 (4), 37–56.

Hackworth, J. and Rekers, J. 2005. Ethnic packaging and gentrification: The case of four neighborhoods in Toronto. *Urban Affairs Review*, 41(2), 211–36.

Han, J. 2004. Doubts on forced administrative nationalization of land. *Finance*, 18, 95–6.

Harvey, D. 1985. *The Urbanization of Capital: Studies in the History and Theory of Capitalist Urbanization*. Baltimore, MD: Johns Hopkins University Press.

Harvey, D. 2005(a). *A Brief History of Neoliberalism*. Oxford: Oxford University Press.

Harvey, D. 2005(b). *Spaces of Global Capitalism: Towards a Theory of Uneven Development*. London: Verso.

He, S.J. 2007. State-sponsored Gentrification Under Market Transition-The case of Shanghai. *Urban Affairs Review*, 43(2), 171–98.

Healey, P. and Barrett, S.M. 1990. Structure and agency in land and property development process: some ideas for research. *Urban Studies*, 27(1), 89–104.

Ho, P. 2001. Greening without conflict? Environmentalism, NGOs and civil society in China. *Development and Change*, 32(5), 893–921.

Hsing, Y-t 2010. *The Great Urban Transformation*. Oxford: Oxford University Press.

Hu, Y., de Roo, G. and Lu, B. 2013. Communicative turn in Chinese Spatial planning? Exploring possibilities in Chinese contexts. *Cities*, 35, 42–5.

Hubbard, P. and Hall, T.1998. The enterprise and the enterprise of narrative: place marketing and the entrepreneurial city, in *The Entrepreneurial City: Geographies of Politics, Regime, and Representation*, edited by T. Hall and P. Hubbard. Chichester: Wiley.

Hustinx, L. and Denk, T. 2009. The 'Black Box' problem in the Study of Participation. *Journal of Civil Society*, 5(3), 209–26.

ICED 2006. 'CCID policy recommendations', CCICED Update, 9(1). The Secretariat of China Council for International Cooperation on Environment and Development, Beijing.

Jennings, M. Kent. 1997. Political participation in the Chinese countryside. *American Political Science Review*, 91 (02), 361–72.

Johnson, T. 2010. Environmentalism and NIMBYism in China: promoting a rules-based approach to public participation. *Environmental Politics*, 19(3), 430–448.

Jones, P.S. 2003. Urban redevelopment's poisoned chalice: Is there an impasse in (community) participation-based policy? *Urban Studies*, 40(3), 581–602.

Laclau, E. and Mouffe, C. 1985. *Hegemony and Socialist Strategy: Towards a Radical Democratic Politics*. London: Verso.

Leaf, M. 2005. Modernity confronts tradition: The professional planner and local corporatism in the rebuilding of China's cities, in *Comparative Planning Cultures*, edited by B. Sanyal. Abingdon: Routledge, 91–111.

Lei, J.Q. (ed.), 2001, *Transitional Urban Community Organizations*. Beijing: Peking University Press.

Ley, D. 2003. Artists, aestheticisation and the field of gentrification. *Urban Studies*, 40(12): 2527–44.

Li, Y. and Li, Z. 2009. Chinese local state entrepreneurialism: a case study of Changchun. *International Development Planning Review*, 31(2), 199–220.

Lin, G.C.S. 2009. *Developing China-Land, Politics and Social Conditions*. London: Routledge.

Liu, R. and Wong, T.C. 2012. Peasants' counterplots against the state monopoly of the rural urbanization process: urban villages and 'small property housing' in Beijing, China. *Environment and Planning A*, 44, 1219–40.

Luo, X.L. and Shen, J.F. 2008. Why City-region planning does not work well in China? *Cities*, 25(4), 207–17.

Ma, L.J.C. 2002. Urban transformation in China, 1949–2000. *Environment and Planning A*, 34(9), 1545–69.

Ma, W. 2005. The return to the essence to of urban planning. *Urban Planning Forum* 2005(1), 16–20 (in Chinese).

Mowforth, M. and Munt, I. 2009. *Tourism and Sustainability: Development, Globalization and New Tourism in the Third World*. 3rd ed. New York: Routledge.

Neil, S. 1998. Giuliani Time-The revanchist 1990s. *Social Text*, 50, 1–20.

Newman, K. 2004. Newark, decline and avoidance, renaissance and desire: From disinvestment to reinvestment. *Annals of the American Academy of Political and Social Science*, 594, 34–48.

NPCSC (Standing Committee of the National People's Congress), 2007(a). Property Law.

NPCSC, 2007(b). Urban and Rural Planning Act.

Palmer, N., Perkins, D. and Xu, Q. 2011. Social capital and community participation among migrant workers in China. *Journal of Community Psychology*, 39(1), 89–105.

Plummer, J. and Taylor, J. 2004. *Community Participation in China: Issues and Processes for Capacity Building*. London: Earthscan.

Putterman, L. 1995. The role of ownership and property rights in China's economic transition. *China Quarterly*, 144, 1047–64.

Rakodi, C. 2003. Politics and performance: the implications of emerging governance arrangements for urban management approaches and information systems. *Habitat International*, 27, 523–47.

Ren, B. and Hu, Y. 2004. Favoured direction of the scale of the reforms on land taking system. *Finance*, 56–7.

Rowe, P.G. 2005. *East Asia Modern: Shaping the Contemporary City*. London: Reaktion Books.

Shang, C. and Yai, T. 2011. Public involvement requirements for infrastructure planning in China. *Habitat International*, 35, 158–66.

Shaw, A. and Satish, M.K. 2007. Metropolitan restructuring in post-liberalized India: separating the global and the local. *Cities*, 24, 148–63.

Shin, H.B. 2010. Urban conservation and revalorization of dilapidated historic quarters: The case of Nanluoguxiang in Beijing. *Cities*, 27, 43–54.

Shi, T. 1997. *Political Participation in Beijing*. Cambridge: Cambridge Univ Press.

Sun, L., Li, C., Gwilliam, J. and Jones, P. 2012. Challenges to sustainable peri-urban settlement development in China: an analysis by empirical evidence in Tianjin, in *Sustainability Today*, edited by C.A. Brebbia. Southampton: WIT Press.

Sun, S., 2006. The unbearable burden of urban planning in China: The impairment of the pursuit of efficiency on urban planning. *Urban Planning Forum*, 2006(1), 11–7 (in Chinese).

Tang, S., Tang, C., and Lo, C. 2005. Public participation and environmental impact assessment in mainland China and Taiwan: political foundations of environmental management. *The Journal of Development Studies*, 41(1), 1–32.

Taylor, G. 1995. The Community Approach: Does It Really Work? *Tourism Management*, 16(7), 487–9.

Verba, S. and Nie, N.H. 1972. *Participation in America: Political Democracy and Social Equality*. New York: Harper & Row Publishers.

WB (The World Bank), 2011. *Conserving the Past as a Foundation for the Future: China-World Bank Partnership on Cultural Heritage Conservation*. Washington, DC: The World Bank.

Wei, Y.H.D. 2005. Planning Chinese Cities. *Urban Geography*, 26(3), 200–221.

Wei, Y.H.D. 2012. Restructuring for growth in urban China: Transitional institutions, urban development and spatial transformation. *Habitat International*, 36, 396–405.

Wu, F.L. 2008. China's great transformation: Neoliberalization as establishing a market society. *Geoforum*, 39, 1093–96.

Wu, F.L. 2012. Neighborhood Attachment, Social Participation and Willingness to Stay in China's Low-Income Communities. *Urban Affairs Review*, 48(4), 547–70.

Xi'an City Planning Bureau (XCPB), 2007. The master plan of Xi'an City 2008–2012 Xi'an City Government (in Chinese).

Xi'an Muslim Historical District Protection Project Office (XMHDPPO), 2003. Report of Sino-Norwegian cooperative Xi'an Muslim historical district protection project.

Xi'an Statistics Bureau (XSB), 2007. Xi'an statistical yearbook. Xi'an Statics Bureau (in Chinese).

Xu, Q. 2007. Community Participation in Urban China: Identifying Mobilization Factors, *Nonprofit and Voluntary Sector Quarterly*, 36(4), 622–42.

Xu, Y., Tang, B. and Chan, E.H.W. 2011. State-led land requisition and transformation of rural villages in transitional China. *Habitat International*, 35 (2011), 57–65.

Yang, G. and Calhoun, C. 2007. Media, Civil society, and the rise of a green public sphere in China. *China information*, 21(2), 211–36.

Yeoh, B.S.A. and Huang, S. 1996. The conservation-redevelopment dilemma in Singapore: the case of the Kampong Glam historic district. *Cities*, 13(6), 411–22.

Yep, R. 2004. Can 'tax-for-free' reform reduce rural tension in China? The process, progress and limitations. *The China Quarterly*, 177, 42–70.

Yin, R.K. 1989. *Case Study Research: Design and Methods*. California: Sage.

Zhai, B. and Ng, M.K.,2013, Urban regeneration and social capital in China: A case study of the Drum Tower Muslim district in Xi'an. *Cities*, 35, 14–25.

Zhang, T. 2000. Land market forces and government's role in sprawl. *Cities*, 17(2), 123–35.

Zhang, T. 2002. Decentralization, localization, and the emergence of a quasiparticipatory decision-making structure in urban development in Shanghai. *International Planning Studies*, 7(4), 303–23.

Zhang, X. 2004. *Designing a Geographic Visual Information System (GVIS) to Support Participation in Urban Planning*. Unpublished PhD thesis, University of Salford.

Zhao, P., Lü, B. and Woltjer, J. 2009. Conflicts in urban fringe in the transformation era: An examination of performance of the metropolitan growth management in Beijing. *Habitat International*, 33(4), 347–56.

Zukin, S. 1982. *Loft Living: Culture and Capital in Urban Change*. Baltimore, MD: Johns Hopkins University Press.

Chapter 9

A Pedagogical Approach to Designing the Future of China's Urban Fringe

Rebecca Kiddle, Joon Sik Kim and Bing Chen

To safeguard the overall quality of the development of urban and rural areas, as increasingly addressed in China's strategic policy documents, there is an urgent need to provide a new vision for planning education, nurturing an inter-disciplinary learning environment that can promote critical thinking as a basis for action or intervention. The urban and rural nexus highlights an area of particular tension as it works to house existing villagers alongside the rising middle classes keen for a more suburban/rural aspect (see Sturzacker and Law in this volume). This challenges planners to think beyond the scope of statutory systems and consider planning as an activity that professionals facilitate, rather than own or monopolize. The planning education system should, therefore, equip prospective planners with not only professional knowledge, but the capability to involve a range of stakeholders in more genuinely collaborative ways. On the urban fringe where very diverse social groups and needs meet, this ability to involve the range of stakeholders in decision-making processes is all the more important.

This chapter evaluates an inter-disciplinary pedagogical model for teaching contemporary urban planning and design using the case study of an international workshop held at the Department of Urban Planning and Design, Xi'an Jiaotong-Liverpool University (XJTLU-UPD), in collaboration with the International Laboratory of Architecture and Urban Design (ILAUD): designing the future of the system of rural villages around Tai Lake in Suzhou. The chapter considers contemporary Chinese planning education and identifies areas in need of augmentation and further development. Then, focussing on the workshop itself, the pedagogical model is detailed and then evaluated with respect to the strengths and weaknesses of teaching in a way which encourages students to work inter-disciplinarily and in an intensive educational setting. Finally, recommendations are made for improvements to the model that may be applicable more generally for improvements to teaching and learning practice in Chinese planning courses and beyond.

Challenges in Urban Planning and Design Education in China

One of the most exciting prospects for those studying disciplines such as architecture, urban planning and design and landscape architecture is that the very environment, village, town, city or mega-city they live and study in offers the raw data on which they can feed their inquiring minds. This chapter explores pedagogy which fosters this 'real-life' student experience, focussing on a case study of an international workshop which took place in Suzhou, China, at Xi'an Jiaotong-Liverpool University (XTJLU).

Mirroring China's urban transition, planning and design education in China is under transformation in order to cope with new issues arising from such processes. This chapter firstly considers these challenges and the model of education advocated by the Department of Urban Planning and Design (UPD) in XJTLU to respond to these challenges. A case study, a partnership project between XJTLU and ILAUD, an Italian-based organization: 'The International Workshop: Critical Planning for Chinese Cities', is analysed in order to highlight best practice and areas for improvement with respect to this learning process. Specifically, the challenges inherent in dealing with China's urban fringe and how pedagogy might respond to these are assessed.

In-depth interviews and participant observation were the two methods used in the chapter. In-depth interviews were undertaken with three participants from XJTLU. All of the authors of this chapter were involved in the workshop as studio tutors and participants and the discussion below draws on their observations. Chinese settlements are faced with an uncertain future. Issues such as pollution, mass urban migration and the ever-widening gap between rich and poor continue to demand the attention of those concerned with planning and designing the built and natural environment. It seems that the traditional emphasis on design-led planning, evident in Chinese planning agencies and, in turn, in Chinese planning education may need to be further bolstered by an approach that takes into account if it is to cope successfully with this on-going, rapid transformation.

Urban and Rural Planning (*chengxiangguihuaxue*) has been an independent discipline in China's higher education system since 2011. Previous to this, it was named *Urban Planning* (*chengshiguihua*) and was categorized as a sub-discipline of architecture. From the 1980s to 2010, urban planning and design in China have been largely associated with physical design. This focus is reflected in the fact that 65 per cent of the existing planning and design education programmes in China were developed from architecture-related disciplines, 15 per cent from engineering-related disciplines (for example survey, environmental science and so on), 15per cent from science-related disciplines (for example geography and so on) and 5 per cent from horticulture-related disciplines (Zhao and Lin 2001). Prior to 2011, urban planning had been interpreted as 'urban design' (*chengshisheji*) where successful graduates were equipped with knowledge and skills that were necessary, but often insufficient, for designing places (for example drawing skills). The lack of understanding of the social sciences and the lack of ability to think critically (or more precisely, the lack of training in critical thinking) has resulted in urban designers who focus on the physical design of a site in isolation of the social, economic and environmental issues that are inherent in these developments. In the quest for expediency and in response to restrictive government regulations, many city projects are formulaic in plan, each one looking very similar to the next.

As a result, China's strategic development plan recognizes there is an urgent need to foster an inter-disciplinary learning environment that can promote critical thinking as a basis for action or intervention, to safeguard the overall quality of the development of urban and rural areas.

However, this situation has changed recently. China's latest strategic development plan outlines a shift in focus from physical design to spatial planning in order to reflect the importance of the integrative development of both urban and rural areas and a balanced planning of resources. Mirroring the above changes, the existing planning education system in China is faced with challenges – some new ideas (for example transition towns) that have been proved to be useful in planning urban-rural fringes in Western countries have not been introduced to China yet; some concepts from the West (for example a bottom-up approach in planning processes) have been misinterpreted by Chinese planners or educators; some planning principles (for example collaborative planning) have been successfully introduced to China but there is a lack of evidence showing the implementation or the usefulness of such theories in practice and so on. Obviously it takes time for planning schools to modify their curricula in response to these new needs.

To facilitate the education reform as addressed above, there is now an urgent need to foster an inter-disciplinary learning environment that can promote critical thinking as the basis for action or intervention. Learning strategies, such as research-led pedagogy, are beneficial to this transformation (Chen 2013) as they place the onus on the learner to develop theories and responses to a given situation independently of the teacher.

In response to these challenges, the Department of Urban Planning and Design (UPD) at XJTLU has developed a model of degree-level education that seeks to draw on best practice planning education worldwide, being a joint venture between Xi'an Jiaotong University, China, and the University of Liverpool, UK.

XJTLU-UPD now offers a combined planning programme over four years at undergraduate level, covering both spatial and specialist elements (referring respectively to spatial and specialist planning education addressed by the Royal Town and Planning Institute (RTPI) in the UK (see Chen 2012, 2013 for details).

Like other planning schools in China, UPD is faced with the challenge of developing graduates who have transferable skills and are able to draw on knowledge and skill from a range of disciplines. In addition, they should be able to make connections between theory and practice in order that they can make the best possible urban planning and design decisions. The course is predicated on the idea that the acquisition of knowledge and skills should not be static experience, rather it is important for all graduates to have the ability to both pursue and use new knowledge throughout their careers (see Miller *et al.* 2012). Finally, the hope is that students graduate with the ability to communicate cross-culturally (see Reeves 2009).

Consequently, UPD draws heavily on contemporary planning education in the UK. The UK's RTPI has been engaged in a programme of radical evolution since 2001. Its New Vision of Planning seeks to build capacity within society and its institutions so that the responsibility can be shared among all actors through a participatory decision-making process (RTPI 2001). The New Vision of Planning provides core principles to encourage planners and designers to think beyond the scope of statutory systems:

- 'Spatial – dealing with the unique needs and characteristics of places
- Sustainable – looking at the short-, medium- and long-term issues
- Integrative – in terms of the knowledge, objectives and actions involved
- Inclusive – recognising the wide range of people involved in planning' (RTPI 2001).

Specific issues arising in current planning practice in China such as the promotion of integrated urban and rural development has also been taken into account in the detailed curriculum design. Under such a planning and design education system, students are expected to be equipped with not only professional knowledge, but also the 'soft skills' needed for planning cities such as the capability to involve a range of stakeholders in more genuinely collaborative ways. The need for these kinds of skills with respect to planning and China is articulated by Bosselmann *et al.* (2012). Whilst talking in this chapter about water villages in the Delta Region, these thoughts could equally relate to urban fringe areas across China:

> The villages could play an economically viable and socially important role as distinct districts within the new cities. To date, there are no models for such successful integration of water villages in the Delta. However, if such an approach could be articulated and disseminated, it may be possible to avoid some future social conflicts, and preserve the unique cultural and environmental attributes of such villages while the surrounding landscape transforms (Bosselmann 2012, p. 250).

The workshop aimed to allow students to develop their 'soft skills' in addition to their technical knowledge and skill base, to seek solutions for the successful integration of an urban fringe site in Suzhou. This chapter uses the international workshop held at XJTLU in 2012 as a case study, exploring an inter-disciplinary pedagogical model for teaching contemporary urban planning and design and evaluates its usefulness in promoting the explicit integration of knowledge, skills and values, thereby facilitating creative planning.

Case Study: International Workshop

The international workshop 'Critical Planning for Chinese Cities' (CPCC) was held at XJTLU-UPD in collaboration with the ILAUD. The first event in 2012, 'Designing the future of the system of rural villages around Tai Lake in Suzhou', brought academics and students from all over the world (namely École Polytechnique Fédérale de Lausanne, South China University of Technology, Suzhou University of Science and Technology, Università degli Studi di Ferrara, the University of Liverpool, the University of Newcastle and Wuhan University). The success of the 2012 workshop led to a second CPCC workshop in 2013. This chapter, however, focusses on the experience of the first 2012 workshop.

The overall theme of the workshop was 'urban and rural conflicts' and the study case was the 'system of rural villages around Tai Lake in Suzhou'. Within this a specific theme was drawn out of a hat for each group to respond to. These were: (1) A Quality Public Realm; (2) Accessibility and Economics; (3) Agricultural Landscapes; (4) Place Identity and Tourism; (5) Conserving Dongcun's Heritage; (6) Improving Public Amenities; (7) Green and Blue Systems; and (8) Transition Towns. Students worked in eight groups of five or six to develop, throughout the week, a design and planning proposal for their particular site and responding to their particular theme.

The rationale for the workshop was fourfold. Firstly, Suzhou and its surrounds offered participants a case study which exemplified the urban contradictions of the current urbanization model in China. How do we attract tourists, keep tourists away, preserve heritage and maintain livelihoods on the urban fringe of one of China's most prosperous cities?

Secondly, and related to this, organizers were keen to reflect on the impact of modernization in terms of the social and environmental costs to China. Organizers felt that in order to more fully understand the urban and rural transformations taking place in China, it would be advantageous to 'compare and contrast China and Western countries in terms of old and new trends, levels of convergence/ divergence, critical theoretical frameworks and eventual planning solutions' (XJTLU, 2012).

Thirdly, in line with the model proffered by ILAUD, the workshop sought collaboration between academics and students from different countries and different disciplines with the aim of inspiring, challenging and, at times, reforming opinions and practice. This 'East/West' cooperation was predicated on the mission of XJTLU which is to act as a bridge between East and West and encourage the internationalization of higher education in China.

Finally, the workshop allowed for 'the experimentation of new and innovative teaching and learning approaches' (XJTLU, 2012).

The students were at different levels of undergraduate study, with a small number being postgraduate level students. The working language of the workshop was English, though students often used Chinese when working together in a studio setting. All students, apart from those from XJTLU study in Mandarin in

Figure 9.1   Learning by doing during the intensive week of the workshop

their institutions, spoke English to varying levels of proficiency. The students had a studio space in which they could work together and access the internet and other resources such as maps, plans and a basic outline of the sites and the issues of concern (Figure 9.1).

Students also came from different built environment disciplines: urban planning and design, architecture and landscape architecture and different education backgrounds, that is, some had been schooled in the traditional Chinese education system whilst others had experienced the hybrid XJTLU model of education.

Students were formed into multi-disciplinary teams and expected to work together on the given sites under the supervision of a group of international academics (including scholars from architecture, urban planning and design, landscape architecture, urban economics and so on). Each team needed to conduct an on-site survey, defining a place-based development strategy supported by design simulations and visualize their proposals through graphs, sketches and texts within the 9 days of the workshop.

The first few days of the workshop were devoted to outlining the workshop themes, visiting the sites (Figure 9.2) and a mini conference where the invited academics gave presentations on issues of relevance to the themes to be explored over the coming week. Many of these talks considered case studies, theory and practice developed in the 'West' with students needing to translate, or not, as

Figure 9.2   The field visit to Xishan Island in Tai Lake during the workshop

the case may be, these ideas to this Suzhou context. The remainder of the week was devoted to students working in their assigned groups to develop proposals with respect to their particular theme. Academics provided guidance and asked questions intermittently along the way and two interim reviews were asked of the groups with academics in attendance to offer feedback and critique.

Apart from facilitating collaboration between different universities, the workshop provided an opportunity to explore the advantages and disadvantages of this way of teaching. The following outlines pedagogical issues that were highlighted by this process.

Pedagogical Analysis

Developing built environment professionals that can respond adequately to the challenges of China's growth and development, such as how best to consider China's urban fringe (the geographic focus of the workshop) requires a tailored pedagogical approach. Sokman *et al.* (2012, p. 44) write, 'fringe landscapes are complex, and existing planning policies are trying to compartmentalise land uses to a specific, clearly classified and static category without considering the equivocal, synergetic and dynamic interactions that present themselves on the edges of cities'.

182 *Urban China's Rural Fringe*

The workshop aimed to pedagogically enable students to systematically reflect on these dynamic interactions by allowing them to visit the site, enabling them to observe the local level situation first-hand. Many also were able to interact and canvas local people's opinions on the development situation. To allow students to respond to the complexities inherent in urban fringe development, three teaching and learning strategies were used in the workshop. The first was a promotion of collaborative and active learning. The premise here is that in order to respond effectively those involved in the decision-making processes need to be well-equipped to work with others in a meaningful and effective way. The second strategy purported the value of inter-disciplinarity, that is, that in addition to securing collaborative working skills, those responses to urban-fringe development problems that reflect input from a range of different disciplines working at different spatial scales are more likely to represent a sophisticated response to these issues. Lastly, and perhaps most contentiously, was the inclusion of 'Western' ideas for students to consider in their 'Eastern' locale. This chapter considers the relative success of this strategy in relation to this urban fringe site.

Collaboration: Social and Active Learning and Critical Thinking

A consideration of issues to do with the urban fringe in China requires a sophisticated response. This contested space has a multitude of stakeholders ranging from the existing local peasant population through to the central and local government who look to the urban fringe to provide an agricultural resource for its urban and suburban neighbours. In order to achieve this sophisticated response planners, designers, architects, landscape architects, politicians, economists and so on must work together in new and potentially uncomfortable (to start with) ways. The workshop, in part, allowed students and academics to make small steps in this regard.

Social or collaborative learning as a pedagogical concept has been influenced throughout history by theorists such as John Dewey (from the late 1800s to the early 1900s), Maria Montessori (whose focus was child development during the early twentieth century) and Jean Piaget (also working throughout the twentieth century). However, one of the key protagonists of a more recent shift towards the promotion of social learning pedagogies is Soviet psychologist, Lev Vygotsky. Editors of a collection of Vygotsky's writings assert that:

> In stressing the social origins of language and thinking, Vygotsky was following the lead of influential French sociologists, but to our knowledge he was the first modern psychologist to suggest the mechanisms by which culture becomes a part of each person's nature. Insisting that psychological functions are a product of the brain's activity, he became an early advocate of combining experimental cognitive psychology with neurology and physiology. (Cole and Scribner, 1978, p. 6)

A Pedagogical Approach to Designing the Future of China's Urban Fringe   183

Vygotsky's view was that all learning is socially constructed and that it is through language and speaking to others that we create meaning and significance in what we learn. That is, 'meanings grow out of social encounters; participation in social interactions is, then, central to the learning process. It is through these interactions with others that we construct our learning' (Kiddle 2011, p. 56). In addition, learners bring their cultural and social understandings to bear on the learning process: 'Language, the very means by which reflection and elaboration of experience takes place, is a highly personal and at the same time a profoundly social human process' (Jon-Steiner and Souberman 1978, p. 126).

Stokman *et al.* assert the importance of these social encounters with respect to planning process on the urban fringe in Beijing. They write:

> It becomes clear that rapid land-use change processes are closely connected to the adaptive and inventive connections between people and the land. Thus a new management system leading to sustainable development and design of the green belt can only be achieved by designing new ways of interaction between the different actors and the land. (2012, p. 30)

The international workshop sought to offer an opportunity for meaning and, ultimately, design and policy solutions to be developed through interactions with others and the range of experiences, both social and cultural, different participants brought to the tasks involved.

This seemed to prove fruitful for many involved, particularly with regard to interactions with scholars from different cultural contexts and academic backgrounds and the local residents from the site the students focussed on for the project. One student commented on the value in hearing a range of different perspectives:

> During the international workshop, we also did a series of international seminars with scholars from all over the world. They were from Liverpool, Newcastle, Italy and China. They brought us a lot of new ideas both from both a non-Chinese and Chinese contexts. At the seminar ... firstly, they presented their ideas and their research work and then we discussed together to share ideas. Actually, I really enjoyed this environment and the process of brain-storming. (Participant 2)

Others highlighted the fact that they got to interact with local people and government decision-makers and that this meant they could locate their projects in the reality of the lives of people who would need to inhabit these spaces. In addition, this helped them to conceptualize the projects in ways that would be taken seriously by decision-makers:

> On the first day of the international workshop, we spent a whole day ... time on site visit ... and field survey for the targeted area. It was good to see what is

184 *Urban China's Rural Fringe*

happening on site and talk to local people. All of our work in the [subsequent] workshop was done based on our site investigation. It was quite a good opportunity for us to explore how things can be done on the ground. (Participant 2)

During the first day of the workshop, we went to a rural village [for site investigation]. It was really fresh experience for me. Because I grow up in urban areas, it was the first time I went to an old village in Suzhou to see actually what problems exist in rural areas in China. (Participant 1)

This was also first time to present my design work to outside of university. I can really see what the government's interests in this area are. In my future career, our clients will be the government so it is very important to know what the government's interests are. These two things were quite helpful for me, especially for future work. (Participant 2)

However, the process was not always trouble-free or without the need to self-reflection. One student highlighted the fact that those coming from universities where the pedagogical approach was more didactic and less focussed on social constructivist approaches found it more difficult to work in groups, across disciplines:

When we started Year one at XJTLU, we were taught in small groups. We discussed and negotiated with each other. We know how to work in a small group. During this workshop, I found that students from other universities were shy in expressing their ideas. They speak only when I asked them what they think. I think we are better at working as a group. (Participant 1)

Another student highlighted the fact that differences in age, experience and background became evident in his group but, as outlined in below, he could articulate the value in terms of content knowledge and skills that the different group members brought to the task:

This kind of activity [international workshop] is not very common in China because it combines European knowledge with very traditional Chinese practice. Many students from different universities came to the workshop. In my group, I had four group members who came from different [Chinese] universities and they were more senior students [than me]. This was a very good chance for me to learn from my group members [who knew more about Chinese practice] but also, it was a good opportunity to show them my English language skills and professional knowledge [that is based on more European approach]. (Participant 3)

One student felt that one of the consequences of working collaboratively is a self-realization for both learners and teachers, of what students do not know, or

A Pedagogical Approach to Designing the Future of China's Urban Fringe 185

to put this in pedagogic terms, the fostering of critical thinking. The collaborative process allowed participants to situate their learning, or lack of learning, in the context of others' understanding:

> On the last day of the workshop, we needed to present our outputs to local government officials who were from the Suzhou Tourism Bureau. This was the first time for me to give an academic presentation in Chinese. I found that I have to improve a lot of things. First thing is terminology. All university students are facing [this issue] because they may come back to China and work in China. We need to learn about Chinese terminology. (Participant 2)

On the whole, the students interviewed asserted the value of a collaborative approach to working. They enjoyed interacting with the range of people the workshop enabled them to interact with and found this at times rewarding and at other times challenging and confusing. In terms of the pedagogic value of this approach to learning it seems that this strategy challenges both learners and teachers to self-reflect on their 'everyday' work in a way that may not have happened if they were not given this opportunity to interact with students from different pedagogic and, in some ways, cultural backgrounds. Students were able to get 'real-time' feedback from the sites' inhabitants and local decision-makers which fostered an authenticity in the process that they would not generally have received in their daily university education.

However, it is also clear that collaborative learning does not just happen. Participants need clues as to how to work with others. Explicit 'rules of engagement' are needed so that students, and staff, have the confidence to take part and contribute their unique cultural perspectives on the problem at hand. In addition, the nature of the teacher/learner relationship may need to be redefined and advertised at the outset. That is, moving from the scenario where the teacher dictates what is learned, to a more reciprocal relationship, where the distinction between teacher and learner is blurred: both parties construct their learning with each another through their specific cultural lens. The instructor still has an important facilitation role in asking questions, providing guidance and creating an environment for learners to arrive at their own conclusions.

Ground rules can be set to encourage students to learn from each other through a process of face-to-face meetings, each by bringing their own expertise to the group. Student participants reported that they could see that students from different disciplines and educational backgrounds had different strengths; however, they had to learn this gradually through a rather stressful process of working together. Had the 'rules of engagement' and the possible benefits of such a way of working been more explicitly detailed at the beginning of the workshop this may have eased some of the tension.

The mini conference which took place at the start of the workshop was helpful in this regard, providing not only international perspectives on the study topic to workshop participants, but also in creating a better environment for debate in the workshop. European and Chinese scholars presented their work and after each presentation there was a 'discussion' session rather than a 'Q&A' session. This helped to set the tone for the remainder of the workshop which said that 'debate and questioning was okay'. For some students, this was their first opportunity to experience this kind of pedagogy. It would seem advantageous to continue with this course structure for future workshops and potentially enhancing the 'mini conference' in order that it serves as a forum in which to define the individual foci or each work group.

In order to avoid unnecessary conflict between students from different disciplines and educational backgrounds, one possibility would be to provide them with a set of questions that they could use as a guideline in group discussions to involve all group members.

From student accounts above, the workshop did offer such a forum to learn these skills of collaboration, though there is potential for this to be outlined more explicitly to give students the confidence to collaborate. Being able to facilitate collaboration among peers and with community groups such as the existing residents is a key skill for built environment professionals working on sites which hold the potential for conflict both within the community and between the different worldviews held by those skilled in different disciplines.

A Joined-up Response to the Urban Fringe

As mentioned above, one of the aims of the workshop was to give students and scholars the opportunity to consider an urban problem with people from other disciplines. However, Wagner *et al.* write: 'Despite the increasing focus on the importance of inter-disciplinary research, the full potential has not been realized, and the barriers to inter-disciplinary work remain high' (2012, p. 182).

It is important here to be clear why inter-disciplinarity is important. The rationale for inter-disciplinary collaborations is complexity: complexity of systems and structures. Newell writes:

> The phenomena modeled by most complex systems are multi-faceted. Seen from one angle, they appear different than they do from another angle, because the viewers see facets (represented as sub-systems) where different components and relationships dominate. (2001, p. 2)

Indeed, it is clear that cities, and in this case, the city fringe are complex systems and warrant inter-disciplinary consideration, with architects, planners, urban designers and landscape architects each approaching the problem of the city from a different angle. For some, the interactions between ecological and human systems are key. For others, the building form and situation are central. But how best to achieve the moulding and meshing of ideas to create a whole that's more than the sum of its parts? Stokman *et al.* note in relation to Beijing's urban fringe

A Pedagogical Approach to Designing the Future of China's Urban Fringe 187

that rather than separating the open space within the urban fringe from the built-up area, these should be considered together as connected space (2012, p. 38).

The workshop structure forced different disciplines to work together, at times causing conflict and frustration amongst students, some feeling they were misunderstood, others just not understanding. As outlined above, no interviews were undertaken with student participants outside of XJTLU which may not therefore be reflective of the wider group's views. However, observations and final verbal feedback from all students suggested that they found this interaction difficult but ultimately rewarding. One participant commented on the contrast between their everyday classroom experience which entailed interactions with only other urban planning and design students as compared to the workshop which enabled them to work with a range of disciplines. The student, perhaps over-emphatically, identifies one of the benefits of the project as knowing how projects would work in reality:

> International workshop was a fantastic experience, because it was quite different from what we learnt and what we get in the ordinary classroom. First thing is that we work together with students and teachers from different disciplines. In my group, there were students from urban planning and architecture departments. Now, I know how the real project works and how architects and urban planners work together. ... For example, my group proposed a new bridge to connect to the island [project site]. This idea was from the architecture students. The architecture students were really focused on how it would look like and what materials needed to be used. However, planning students were looking at how this new bridge would affect the surrounding areas and what are the benefits of this bridge for this region. While planners approached from bigger aspects, architects thought about more detailed things. (Participant 2).

Another student highlighted the difficulties of working with others from other disciplines and the need for negotiation skills:

> Actually, it was my first time to work with students and teachers from different schools. In my group, except me [planning discipline], all are from architecture departments. During the working process, we had many conflicts. It meant we had to learn how to cooperate with each other and how to negotiate to achieve agreement. After all, we became good friends and still keep in touch with each other. (Participant 1).

Whilst, on the whole, the conflicts seemed to have been overcome in this group, there may be opportunities for further improvement in future workshops of this kind. Possible ways to improve the inter-disciplinary component of the workshop drawn from the literature are outlined below.

Wagner *et al.* concluded in their analysis of an inter-disciplinary course on landscape genetics that a preparation meeting was essential to the success of the course: 'A multiday preparation meeting is essential to initiating a distributed inter-disciplinary course, because it allows faculty to develop the common ground, integration across topics, and technical skills necessary for them to teach the course' (2012, p. 186). Whilst the landscape genetics course was a longer offering, the principle of preparatory meetings is a good one. This issue was raised by one of the ILAUD members at the final summary meeting of the workshop, saying that in previous workshops a preparation meeting had taken place and had worked well to prepare faculty.

In addition to a pre-meeting, a post-workshop meeting might be of benefit to the overall process and to ensure that any best practice and areas for improvement can be highlighted and recorded whilst it is fresh in the minds of participants and organizers. In addition, according to Wagner *et al.*, these 'synthesis meetings', as they call them, allow for on-going networking with the group: 'A synthesis meeting is an essential element, both for the success of group projects and for networking' (Wagner *et al.* 2012, p. 187).

Thirdly, with respect to the workshop itself, it may be advantageous to incorporate peer review more concertedly into the programme. The programme allowed students to take part in a series of interim reviews of their work and whilst students were encouraged to critique other groups' work, the focus was primarily on tutors giving feedback. There may be opportunities to foster further, more formal peer review opportunities amongst the students to add to the learning process. An archive of the lecture material and workshop outcomes may be helpful to allow students to refer back to the materials so that they can reacquaint themselves with the proceedings and outcomes of the workshop. Websites are useful in this regard, enabling access wherever participants are.

Facilitation of this inter-disciplinarity was key to the success of the workshop, enabling groups to work together through the management of face-to-face conversations in meetings (Susskind *et al.* 1999). Certainly, effective facilitation can encourage group participants to work together to maximize joint gains, even in an intensive setting like the workshop. In order to enable this to take place more easily and given the shortage of time in the workshop, one possibility may be to engage the services of a trained facilitator. Another possibility is that workshop tutors could play a facilitative role and train students on how to work collaboratively before the group work starts. Possible ground rules for facilitation include:

1. Group participants should understand and have mutual respect for each other's viewpoints;
2. Group participants should represent the interests and expertise of their discipline rather than an individual's personal opinion; and,
3. Group participants should set a time limit in discussing the issues and making an agreed decision.

The ability to collaborate and involve a range of views in the decision-making process is crucial to approaching (or facing) the planning challenges of the urban fringe. As alluded to previously, stakeholders such as the local government, existing villagers (who tend to have lower incomes) and the new rising middle classes all have a stake in this ambiguous area that sits between the countryside and the city. In order to be able to respond to this variety of needs in a sophisticated way, planners will need to be able to collaborate with other disciplines, including architects, landscape designers, economists, business owners and politicians.

The workshop brought together architects, landscape designers and urban planners and designers, however there may be an argument for widening the scope of student participation to include social scientists such as economists, environmental scientists and sociologists, for example.

Working Cross-culturally: Transferable Concepts?

One of the points of interest in the workshop and also a key source of angst that proved quite difficult for students to overcome was the fact that they felt they were being asked to consider 'Western' concepts in relation to a Chinese context. The point of doing this was to give the students a range of 'tools' developed in different political, economic and cultural contexts to use in their considerations of the urban fringe with the hope that ideas from elsewhere might stimulate the production of 'new' ideas relevant to the Suzhou context.

As an example, as outlined earlier, a theme given to one group was 'Transition towns' a movement taking place worldwide which according to their New Zealand site:

> brings people together to explore how we – as communities – can respond to the environmental, economic and social challenges arising from climate change, resource depletion and an economy based on growth. We don't look for anyone to blame or anyone to save us, but believe our communities have within themselves the innovation and ingenuity to create positive solutions to the converging crises of our time. (Transition Towns NZ website 2013).

Students found this an incredibly difficult concept to think about in relation to their site on the urban fringe of Suzhou, despite the fact that the motivation behind transition towns, as outlined above, is relatively wide-ranging and, potentially, all encompassing. If criticisms of this theme focussed on it being too broad or that solutions would be more likely to be operational in nature as opposed to proposals that required a designed solution, this would be understandable, however, in the main, these were not the students' concerns. Rather, they felt that the notion of Transition Towns held little or no relevance to their Chinese site. This group's struggle epitomized the potential for conflict inherent in transferring ideas from one context to another.

It was clear that participants needed a set of tools or a framework to enable them to make decisions around how and what to practically translate from one context to another. To this end it may be advantageous, where possible, to allocate groups and themes ahead of time to enable participants to investigate the theme and its possible application to the local context more generally before coming to the workshop.

Another possibility here is for tutors to deliver a predefined framework to students to guide their thinking around the translation of these issues in relation to physical space design and process-based outcomes. For example, the 'embodied translation' framework developed by Scott Townsend (2009) in relation to language itself makes a distinction between direct translation which is 'based on preserving the fidelity of the message as literally as possible' and 'embodied translation' which is a performative act (Townsend 2009, p. 51–2). That is, direct translation can be difficult and, indeed, potentially not preferable in the context of the built environment, however, an 'embodied translation' of ideas which integrates the translators' own experiences allows for a more fruitful, and arguably, more grounded translation.

Townsend, in talking about language translation, goes on to say that the person trying to translate can find that if the schema of a particular story is outside the cultural experience of the translator, they might find this hard to grasp. This may require someone from the culture from which the story, or in our case concept, came to explain the logic of it. Translation, then, becomes discursive with the values represented in the story exposed as a construction rather than as unconsciously accepted (Townsend 2009, p. 53). When this happens, the new user of the concept can use the deconstructed parts of the concept in a way which is more grounded in local realities.

The ability to work cross-culturally (that is, across different learning cultures) was hindered by not only the pedagogical histories of the students, but by the types of knowledge received by students in their learning experiences prior to the workshop. This conflict was highlighted in the student interviews with students picking up on differences in the learning content offered by the respective institutions to which the students belonged, influenced by the different contexts from which their tutors had come. At XJTLU, urban planning and design is taught with its basis in the social sciences, as in Europe. This can be compared with the way urban planning is conceptualized in China, as an offshoot of architecture and design disciplines. This meant that it became clear through the course of the workshop that students who attended the more traditional Chinese universities had a better knowledge of Chinese regulations related to the built environment and had better technical design skills, but seemed less used to discussing, sharing ideas and debating issues, so group discussions tended to be dominated by XJTLU students:

> The educational system in our university [XJTLU] is different from traditional Chinese universities. Our teachers have an international background, therefore the focus [in the class] is a little different than what other Chinese universities are doing. For example, in the UK and in Western countries, they don't have massive construction projects, but we have [in China]. So, students from other Chinese universities are trained like urban designers rather than urban planners.

A Pedagogical Approach to Designing the Future of China's Urban Fringe   191

> When we face a problem, they are trying to find a solution with physical design such as designing buildings and building parks. . As soon as we got the group topic, they actually went to drawing board ... For us [XJTLU], we sometimes try to find a solution to do with social aspects. This includes how to negotiate with local people and cooperate with local government to tackle this problem with communication or by making policies. This is how we [XJTLU] are different from them. (Participant 2).

This was a common theme with the two other students interviewed, both highlighting these skill differences:

> I think we [XJTLU] are better at strategic thinking, oral presentation, and teamwork. This is because the majority of coursework we did in the class was group projects. For other Chinese university students, they are better at technical drawing and computer software skills which we need to improve. (Participant 2).

> I think there is a gap between Chinese students and students who have learned in this university [XJTLU]. I found difficulties when I need to translate Chinese to English, or English to Chinese. Chinese university students have learned very high level technical terms in Chinese which are difficult to find in a normal English dictionary. That is a kind of gap, I think. (Participant 3).

Students spent considerable time synchronizing academic and professional planning terminologies between Chinese and English language. As a time-saving measure, it may be helpful to provide an English-Chinese and Chinese-English terminology dictionary in the relevant fields to facilitate efficient interaction and understanding in the short time-frame of the workshop.

Despite the fact that students found it difficult to translate ideas and concepts from one locale to another, this could prove a valuable process if they are given aids with which to translate such as a predefined framework and something as basic as a dictionary of terminology.

Conclusion: Recommendations for the Future Practice

This chapter has focussed on the pedagogical lessons learned from an inaugural international workshop held at XJTLU which involved its own students as well as students from a range of different Chinese institutions. Three pedagogical concerns were outlined, including the ability of such a learning exercise to offer a positive collaborative and critical learning experience; the value of working across and with people of other disciplines; and the value of translating ideas from one context to another.

The workshop was organized with students from different educational systems and diverse disciplines and as such it was critical to encourage students to work as a group to solve problems and make decisions together. In order to maximize synergies in the international workshop, it was important to create an environment that enabled participants to share their experiences and knowledge in a collaborative way. Ideally, the group would work together using a consensus-building process. All group participants would engage in a joint fact-finding task to evaluate current issues offered up by the study case and discuss freely to reach an implementable solution agreed to by all participants.

When students participated in the group work, it was found that students from different educational frameworks had different approaches to group discussion. Although they are all Chinese students, students who had been taught within the XJTLU educational model tended to be more active in group discussions than students from Chinese universities who were more likely to listen and observe the discussion rather than get involved actively. Conversely, students from more traditional Chinese universities had better knowledge of the local planning regulations and terminology than students from XJTLU and were therefore able to offer a more grounded perspective on the problem. The challenge in the international workshop was how to encourage XJTLU students to learn from those taught in more traditional Chinese universities and how to encourage students from Chinese universities students to express their opinion more actively in the group.

Student participants saw value in hearing a range of perspectives on a particular issue, however their ability to synthesize this information and develop context-specific solutions based on these ideas, whilst working with others, was not without its problems. Possible strategies which might enable students to work together more efficiently and effectively include developing a set of ground rules which makes clear the facilitative role of the tutor and sets out the ground rules for engagement with fellow group members.

Students also saw the value of working across disciplines despite finding the different approaches of their group members difficult at times. A range of possible additions to the process might be helpful in responding to these difficulties. These include the establishment of a pre-meeting prior to the workshop in order to establish a clear sense of direction for the workshop, a synthesis meeting to consolidate learning from the workshop, the addition of formal student peer review to encourage further learning possibilities, the establishment of an archive to allow participants to go back and re-look at the workshop material post-workshop and the training of staff or student facilitators to model effective inter-disciplinary debate.

Observation of the workshop showed that all students found it difficult to translate concepts born in cultural contexts other than their own to a local site. This caused friction in some groups. To manage this, a number of strategies are available: firstly, where possible, group members and themes could be identified prior to the beginning of the workshop so that students have a chance to investigate the theme in detail before arriving at the workshop; secondly, there may be a need for the development of a predefined framework that students could use to guide their translation of the concept from one cultural context to another.

Finally, the workshop showed that students from traditional Chinese universities tend to excel at physical space design and relevant skills (for example sketch, CAD and so on), but can lack the ability to link the space with local sustainable development (including managing social, economic and environmental concerns from the short-, medium- and long-term perspectives). Students from XJTLU had a better understanding of sustainable, integrative and inclusive planning principles, but their technical skills were not as sophisticated. Both skill sets are needed to respond to the vision set out in China's strategic development plan (Wei and Zhao 2009). Therefore, it is important for these academic institutions to learn from each other and develop their own pedagogic approaches in line with their articulated educational philosophies. Cross-university activities, such as the international workshop, are certainly of benefit to this.

The workshop, by student accounts, improved their understanding of the importance of inclusive teamwork and the role they and others will play in relation to each other in the development of sustainable practices and the procurement of resilient urban-rural fringes. This student-led research-based learning process also provided an opportunity to explore how different disciplines contribute to problems and solutions in a collaborative design process (Chen 2012). By working in a multi-disciplinary environment like this, students can achieve a holistic appreciation of important urban fringe concerns (for example sustainability, resilience and so on). The hope is that students continue to improve their ability to think holistically and apply their thinking in facilitative ways that ensure local community groups are included in meaningful ways alongside the political and economic decision-makers.

Acknowledgements

This work was, in part, supported by the 2013 Jiangsu Philosophy and Social Sciences Research Funding Programme (Ref: 2013SJD880110).

References

Bosselmann, P.C., Kondolf, G.M., Jiang, F., Bao, G., Zhang, Z. and Liu, M. 2012. The Future of a Chinese Water Village. Alternative Design Practices Aimed to Provide New Life for Traditional Water Villages in the Pearl River Delta. *Journal of Urban Design*, 15(2), 243–67.

Chen, B. 2012. Planning Education for Sustainable City Transformation: The programme design and education reform in the XJTLU Department of Urban Planning and Design. Paper to *Humanistic Planning Creative Transformation: Proceedings of China Urban Planning Education Conference*. Wuhan: 19–22 September 2012. Beijing: China Architecture and Building Press, 360–67.

Chen, B. 2013. The Research-led Pedagogy in Contemporary Planning Education. Paper to AESOP-ACSP Joint Congress *'Planning for Resilient Cities and Regions' Conference Proceeding*. Dublin, 15–19 July.

Cole, M. and Scribner, S. 1978. Introduction, in *Mind in Society: The Development of Higher Psychological Processes*, edited by L.S. Vygotsky. Boston, MA: Harvard University Press.

John-Steiner, V. and Souberman, E. 1978. Afterword, in *Mind in Society: The Development of Higher Psychological Processes*, edited by L.S. Vygotsky. Boston, MA: Harvard University Press.

Kiddle, R. 2011. Learning Outside the Box: Designing Social Learning Spaces, PhD Thesis, Oxford Brookes University.

Miller A., Sharp J. and Strong, J. (eds) 2012. *What is Research-Led Teaching? Multi-disciplinary Perspective*. London: CREST.

Newell, W. 2001. A Theory of Interdisciplinary Studies in Issues in Integrative Studies, No. 199 pp. 1–25.

Reeves, D. 2009. Future scoping – developing excellence in urban planners. *Australian Planner*, 46(1), 28–33.

RTPI (Royal Town Planning Institute), 2001. A New Vision for Planning: Delivering sustainable communities, settlements and places [Online]. Available at: http://www.rtpi.org.uk/education-and-careers/learning-about-planning/what-planning-does/rtpi-vision-for-planning [assessed: 10 March 2013].

Stokman, A., Rabe, S. and Ruff, S. 2012. Beijing's New Urban Countryside – Designing with Complexity and Strategic Landscape Planning. *Journal of Landscape Design*, 3(2), 30–45.

Susskind, L., McKearnan, S. and Thomas-Larmer, J. (eds) 1999. *The Consensus-Building Handbook: A Comprehensive Guide to Reaching Agreement*. Thousand Oaks, CA: Sage.

Townsend, S. 2009. Cross-cultural Metaphor and the Online Environment: Projects – 2006–2008, Berlin, Tokyo and the US. *International Journal of the Book*, 6(2), 51–60.

Transition Towns, Aotearoa New Zealand. Available at: http://www.transition towns.org.nz/node/1667 [accessed: 20 September 2013].

Wagner, H.H., Murphy, M.A., Holderegger, R. and Waits, L. 2012. Developing an Interdisciplinary, Distributed Graduate Course for Twenty-First Century Scientists. *BioScience*, 62(2), 182–8.

Wei, Y. and Zhao, M. 2009. Advancing Normative Urban Planning Education in China: A study of educational institutions and urban planning curricula. *China City Planning Review*, 18(3), 42–9.

Xi'an Jiaotong-Liverpool University, 2012. Workshop Handbook: Designing the Future of the System of Rural Villages around Tai Lake in Suzhou, 19–29th October 2012.

Point of View

Paolo Ceccarelli

In presenting the results of a research project on the urban and rural fringe recently carried out in the region of Suzhou and in examining a number of interesting case studies in the Yangtze and Pearl River Deltas or in other regions of inland China, this book gives a useful contribution to a better understanding of current urbanization processes in China. While urban fringes are an important component of the structure of contemporary Chinese cities, both in spatial and socio-economic terms, they haven't been really studied thus far.

However, the issue of the new characteristics and role of urban fringes does not involve only large Chinese cities. The urban fringes of most of the biggest cities around the world have gradually taken on new characteristics and roles that are different from the original ones. They are no longer a chaotic and undefined peripheral component of the urban system, areas of loose transition from the city to the countryside or marginal areas where different, inconsistent and possibly conflicting activities are located. They are not even the mainly residential low-density areas made of individual houses of North America or the high-density and low-cost housing on European peripheries. Present urban fringes are in many respects a new dynamic and interesting reality in themselves: a phenomenon that is well exemplified by the case studies presented in this book and that was directly explored in the workshop 'Designing the future of the system of rural villages around Tai Lake'. The new urban fringes are areas undergoing a continuous process of change, with a mixed and loose age, social and income structure and a wide range of different economic functions. For many aspects they also are the nursing ground for newly emerging social groups.

The 'onion ring' pattern which characterized the growth of the cities in Western countries during the Industrial Revolution and which was based on a sequence of steps – creation of an external fringe of the existing city, progressive stabilization of this fringe, creation of a new fringe that in turn is stabilized and so on – has changed. And the approach adopted in the last two centuries by planners can no longer be used to create stable and safe borders for the city by planning green belts or peripheral boulevards (as a reinterpretation of the ancient city walls).

Since the new urban fringes epitomize most of the specific features of the contemporary city, they are laboratories for the study and understanding of the processes of change that take place in it. This suggests the opportunity to explore ways to assign a role to the urban fringes that preserves their internal dynamics and allows for constant possibility of change. In this way they become a potential testing ground for a different approach to the problems of the entire city.

How does one deal with the issues of the development of these areas where a variety of factors make an orderly development extremely difficult?

Possibly the first decision to be taken is to consider their lack of definition, their disorder and their dynamism as an asset, a resource. They are not negative urban components that must be brought to a standard condition and eventually limited. On the contrary they are elements upon which new strategies, new spatial structures, new morphologies can be based. Urban fringes are areas in which the transformation is driven not only by big economic interests and political agendas, as in the established parts of the city or in the still undeveloped ones. They are a blend of elements such as: traditional economic and social structures, new functions and new businesses, small and big enterprises in advanced sectors, social groups with different incomes, parts of the architectural and historic urban heritage, new construction projects and planned spatial developments.

They are in fact still one of the major fields of experimentation and change within urban structures, and represent the existence of different ways and forms of urban organization. Two examples can help us to understand the opportunities they offer:

- Firstly, in urban fringes one can still have the chance to test new small-scale economic initiatives related to creativity and individual commitment. Urban fringes are a key resource in any society as incubators of innovation.
- Secondly, in urban fringes there is a wide range of housing answering to the residential needs of different types of families. It represents an opportunity to experiment and develop technical solutions and policies that go beyond the rigidity of the solutions offered by large-scale housing projects.

In summary, we can say that urban fringes are still in many ways a laboratory where processes that are lost elsewhere can be still studied, and solutions that cannot be designed and implemented in other urban systems can be imagined. It is not a minor issue and it is a quality to be considered as strategic. Basically, in the urban fringes there are opportunities to carry on experimental projects for the organization and management of space that can be applied to other cases, and at a larger scale. It is a practice that has been and still is successfully used in China, mainly in the field of economic policies.

What can and must be, then, the technical approach for the study of these issues and for their appropriate solution? I think that ILAUD can give a positive contribution to a better understanding of the urban fringes and the problems they face in three ways. The first one is to approach issues without a preconceived idea of how they should be solved. Answers should emerge through a careful analysis of the specific situation and an attentive listening of ideas, doubts, expectations and suggestions by local actors. This implies an open-minded approach based on the assumption that in the process of planning and design there are not just a few experts who know and 'own' the knowledge to be taught. It also implies a different conception of how knowledge is produced. The second way is by using design as a tool for a critical analysis and assessment of a specific situation. To elaborate on a project for a given area it is necessary to know it in depth, to identify its problems, to assess its potential and then to suggest solutions that can be implemented. This project can be then used as a tool for exploring a specific case and for analysing the pros and cons of its process of change. It is not necessarily the best and only solution to a problem. The use of design as a critical knowledge device that by trial and error helps to find acceptable answers is particularly suitable for studying the urban fringes. As has been said before, solving issues emerging at the urban fringes requires an experimental method and a non-conventional approach. This type of free exploration is a basic ILAUD principle. These two approaches correspond to the ILAUD assumption that the best way of learning is by doing. The third contribution comes from the very nature of ILAUD as an international association of different schools and research centres. In developing a project, ILAUD can bring different perspectives on conceiving a problem, a range of values belonging to different cultures and different design and planning skills. It is a cultural resource that can play an important role in approaching problems in an original and alternative way.

Conclusions

Giulio Verdini

The rural fringe of urban China is today the liminal space in fast-growing cities where the tension of development shows its more dramatic effects. Such tension is the direct consequence of the current institutional configuration of the country that stimulates the city's appetite for unabated urban growth. This is the reason why the institutional dimension of the rural-urban fringe appears to be by far one of the most critical issues of the current urbanization of China. At the same time, the high rate of rural to urban conversion does not just imply the loss of agricultural land around the main emerging cities, but also the reshaping of peri-urban livelihoods and the alteration of a highly dense inhabited rural fringe. In this respect, the environmental concern lying behind the urban growth cannot be distinguished by broader socio-economic considerations. This is indeed a consequence of the nature of the Chinese fringe already interpreted in this book as a dense web of relations, rather than a relatively empty, open space, shaped by conflictive/cooperative actors and by a peculiar city governance system, as presented in Chapter 1.

Throughout the book the multi-faceted complexity of the Chinese urban-rural fringe (actors and dimensions) emerges as a distinctive element of the country, at least in its fast-growing regions. This is determined by the particular way the state interacts with the market in city development in relationship with land property ownership (Chapter 2) and by the changing nature of the Chinese middle class that is increasingly turning to the countryside to fulfil their new demands of housing (Chapter 3) or of leisure and tourist activities (Chapters 5 and 7). However, such complexity results in difficult acknowledgment and consequently of difficult management. The reason is mainly ascribable to the articulated morphologies of cities in relationship to their central or intermediate role played within the current administrative structure (Chapter 4) or to the main spatial planning representation and policy discourses which are still primarily urban-centred and not entirely capable of capturing the specificity of such an environment (Chapter 6). Finally, the specificity of contested places in China, regardless of their specific location in the fringe or the inner city areas, are still hard to be properly addressed due to the lacking of effective participation mechanisms (Chapter 8).

Overall, these contributions, in showing preliminary evidence of mutual beneficial synergy between the urban and the rural realm, especially in social and economic terms, provide arguments to challenge a mono-directional and pro-growth Chinese model of development, highly relying on urban expansion. Despite the mentioned limitations, there are promising seeds for a better reconsideration of the rural fringe in future sustainable urban development scenarios. These scenarios are mainly related to fast-changing behaviours and values of an emerging middle class in search of a better balance between economic achievements and overall quality of life. However, in touching upon the nerves of the urbanization process of the Chinese rural fringe, some questions remain open still, as the research papers bear testimony. In summary, these issues are mainly related to two broad considerations that set the agenda for future research in planning in this part of the world: on the one hand, the existence of institutional limitations that prevent, very often, achieving fairness in whatever urban transformation process and, consequently, a meaningful involvement of all actors affected by development. The removal of this barrier could pave the road for more socially and economically inclusive patterns of development, with positive environmental externalities in urban management. On the other hand, there is the existence of a discourse of urbanization, primarily shaped by the leading elite, tightly related to the aspiration (or ideology) of modernization, which often prevents considering the rural areas as an important component *per se* of the sustainable functioning of the city. While the former implies innovating the practices of the planning and design of the rural fringe in more bottom-up and cooperative terms, the latter implies building innovative capacities and skills more suitable to deal with the specificity of the Chinese fringe areas.

This brings us to another fundamental conclusion of this book that has been addressed by implementing an experimental teaching experience carried out during the international workshop in Suzhou (Chapter 9) in cooperation with ILAUD (point of view): besides the research outcomes and their dissemination among practitioners and policymakers, the teaching agenda of the urban planning and design discipline in China needs a Copernican revolution, especially when dealing with subjects in need of reconceptualization, like the rural fringe and the urban-rural linkages. This would require a formation for future architects, urban designers and planners, less relying on pure technical skills (where and how to allocate the next urban addition) and more open to the social science influence. In broader terms this would imply the experimentation of healthy and sometimes 'off the beaten track' interdisciplinary approaches.

Index

References to illustrations are in **bold**.

agricultural land
    loss of 82, 199
    state expropriation of 19
    urbanization of 87
        preservation of 9
Agricultural Land Protection Law (1994) 122
agricultural parks 10
agriculture
    collectivization 46
    multifunctional 8

Beijing 19, 61, 66
    green belt(s) xv
Beijing Capital Region, rural tourism 84
bourgeoisie, Chinese 5
Brown, Lester 18

China
    development pattern 1–2
    mega cities 19, 61
    regional differences xv–xvi
    strategic development plan 177
    urban population 34
    urbanizing xvi, 6, 7, 8, 35–6, 62, 109
Chongqing xvi
    CURD development 23
    government expenditure 23
    land ticket trading 22–6, 28
    population decrease 23
    social instability 24
    urban-rural gap 23
    urbanization 23
Chuodunshan Village *see under* Suzhou
cities
    China, classification 66
    global 63
    see also mega cities; SMCs
city boundary, fluidity of 117
city-space 116, 119, 124
    definition 116fn4

class identity, formation 38
    see also middle classes
CNTA (China National Tourism
        Administration), initiatives 83
Confucianism 152
countryside
    'building the new countryside' 65–6,
        67, 83, 87, 88–9, 100, 105
    Chinese
        1949-1980s 46–7
        dynastic era 44–5
        historical perception 44–7
        industrialization of 93
        new-old 54–7
        Opium Wars era 45–6
        pastoralism, vs modernism 48
        present day 47, 48–54
    differentiated 33
        China and the West 34–6
    English
        clientelist 35
        middle-class incomers 36
        narratives 34
        pastoralism vs modernism 34, 49
        paternalistic 35
        preserved vs contested 35
        typology 35
    new, rural tourism policy 83, 88–9
    urbanization of 127
CPC (Communist Party of China) 46
CPCC (Critical Planning for Chinese
        Cities) workshop xvii, 179–93, 200
    benefits of 187
    case study 179
    collaborative learning 182–6
    critical thinking 185
    cross-cultural transferability 189–91
    facilitation, ground rules 188–9
    inter-disciplinarity 182, 186, 187–8, 192
    participants 179, 180

pedagogical analysis 181–91
problems 187–8
rationale 179
site visits 180, **181**, 183–4
studio space 180, **180**
tasks 180
themes 17
Western ideas 182
CURD (Coordinated Urban-Rural
Development) 21–2
Chongqing 23

Dayuwan Tourism Development Company
142
Dayuwan Village (Wuhan) 133
architectural forms 139, **139**, 141
artistic decoration 139–40
development 135–6
Fengshui pattern 137, **138**, 139
funding, lack of 142
history 137
land area 137
Miss International Tourism,
competition 142, 143
National Folk Culture Festival 142
National Historical and Cultural status
140, 141
population 137
preservation programme 140–1, 142,
145
rural tourism 136–7, 142
activities **143**
elements 144
scenic area 142
secluded location 136, 144
stakeholders 141–2
de Carlo, Giancarlo xvii
Dengfeng city xvi, 62
built area and water system **74–5**
destruction in **70**, 72
kung fu capital 67
location 67
new city site **69**
new residential area **71**
population 67
UNESCO world heritage site 67
desakota phenomenon 3, 120
Donald, S.H., and Zheng, Y. 38

DTMD (Drum Tower Muslim District)
area 151
case study
findings 156–7, 168–9
interviews 156
research methodology 156
residents' views 157–9
government manipulation 159, 162
Hui people 152
landlords 160
location **151**
mosques, centrality of 158
neighbourhoods 152
plans **154**
population 151
private property 152
reconstruction **160**
redevelopment 152–6, 161
disparities 163
public participation, lack of 163–5
residents/government
interaction 165–6, 168
passive chain reaction **166**
run-down houses **154**
Urban Residents Committee, role
161–2, 165
Dujiangyan city xvi, 62
built area and water system **74–5**
location 67
new city site **69**
population 67
UNESCO world heritage site 67

England, counter-urbanization 48

farmers
destruction of homes 72
dispossessed
compensation 7, 24, 25, 26
numbers 4
farm tourism 85
land rights 7
peri-urban 7, 9, 11
relocation 3, 25, 67
suburban 135
food security 17, 18, 19, 81
Foshan town 116
Friedmann, J., *China's Urban Transition* 2

gentrification, inner city 41–4
Global South xv
Great Famine(1959-61) 18
'Great Leap Forward' 46
Green Belt
    Beijing xv
    UK 54–5
Guangdong Province 20
    administrative readjustment
        (1981-2011) 125
Guangzhou 24, 61, 66, 114

household registration system 23, 26, 28,
    35, 47, 92
housing EXPO (2009), exhibitors 52
Hui people 152
hukou system 2, 4, 26, 46–7, 57, 128
    and distribution of PRD population **126**
    purpose 35–6

IDB (increasing and decreasing balance)
    implementation 21
    policy 20–2
ILAUD (International Laboratory of
    Architecture and Urban Design)
    175, 176, 179, 188, 196, 197, 200
    de Carlo, Giancarlo, founder xvii

Jiangsu Province, rural tourism 86
Jingjinji Region 18
Jinshi Village *see under* Suzhou

Land Administration Bureau 121
Land Administration Law 19, 121, 122
land ownership 199
    and land ticket trading 25
    rural 7, 19, 27, 113
    urban 7, 113
land resources
    threats to 17
    see also agricultural land; rural land;
        urban land
land ticket
    reform 17
        proposal 26–9
    trading
        Chongqing 22–6, 28
        constraints on 25

and land ownership 25
market role 25
potential 24
landscape
    agricultural 7, 81, 85, 95, 98, 100, 105
    cultural 87, 145
    genetics 187–8
    natural 86, 90
    rural xvii, 19, 24, 81, 82, 87, 89, 93,
        98, 134
    urban 12, 41, 62, 66, 72
land-use rights
    mechanisms 122
    sale, Shenzen 122
    transference 122
learning
    by doing xviii, **180**
    collaborative 182–3, 184–5
    see also pedagogy
Lee, C.K. & Yang, G. 56

mega cities
    Asia 3
    China 19, 61
        populations 65
    see also SMCs
middle classes xvi, 37–44, 199
    dispotif concept 39
    English countryside, incomers 36
    identity production 38
    perspectives
        combinationist 38
        Marxist 37–8
        post-structuralist 39
        statistical-survey 37
        Weberian 38
    property market 40
    studies on 37
Ming Dynasty 152
Ministry of Environment Protection 18
Ministry of Land and Resources 17, 18, 21
modernization, and urbanization 200
Murdoch, J. 48
    The Differentiated Countryside 34

Nankun Village *see under* Suzhou
National Folk Culture Festival, Dayuwan
    Village 142

National Land Development and
Consolidation Plan (2001-10) 17
National People's Congress 122
National Urbanization Plan 9
neo-liberalism, and risk 39
NGOs (Non-Governmental Organizations)
165

pastoralism
Chinese 50–4
vs modernism
Chinese countryside 48
English countryside 34, 49
Pearl River Delta (PRD) xvi, 2, 5, 18
population distribution, by hukou **126**
rural tourism 84
rural-urban edge 126–8
rural-urban interactions 112
SEZs 112
urbanization 125
revenue 123–4
pedagogy 181–91
Dewey, John 182
Montessori, Maria 182
Piaget, Jean 182
research-led 177
Vygotsky, Lev 182–3
see also learning
Pickowicz, P.G. 56
planning
centralized 117
Chinese system 22, 115, 1, 164, 167,
176
collaborative 26–7, 27–8, 29, 175
communist 112
core principles 178
degree, Xi'an Jiaotong-Liverpool
University 177
education system 177
modernist 115
soft skills 178
see also CPCC workshop; spatial
planning; urban planning
population
distribution, PRD **126**
rural, decrease 19
urban, growth 4–5, 18
poverty, alleviation

and rural tourism 105
and SMCs 63–4
PRD *see* Pearl River Delta

Ren, H., *The Middle Class in Neo-Liberal
China* 39
RTPI (Royal Town and Planning Institute
UK) 177
New Vision of Planning, core
principles 178
rural fringe xvi
actors 4–6
concept 1
economic dimension 9
floating population 4, 92
typologies 6
urbanization of 2, 3, 7, 36, 200
see also urban fringe
rural heritage
conservation 12, 82
definition 82
and rural tourism 82, 85, 104, 105
Yangtze River Delta, external threats
87
rural households, numbers 4
rural industrialization 2–3, 7
rural land
collective ownership 7, 19, 27, 113
cultivated
metal contamination 18
requirement 18
totality 17–18
management 17, 19
see also urban land
rural land consolidation 17–20
factors shaping 17
grievances 21
participation model 27
and urban development 21
rural tourism 8, 33
agricultural tourism 85
Beijing Capital Region 84
China Rural Tourism Year 1998: 83
Dayuwan Village 136–7, 142
development 83–4
economic activities 3, 81, 85
farms 85
geographical distribution 84

'Golden Week' policy 83
Jiangsu Province 86
'National Demonstration Sites for
    Rural Tourism' 84
and new countryside policy 83, 88–9
Pearl River Delta 84
as rural diversification 56, 81
and rural heritage 82, 85, 104, 105
Shanghai 86
Sichuan Province 84
themes 85
Yangtze River Delta 49, 82, 84, 85–9
Zhejiang Province 86
see also Suzhou
rural-urban
    continuum 111
    hybridization 120
    integration discourse, distortion
        120–6, 128
    interactions 11–12, 116–20, 199
        in PRD 112
    migration 47, 56, 57
rural-urban edge 109–10, 114
    in institutional bodies 119
    meaning 110
    PRD 126–8
    and spatial planning 111–13
    Zhaoqing city **115**

science parks, urban fringe 8
SEZs (Special Economic Zones)
    Master Plan 123
    PRD 112, 121
    Shenzen 122–3
Shanghai 4, 12, 19, 61, 66
    density 36
    Master Plan 10
    rural tourism 86
    Songjiang new city development 41, 51
    suburban expansion 36
    Windsor Island, Thames Town **40**, 41
    Zhujiajiao water-town **50–1**, 51
Shenzen
    land-use rights
        revenue 123
        sale 122
    SEZ 122–3
Sichuan Province, rural tourism 84

Silk Road 53
SMCs (small and medium-sized cities)
    China
        competition between 70
        development 65
        impact analysis 73, **74–5**
        intermediation 76
        numbers 66
        populations 65
        see also Dengfeng city;
            Dujiangyan city
    definition 64–5
    and fight against poverty 63–4
    and poverty alleviation 63–4
    role 62
Song, Mount **68**
Songjiang new city development 41, 51
spatial planning 8, 110, 124, 177
    decentralization of 147
    PRD 109
    public participation 148–9
        benefits of 149
    and rural-urban edge 111–13
State Bureau of Cultural Relics
    133, 134
Suzhou 12, 82, 89–104
    case studies
        list 92
        locations **91**
    Chuodunshan Village 100
        aerial views **101**
        canals and footpaths **102**
        public spaces **102**
        restaurant 100, **103**
    countryside
        deterioration 90
        houses **89**
    field surveys 90, **91**
    Jinshi Village
        abandoned houses **96**
        aerial view **94**
        ground view **99**
        unoccupied shop-houses **95**
    Nankun Village
        aerial view **97**
        bay view **97**
        houses 95, **97**, 98, **98**
        silk production 95

prefecture, map **93**
rural tourism 98
    community involvement 100, 104
    Xitang Village, view **99**

Tai Lake village 179
    Xishan Island **181**
Tang Dynasty 52, 53
Tongji Design Institute 72
Tongli water-town 5, 136
tourism, Xi'an City 151
    see also rural tourism

UK
    Green Belt 54–5
    urban population 34
    see also England
Urban Conference, Third National
    (1978) 65
urban design, urban planning as 176
urban expansion 17
urban fringe
    approaches to 186–7
    development 40–1, 195–6
    experimentation 196–7
    as liminal space 199
    planning workshop 179–93
        see also under CPCC workshop
    science parks 8
    see also rural fringe
urban land
    ownership 7, 113
    state ownership 19, 113
    see also rural land
urban planning
    pedagogical model 175
    as urban design 176
    workshop 176
urban population
    China 34
    UK 34
    USA 34
    world 61
urban sprawl 9, 17, 19, 36
urban-rural
    divide 4, 46, 47, 109
    income gap 24
    interaction xvi, 1, 109

urbanization
    of agricultural land 87
    Chongqing 23
    compulsory 7
    counter-
        England 48
        USA 55
    of the countryside 127
    green 53, 54, **54**
    growth 18–19, 33
    and modernization 200
    passive 7
    Pearl River Delta, revenue 123–4
    purpose 72
    of rural fringe 2, 3, 7, 36, 200
    waves 119–20
URCs (Urban Residents Committees) 150
USA, urban population 34

villages
    'back to villages' movement 46
    historic 10–11, 83
        preservation schemes 134, 142–4
        threats to 135
        see also Dayuwan Village; Suzhou,
            Jinshi Village
    'hollow' 20
    new, relocation to 20
    theme park 48–9, **48**
    water 178
Vygotsky, Lev, on learning 182–3

Wang, J. & Siu Lu Lau 41
water-towns
    new-old **50–1**
    Tongli 5, 136
    Zhouzhuang 5, 136
Wu, F. 40
Wuhan
    advertisement for Eton flats **42**
    Han Mansions development
        42, **43**
    Han Road **43**
    Tiandi real estate development,
        'creative space' **54**

Xi'an Jiaotong-Liverpool University,
    planning degree 177

Xi'an City xvii, 150
    Cultural Renowned City 151
    economic development 151
    GDP 151
    Great Ancient Capital 151
    population 151
    tourism 151
    see also DTMD
Xingqing Palace 52–3, 56
Xuan Zong, Emperor 52

Yangtze River Delta xvi, 2, 12, 18, 36
    map **88**
    rural heritage, external threats 87

rural tourism 49, 82, 84, 85–7
urban agglomeration 85–6
Yuan dynasty 152

Zhang Li, *In Search of Paradise: Middle-Class Living in a Chinese Metropolis* 38
Zhaoqing city
    rural-urban edge **115**
    urban future **116**
Zhejiang Province, rural tourism 86
Zhouzhuang 5, 136
Zhujiajiao water-town **50–1**, 51